MFA HIGHLIGHTS arts of korea

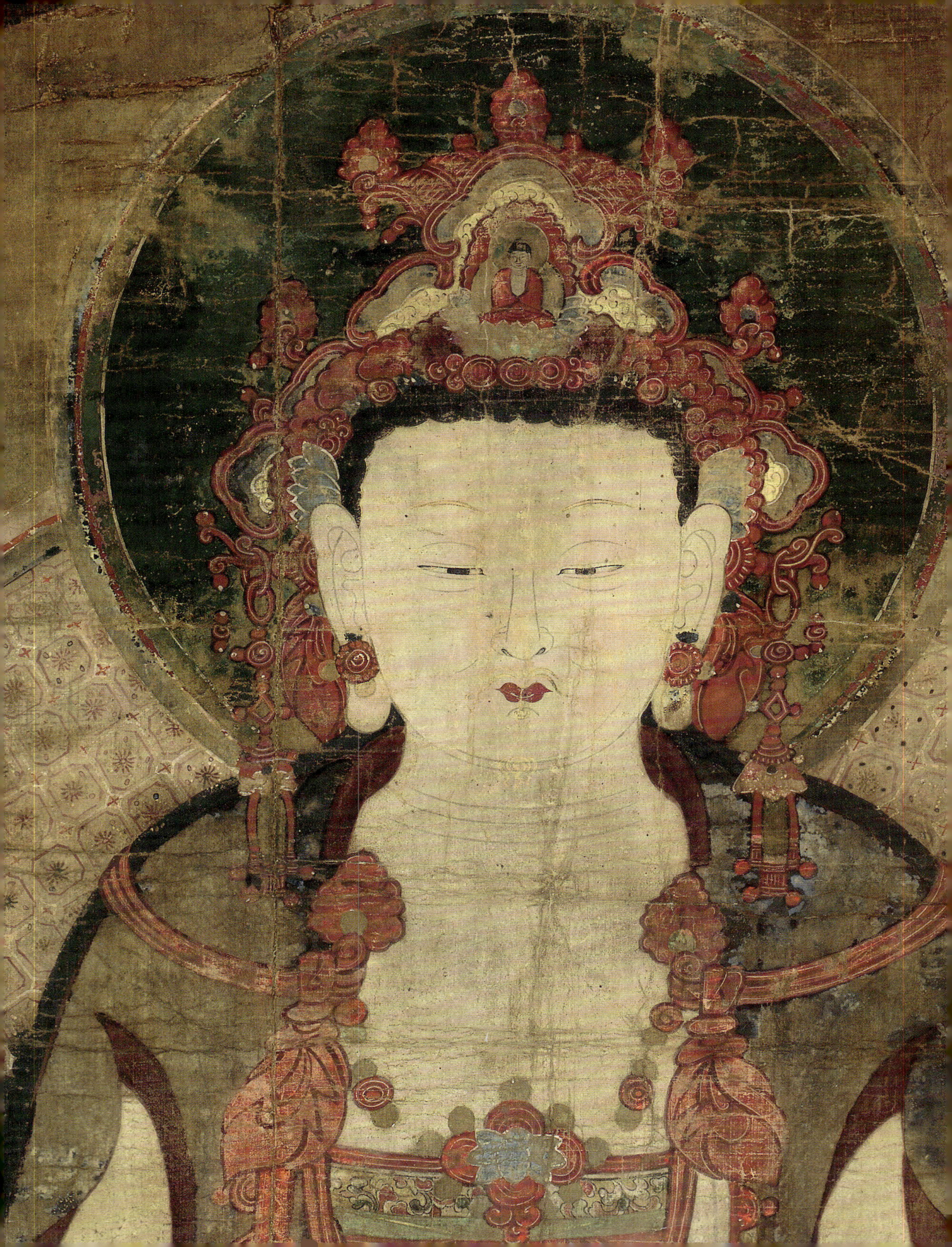

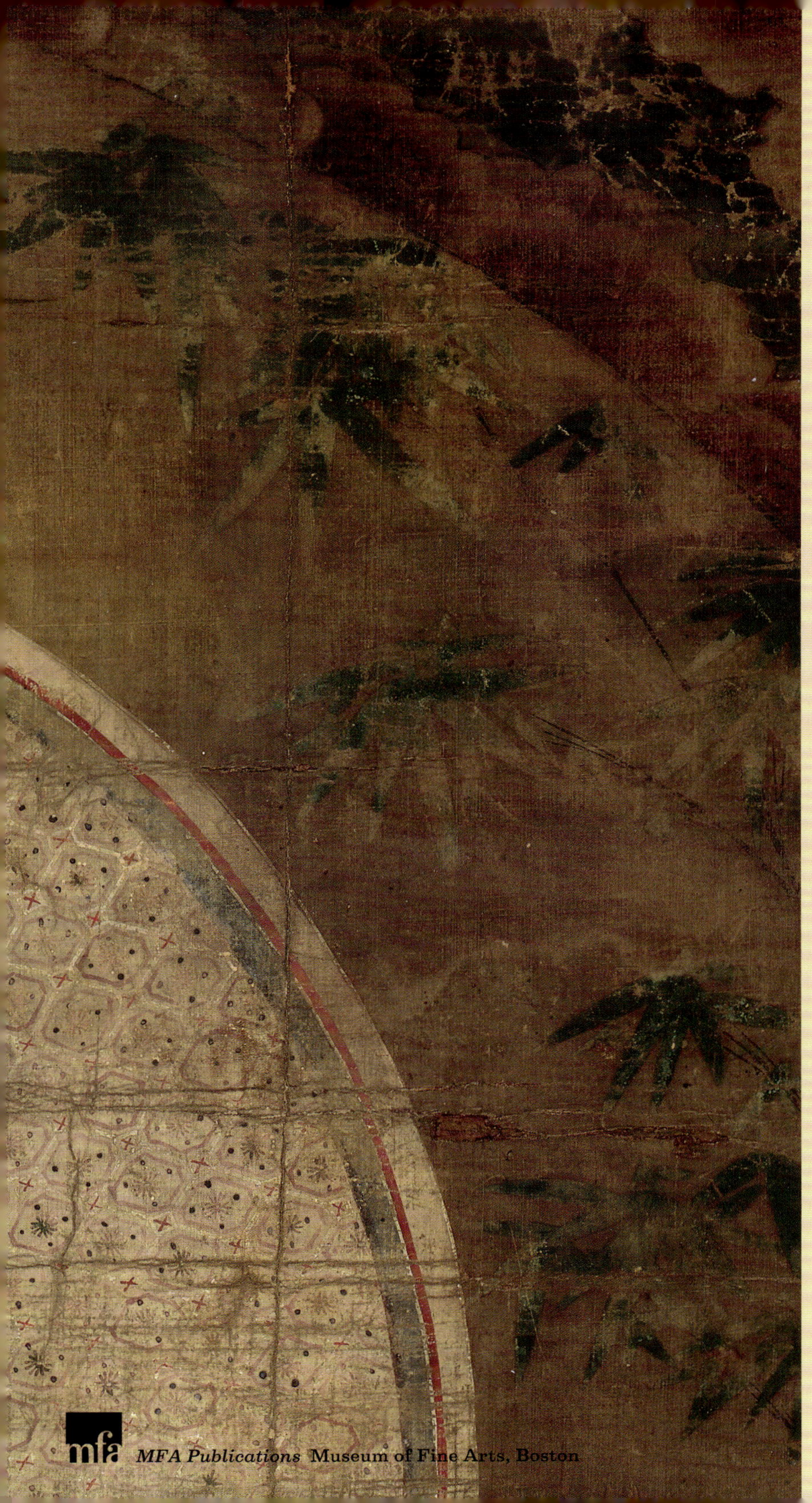

MFA HIGHLIGHTS arts of korea

Jane Portal

with

Suhyung Kim and Hee Jung Lee

MFA Publications Museum of Fine Arts, Boston

MFA PUBLICATIONS
Museum of Fine Arts, Boston
465 Huntington Avenue
Boston, Massachusetts 02115
www.mfa.org/publications

The publication of this book was made possible in part through an award from the National Endowment for the Arts.

ISBN 978-0-87846-788-4
Library of Congress Control Number: 2012937503

While the objects in this publication necessarily represent only a small portion of the MFA's holdings, the Museum is proud to be a leader within the American museum community in sharing the objects in its collection via its website. Currently, information about more than 330,000 objects is available to the public worldwide. To learn more about the MFA's collections, including provenance, publication, and exhibition history, kindly visit www.mfa.org/collections.

For a complete listing of MFA publications, please contact the publisher at the above address, or call 617 369 3438.

All illustrations in this book were photographed by the Imaging Studios, Museum of Fine Arts, Boston, except where otherwise noted.

Edited by Jennifer Snodgrass and Emiko K. Usui
Copyedited and proofread by Kelly Flynn
Typeset by Fran Presti-Fazio
Designed and produced by Terry McAweeney
Series design by Lucinda Hitchcock
Printed and bound at Graphicom, Verona, Italy

Available through ARTBOOK | D.A.P.
155 Sixth Avenue, 2nd floor
New York, New York 10013
Tel.: 212 627 1999 · Fax: 212 627 9484

FIRST EDITION
Printed and bound in Italy
This book was printed on acid-free paper.

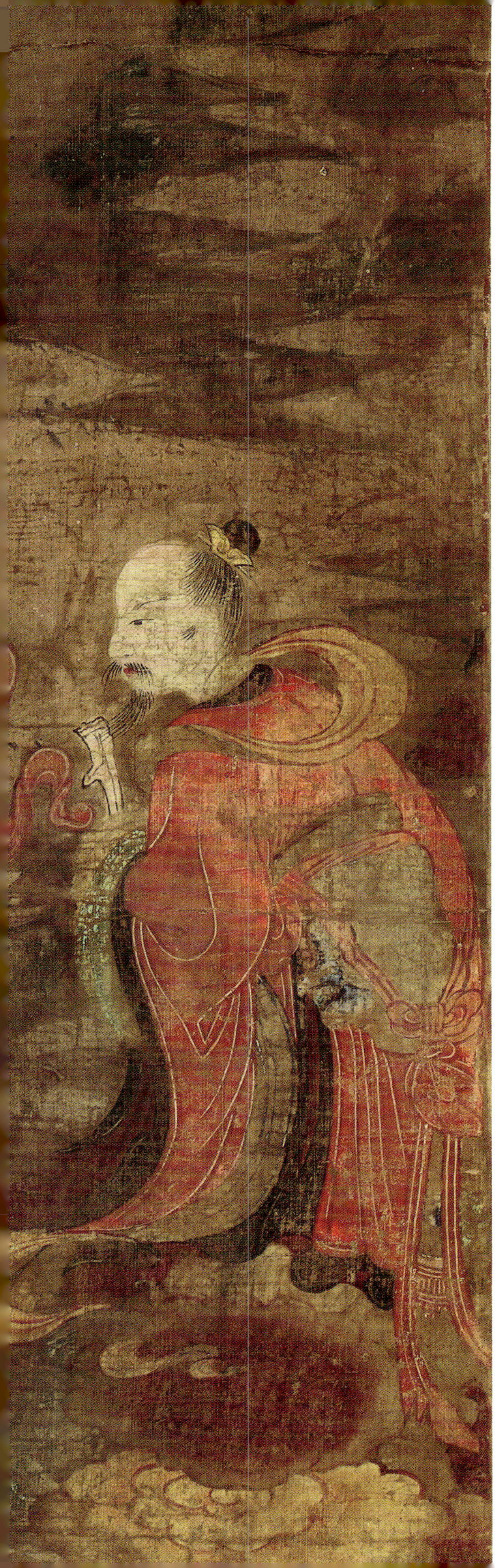

Contents

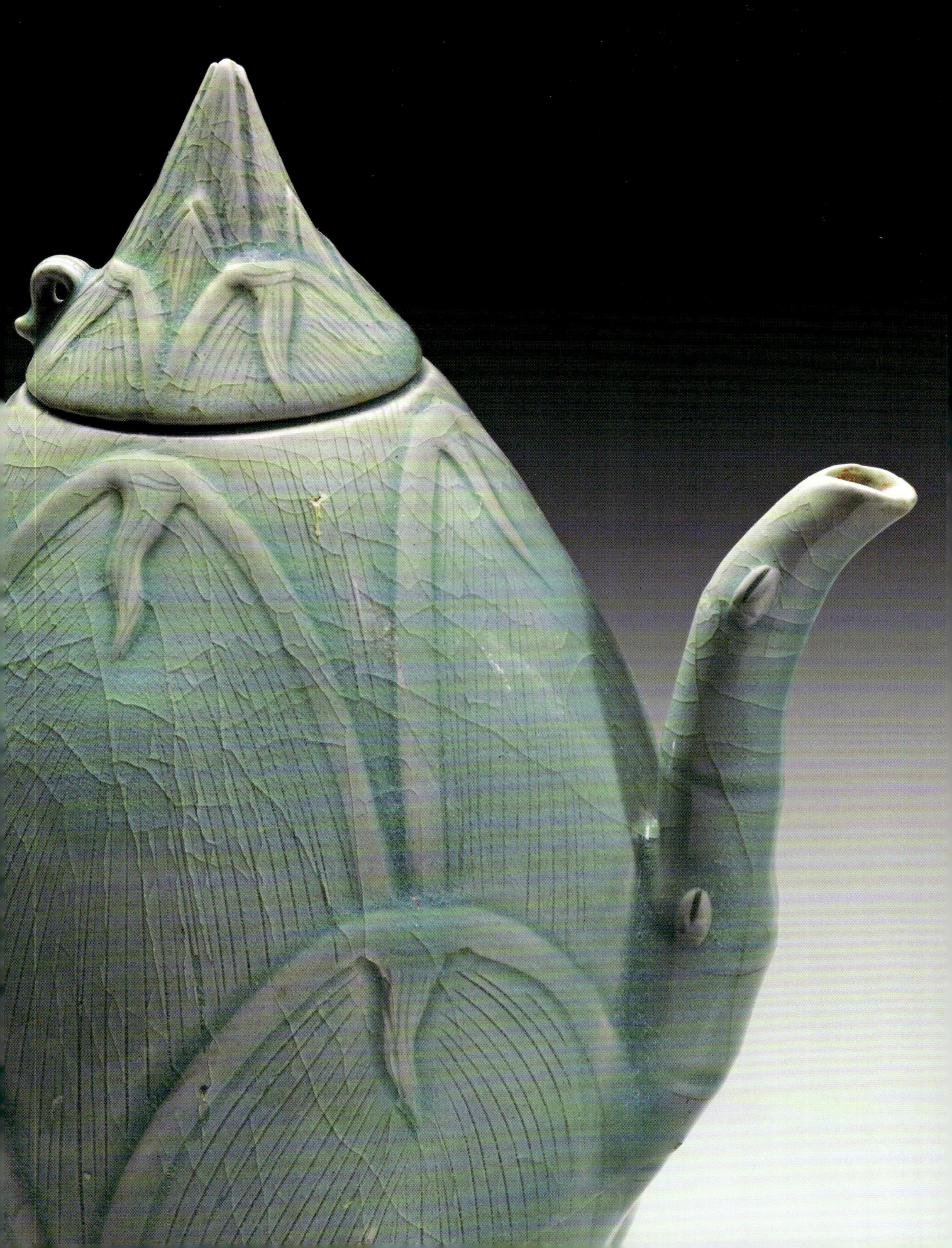

Director's Foreword

Art is for everyone, and it is in this spirit that the MFA Highlights series was conceived. The series introduces some of the greatest works of art in a manner that is both approachable and stimulating. Each volume focuses on an individual collection, allowing fascinating themes—both visual and textual—to emerge. We aim, over time, to represent every one of the Museum's major collections in the Highlights series, thus forming a library that will be a wonderful resource for the understanding and enjoyment of world art.

It is our goal to make the Museum's artworks accessible by every means possible. We hope that each volume of MFA Highlights will help you to know and understand our encyclopedic collections and to make your own discoveries among their riches.

Malcolm Rogers
Ann and Graham Gund Director
Museum of Fine Arts, Boston

Acknowledgments

This book celebrates the superb Korean art collection at the Museum of Fine Arts, Boston, on the occasion of the 2012 renovation of the Korean gallery made possible by support from the Korea Foundation. The Korean collection is one element of the Museum's exceptional Asian collection, a result of the generosity of generations of donors from Boston and around the world.

I am grateful to Malcolm Rogers, Ann and Graham Gund Director, for creating the Highlights series to make the Museum's collection accessible to general readers. I am also grateful to Katie Getchell and Maria Muller, Deputy Directors, who have been great advocates and supporters of my work.

I would like to thank my co-authors Suhyung Kim-Chung and Hee Jung Lee for their hard work and dedication to this project. Also in Art of Asia, Oceania, and Africa, thanks are due to Judy Morillo for her exceptionally well-organized coordination and support, as well as to Angie Simonds and Ellen Takata for their unfailing willingness to help me and to answer queries about the collection. Conservators Pam Hatchfield, Robert P. and Carol T. Henderson Head of Objects Conservation, Abby Hykin, Susanne Gänsicke, Flavia Perugini, LeeAnn Gordon, Jacki Elgar, Philip Meredith, Higashiyama Kaii Conservator of Japanese Paintings, and Jing Gao, Cornelius Van der Starr Conservator of Chinese Paintings, have examined and treated many of the works in this book to their usual high standards. John Robbe has helped in numerous ways and Richard Newman, Head of the Scientific Research Lab, has made illuminating discoveries about the collection, for which I am most grateful. Korea Foundation Intern Dayun Oh carried out some extremely useful research on the paintings collection and updated object files during her three-month stay in 2011 as part of the Korea Foundation's Global Internship Program. Melissa Gallin coordinated our Korea Foundation application for the gallery project, and Tsugumi Maki Joiner, Keith Crippen, and Kyla Hygysian masterminded its execution.

The beautiful photographs by Michael Gould and Saravuth Neou of the Museum's Imaging Studios have enhanced this book, and the editing and production process has been superbly overseen by Emiko Usui and Jennifer Snodgrass with Terry McAweeney and Anna Barnet. The publication of this book was made possible in part through an award from the National Endowment for the Arts.

Former MFA Director Jan Fontein and Robert Mowry, Alan J. Dworsky Curator of Chinese Art at the Harvard Art Museums, have each contributed scholarly advice. I am also indebted to colleagues and friends in Korea, in particular to Professors Insoo Cho, Hongnam Kim, Lena Kim, Youngna Kim, and Insook Lee. Keum-jin Yoon, Director of the Culture and Arts Department at the Korea Foundation, has encouraged and supported my work over the twenty years that we have known each other. Euna Yoo and Ji-yoon Lee have also provided friendship and support over many years. I would like to acknowledge the help and companionship offered by Korean art curators across the world whom I have met over the last twelve years at the Korea Foundation Curators' Workshops. I thank all my colleagues in the Art of Asia, Oceania, and Africa Department and the Asian Conservation Studio for working with me, and finally I wish to acknowledge Trustee and Visiting Committee Chair Nina Burr for her exceptional and invaluable personal support over the past four years.

Jane Portal
Matsutaro Shoriki Chair
Art of Asia, Oceania, and Africa
Museum of Fine Arts, Boston

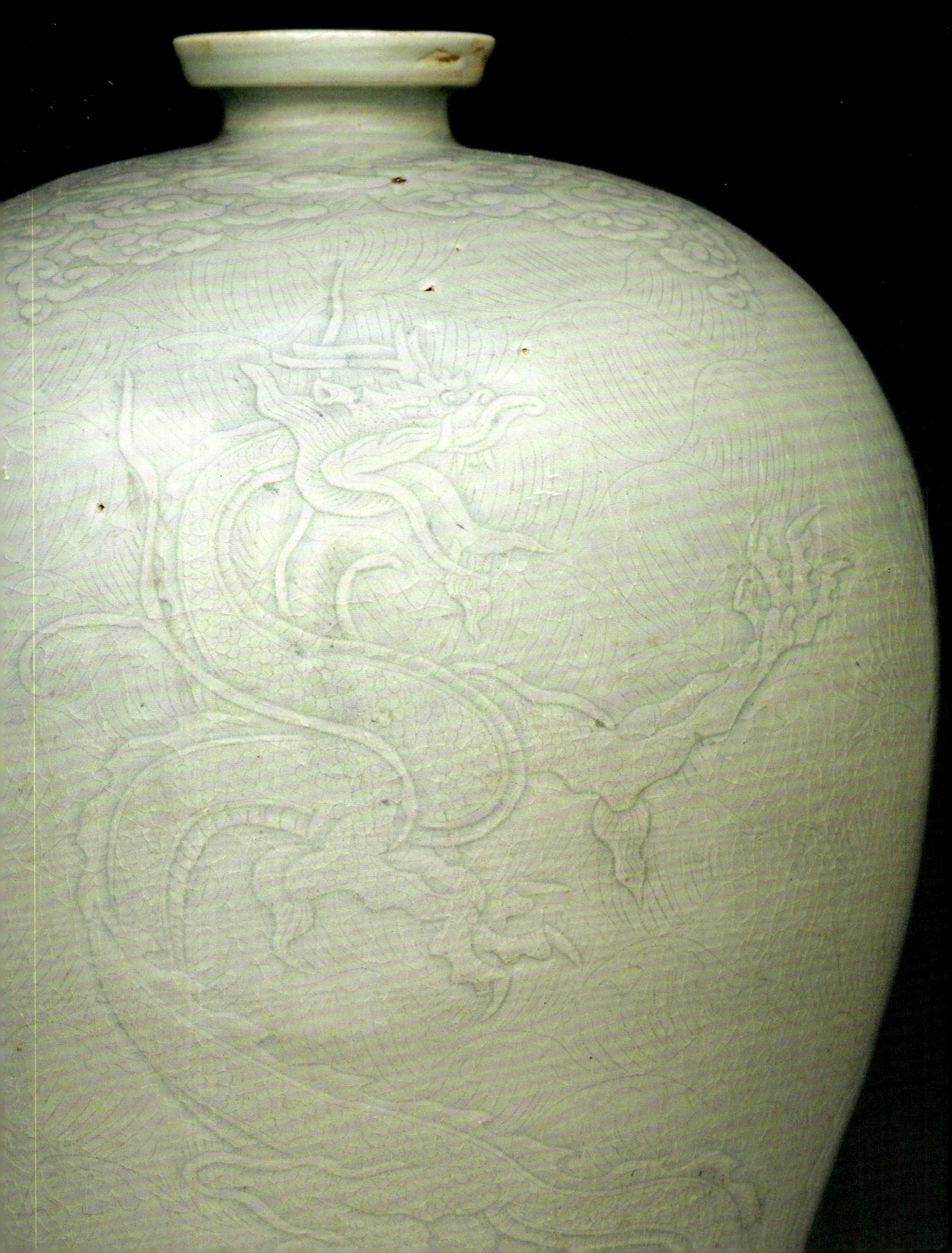

The Story of Korean Art

Korea is a country with a long history, sophisticated culture, and great artistic achievements, but it has remained less well known in the Western world than its neighbors, China and Japan. In fact, Korea was long called "The Hermit Kingdom" because until 1880 Westerners were forbidden—on pain of death—to set foot in the country. Within East Asia, however, Korea played an important cultural, diplomatic, and economic role from early times. Arab traders interacted with what they called "Silla" from at least the ninth century.

This book celebrates Korean art through one hundred works in the collection of one Western museum, the Museum of Fine Arts, Boston. The MFA has one of the finest collections of Korean art outside East Asia, with particularly superb holdings of ceramics and Buddhist paintings. It is also rich in metalwork, lacquer, and ink painting. Many of the things in this book were originally made for everyday use and were not regarded as works of art at all at the time. They tell a story not only about the people who used or collected these objects, but also about the people who made them. For example, Korea is justly famous for its celadons—green-glazed, high-fired ceramics made from the eleventh to fourteenth centuries. These celadons, now highly valued as works of art, provide a glimpse into the courtly lifestyle of the Korean royal family and aristocrats, as well as the tightly organized and controlled manufacturing communities of the potters. The potters were perhaps not exactly slaves, but they were socially inferior to other people.[1] In a sense, these celadons are a way for this otherwise silent underclass to communicate with us today, almost a thousand years later.

This story of Korean art is dependent on several factors: for example, which things survived to tell their tales; which things travelers, scholars, and collectors liked and wanted to collect; which Boston philanthropists over the years felt moved to donate their collections to the MFA; and which things became available on the market for the Museum's curators to acquire. Many celadons survive because they are tough, hardy objects that held up well buried in tombs. Bronze rice bowls, chopsticks, coins, and mirrors also survive in much greater numbers than, for example, silver objects (which were often melted down), lacquer (which needs a certain climate to survive), or paintings or textiles (which were liable to disintegrate).

In addition to works of art, we must consider written texts when telling the story of Korean art. Much of what we know about early Korea comes from historical records in Chinese, Korean, and Japanese, even if those texts show the biases or prejudices of their authors. The two Korean histories *Samguksagi* (History of the Three Kingdoms) and *Samgukyusa* (Memorabilia of the Three Kingdoms) were written in the twelfth and thirteenth centuries, much later than the time periods they cover, so their reliability is limited. The Chinese histories, such as the *Weiji*, in general provide reliable information and stem from a long Chinese tradition of history writing. The Japanese *Nihon shoki* and *Kojiki* can be used as sources of information about the early relations between Japan and Korea but interpretations differ and the Japanese histories were used in the twentieth century to justify Japan's colonization of Korea.

Korea's geographic location has naturally influenced its cultural and artistic development. It is a peninsula reaching southward toward the islands of Japan from the point in East Asia where China meets Russia. A remarkably homogenous people with origins in the Altai region of Siberia inhabit this beautiful, mountainous country. Their native shamanistic religion reflects its Siberian origins in such products as antler-like gold crowns of the Three Kingdoms period (57 B.C.–A.D. 668), and in the worshipping of natural phenomena such as the sun, moon, and mountains. Shamanism was widely practiced in early Korea until the arrival of Buddhism from the fourth through sixth centuries via China.

Buddhism reached a highpoint in Korea from the seventh to the fourteenth centuries. Many of the schools of Buddhism popular in China were transmitted to Korea, mainly by Korean Buddhist priests who studied in China. The most influential of the schools was the Avatamsaka, which sought a synthesis of all Buddhist teachings. Also introduced were the Meditation School (Zen), the Pure Land School, which stressed the importance of prayer, and Esoteric Buddhism, which emphasized ritual. The Confucian philosophy, also from China and based on the moral and ethical teachings of Confucius (551–479 B.C.), dominated Korea from the fourteenth century. The philosophy was manifested in a highly stratified social system with an emphasis on family lineage and male heirs. The legacy of Confucianism can still be seen in modern Korea, for example, in the respect shown for elders and education, as well as in the tendency for men to dominate society. Shamanism is still practiced today, particularly by women, and Buddhism continues to be a strong force with many supporters.

Although the Korean spoken language is part of the Altaic language group, it has a similar word order and grammatical structure to Japanese and shares with it a considerable proportion of loan words from Chinese. The Korean people wrote in Chinese until the sixth century when they started taking down the lyrics of Korean songs using Chinese characters only for their sounds. This system is known as Idu. The Korean phonetic script used today (now known as Hangeul), was not invented until the fifteenth century. It was originally created as a way to help people read Chinese characters. Chinese continued to be used in official and literary works up until the modern period, and as a result many Korean paintings have inscriptions and seals in Chinese characters.

Korea's relationship with China was generally one of a smaller nation to a bigger and more powerful one. Wang Geon, the founder of Korea's Goryeo era (918–1392) in the tenth century, said: "We in the East have long admired Tang [Chinese] ways. In culture, ritual and music, we are entirely following its model."[2] Then in the following Joseon era (1392–1910), Joseon's founder Yi Seonggye described Korea's position vis-à-vis China as *sadae*, or "serving the great." In practice this meant that at least three regular embassies were sent annually to the Ming court, resulting in much trade between the two countries. Korea exported such things as horses, ginseng, furs, ramie, and straw mats in return for imports of silk, medicines, books, and porcelain.[3] Regular envoys from late Joseon Korea were also sent to Japan in the seventeenth and eighteenth centuries. They were accompanied by Korean painters, whose works were greatly admired, collected, and copied in Japan. Many paintings and prints by Japanese artists record the journeys of the official processions as the envoys traveled through Japan to the capital.[4] After the Japanese warrior and ruler Toyotomi Hideyoshi invaded Korea in 1592, Jesuit missionaries, some of whom accompanied the troops, spread news about Korea to Europe. These accounts were followed in the seventeenth century by those of the Dutchman Hendrik Hamel, who was held in captivity in Korea from 1653 to 1666, having been shipwrecked off Jeju Island. After his release, Hamel published the first Western eyewitness report of the country in 1668.

Korea opened up after it signed the unequal Treaty of Ganghwa with Japan in 1876. Diplomatic relations were established between Korea and Western countries, such as the United States in 1882, and there was an influx of Western missionaries, diplomats, and independent travelers, many of whom published their own accounts. They included the Scotswoman Isabella Bird Bishop, who wrote the classic *Korea and Her Neighbours*, and the Americans William Franklin Sands, a diplomat and advisor to King Gojong; Homer B. Hulbert, a missionary; and Percival Lowell, a scientist and traveler. Their eyewitness accounts, published in books and periodicals, introduced their countrymen to a largely unknown area of the world. The photographs accompanying the accounts were also valuable records. Many innovations and modernizations took place in Korea from 1880 until the Japanese Occupation in 1910. After 1910, information about Korea was largely filtered through Japan.

Japanese art collectors have long appreciated Korean art. Since the tenth century, many works have made their way into Japanese private collections as well as Buddhist temples. Japanese tea ceremony practitioners have had a particular interest in Korean ceramics. The scholar and collector of Japanese folk crafts Yanagi Soetsu led the modern movement to promote Korean ceramics in the early twentieth century, but also emphasized what he characterized as their naïve, unsophisticated, and sad aspects:

> In modern art, as everyone knows, the beauty of deformity is very often emphasized, insisted upon. But how different is Korean deformity. The former is produced deliberately, the latter naturally. Korean work is merely the natural result of the artisan's state of mind, which is free from dualistic man-made rules . . . Here lies buried the mystery of the endless beauty of the Korean artisan's work. He simply makes what he wants, without pretension.[5]

Yanagi's statement reflects the ambivalent view—a mixture of admiration and condescension—held by the Japanese toward Korean art at that time. It was paradoxically due to Japanese scholars such as Yanagi (who were necessarily part of the twentieth-century Japanese occupation and subjugation of Korea) that Western potters such as Bernard Leach and Lucie Rie came to know and love Korean pottery and absorb its influence into their work (fig. 1). Leach echoed Yanagi's thoughts when he said,

> [Korean potters] added a quite peculiar fresh flavor of their own. It shows in the material, form, and pattern, all of which they employed in a manner which is at once naïve and cultured. The clays are lovely but they are handled with nonchalance.[6]

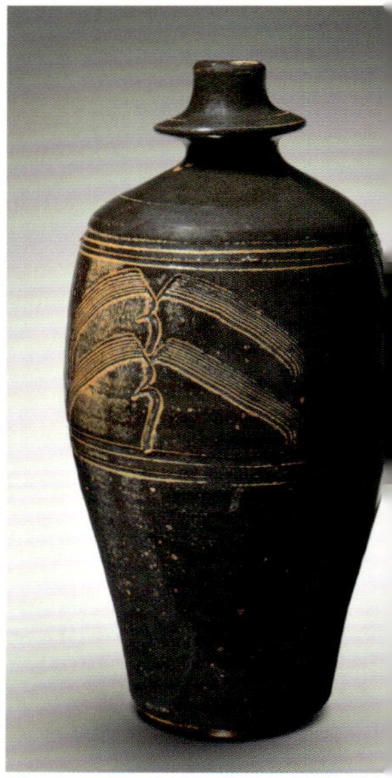

fig. 1. **Bernard Leach (British, 1887–1979).** ***Bottle*****, 20th century. Ceramic. The shape and glazing of this vase are reminiscent of Korean *maebyeong*.**

The MFA's collection of more than one thousand works of Korean art is rich in ceramics. Among them, those usually identified as the most spontaneous or "nonchalant" are the *buncheong* wares of the fifteenth and sixteenth centuries. Buncheong ceramics are made of coarse stoneware covered in slip and decorated in many different techniques. Celadons from the Goryeo period are usually described as refined and elegant, but these wares too can be said to have a nonchalant quality about them, in that they are often not quite symmetrical, and sometimes the relative scale of the different decorative motifs is not realistic. Finally, white porcelains from Korea can also be described as nonchalant because they are often slightly bent or have dips and ridges in them which make them imperfect.

Another strength of the collection, Buddhist paintings, are anything but nonchalant in their execution or deformed in format or style. Korean Buddhist paintings are characterized by refinement and superb quality and technique. Many were taken from Korea to Japan and stored for hundreds of years in Buddhist temples, where they were highly valued as objects of ritual and worship as well as works of great beauty and skill. Metalwork and lacquerware from the Goryeo period are also refined, elegant, and of a high technical quality. It is therefore misleading to follow Yanagi's lead and characterize all Korean art as naïve and unsophisticated.

The Korean collection at the MFA began with a trio of Gilded Age Bostonians fascinated by Japan. Some of the first Korean works to enter the Museum were Buddhist paintings collected in Japan between 1878 and 1889 by devotees William Sturgis Bigelow and Ernest Francisco Fenollosa. The pair traveled there at the suggestion and encouragement of Edward Sylvester Morse, a zoologist from Salem who first went to Japan in 1877 to collect brachiopods. Offered a position at the University of Tokyo, Morse remained for more than two years, during which time he carried out the country's first archaeological excavations. Morse developed an interest in pottery, and his collection of more than five thousand pieces, predominantly tea wares, was eventually purchased by the MFA in 1892. Among them was a group of 112 early Korean ceramics (fig. 2). In addition, some of his friends established the Edward Sylvester Morse Memorial Fund after his death in 1925, and this was used to purchase more Korean ceramics. Although Morse wrote at the beginning of the catalogue of his collection that "a small collection of Korean pottery has been brought together to show in a measure what the Japanese really owe to Korea," in fact he reflects the view prevalent among Western scholars at the time that "it is to China that the Japanese as well as all other nations are indebted for many of the methods of work and styles of decoration in porcelain and pottery." He continued, "Indeed the more one studies authentic specimens of Korean pottery, the more impressed he becomes that . . . Korea gave to Japan nothing beyond a number of industrious potters who, in early centuries, brought the lathe-turned mortuary pottery and later the *mishima* decoration which the Japanese rapidly converted into a highly artistic form."[7] This somewhat dismissive statement includes some truth: funerary stoneware technology was transferred to Japan from Korea from the fourth to fifth centuries, and the stamped slip-decorated mishima or buncheong wares were also taken to Japan in the sixteenth century, when potters left Korea for Japan as a result of the Japanese invasion of 1592, sometimes called the "Pottery Wars." In fact it was due to such Korean potters that porcelain developed in Japan in the seventeenth century.

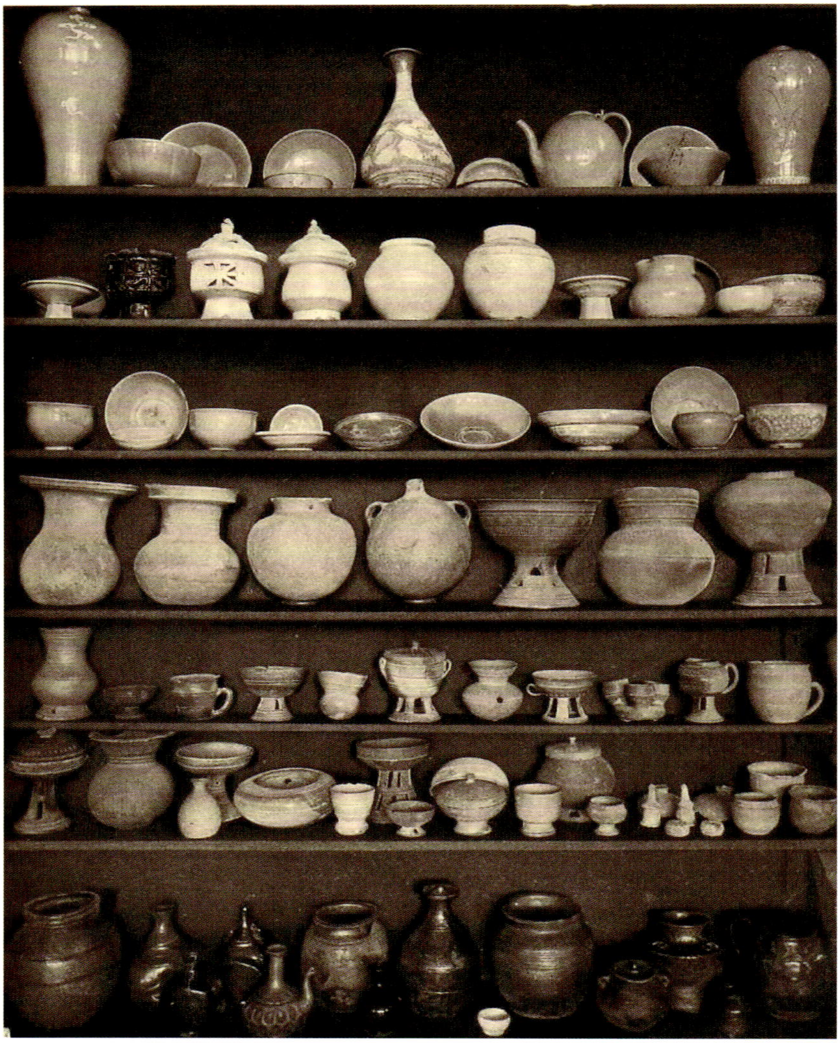

fig. 2. **Early Korean ceramics in the Edward Sylvester Morse Collection, as originally displayed at the MFA.**

Thirty-one pieces of Korean art came to the MFA through Bigelow, who collected them during the seven years he spent in Japan. These include fine paintings, metalwork, ceramics, and lacquer. Whether he knew that they were Korean when he collected them is uncertain, but MFA curators thought at least some of them to be Chinese or Japanese when they accessioned them. Bigelow was the son and grandson of famous Bostonian surgeons but abandoned medicine for Japan, where he lived from 1882 to 1889. Both he and Fenollosa were no doubt inspired by the Centennial Exhibition in Philadelphia in 1876, where many Japanese artifacts were displayed. Bigelow's interests were wide-ranging, and his family's wealth allowed him to amass more than forty thousand works, all of which were donated to the MFA.

Born in Salem, Fenollosa was the son of a Spanish musician. Although he worked as a professor of Philosophy and Political Economy at the University of Tokyo, he became passionately interested in Japanese art, particularly paintings. Paradoxically, it was partly through the efforts of Bigelow and Fenollosa that the modernizing Japanese came to realize the importance of their own ancient culture. Fenollosa's *Epochs of Chinese and Japanese Art*, published in 1913 after his death, was a groundbreaking history of East Asian art. In it, he makes reference to the high quality of early Korean Buddhist art and is much more positive than Morse about the debt Japan owed to Korea. Fenollosa's collection was purchased and donated to the MFA by wealthy Bostonian physician Charles Goddard Weld. It is now known as the Fenollosa-Weld Collection. Twenty-two of these works are Korean.

Bigelow and Fenollosa could not have been so successful in Japan without the aid of their Japanese friend, translator, connoisseur, and advisor Okakura Kakuzō, with whom they traveled widely around Japan. Originally one of Fenollosa's students, Okakura later became advisor and curator at the MFA from 1904 to 1913. Author of *Ideals of the East* and *The Book of Tea*, Okakura was an eloquent spokesperson who could translate the ways of Asia for a Bostonian audience, which included the collector Isabella Stewart Gardner. Okakura established a Special Korean Pottery Fund, through which he purchased celadons and bronze mirrors. And, testimony to his immaculate taste, one of the most important works in the Korean collection belonged to Okakura personally—an exceptional eighth-century gilt-bronze *Medicine Buddha*, which was donated to the MFA after Okakura's death by Edward Jackson Holmes (see p. 37).

A group of sixty photographs of Korea taken between 1882 and 1883 by Percival Lowell, a descendant of the prominent Boston Lowell family, are of great historical significance. Now in the MFA collection, they record his time as an intimate of Korean King Gojong (reigned 1863–1907), of whom he was uniquely allowed to take photographs sitting in Gyeongbok Palace (fig. 3). Lowell had the remarkable experience of being the escort for ten members of Korea's first diplomatic mission to the United States via Japan in 1883 (fig. 4). He spent a decade in Asia and wrote *Choson, the Land of the Morning Calm* in 1886. He later became an astronomer and founded the Lowell Observatory in Flagstaff, Arizona.

The other great collection of Korean art came to the MFA in 1950 as a bequest from Charles Bain Hoyt. It consists mainly of ceramics but also includes some metalwork. Hoyt also collected fine Chinese ceramics, particularly of the Song dynasty (960–1279). His wealth came from an inherited share of the Bain Wagon

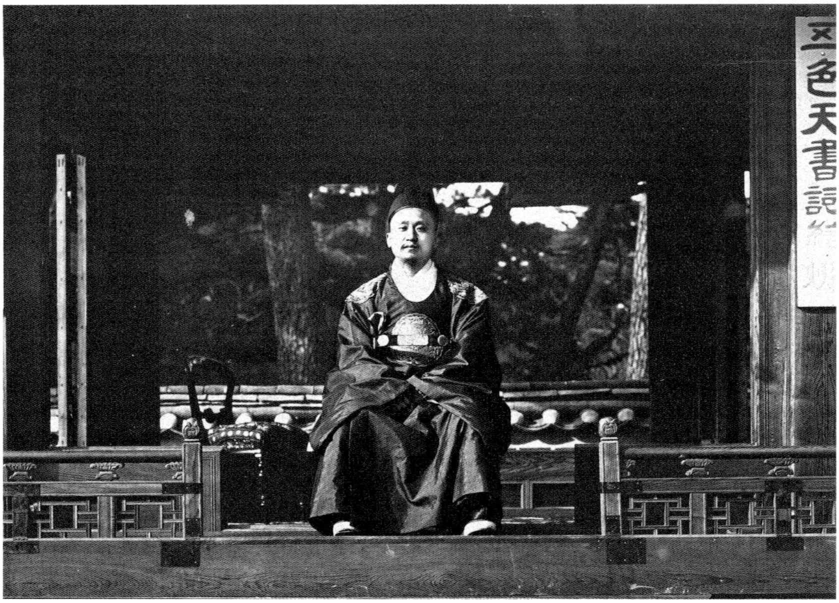

fig. 3. **Percival Lowell (American, 1855–1916).** ***His Majesty the King of Korea*****, 1884.**

Company, which allowed him to spend his life collecting and studying Asian ceramics. He acquired the foundation of his great Korean collection in Paris, where it had been brought from Korea during World War I. An honorary curator at the Fogg Museum at Harvard University and a close friend of the art historian Langdon Warner, Hoyt not only left his collection to the MFA but also established a purchase fund from which the Museum continues to benefit. The Hoyt collection of nearly three hundred pieces has remained relatively unknown, partly because of the restriction he made stipulating that it should not be lent anywhere. It is unparalleled in the United States and perhaps only rivaled in the West by the Gompertz Collection at the Fitzwilliam Museum, Cambridge, England. Whether Hoyt and Godfrey Gompertz, two transatlantic collectors of superb Goryeo celadons, knew each other personally is unknown, but Gompertz definitely knew and appreciated the Hoyt Collection when he wrote his 1963 groundbreaking study, *Korean Celadon and Other Wares of the Koryo Dynasty*, as he included several pieces as illustrations.

Other donors of Korean art to the MFA are Denman Waldo Ross, Robert Treat Paine Jr., and Hervey Edward Wetzel. Ross, one of the major and most wide-ranging donors to the MFA, served as a trustee for nearly forty years, from 1895 to 1934, and donated thirty-nine Korean pieces, some jointly with Bigelow. In more recent years, Jan Fontein, an Asian art scholar who worked at the MFA from 1968 to 1987 (becoming director in 1976), acquired 253 works of Korean art

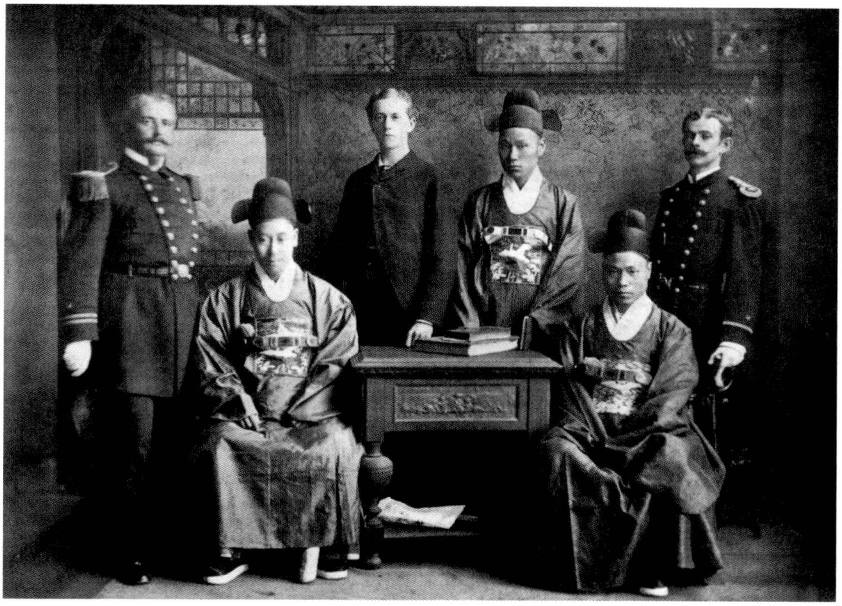

fig. 4. **The Korean embassy to the United States, 1883. Percival Lowell is standing center left.**

and archaeology for the Museum. He also organized the traveling loan exhibition from Korea entitled *5000 Years of Korean Art* in 1980 and opened the first Korean Gallery in 1982, celebrating the hundredth anniversary of diplomatic relations between Korea and the United States.

The city of Boston continues to have a close relationship with Korea, with increasing numbers of Koreans coming to study in the many schools and colleges in the area. In 2003, the Korean National Research Institute for Cultural Heritage carried out a survey of the MFA's Korean collection and as a result there are digital photographs of the entire collection on the Museum's website, making them accessible to a worldwide audience at *www.mfa.org/collections.*

The MFA also continues to acquire Korean art through purchase and donation, in order to keep the collection abreast of the times and reflect today's Korea as well as yesterday's. Thanks to the Korea Foundation, the MFA is able to open a renovated and redesigned Korean Gallery in 2012, which will enable new generations to see and appreciate the beauty of Korean art both past and present, and the efforts of those early scholars, travelers, and collectors.

NOTES

1. Martina Deuchler, "Connoisseurs and Artisans: A Social View of Korean Culture," in *Korean Art from the Gompertz and Other Collections in the Fitzwilliam Museum, Cambridge*, by Yun Yong-I (New York: Cambridge University Press, 2005), 3–11.

2. Martina Deuchler, *The Confucian Transformation of Korea: A Study of Society and Ideology* (Cambridge, MA: Harvard University Press, 1992), 29.

3. Lee Ki-baik, *A New History of Korea*, trans. Edward E. Wagner and Edward J. Schulz (Cambridge, MA: Harvard University Press, 1984), 189.

4. See Burglind Jungmann, *Painters as Envoys: Korean Inspiration in Eighteenth-Century Japanese Nanga* (Princeton: Princeton University Press, 2004).

5. Yanagi Soetsu quoted in G. St. G. M. Gompertz, *Korean Pottery and Porcelain of the Yi Period* (London: Faber and Faber, 1968), 8.

6. Bernard Leach quoted in Gompertz, *Korean Pottery and Porcelain of the Yi Period*, 9.

7. Edward Sylvester Morse, "Korean Pottery," in *Catalogue of the Morse Collection of Japanese Pottery* (Boston: Museum of Fine Arts, 1901), 25–31.

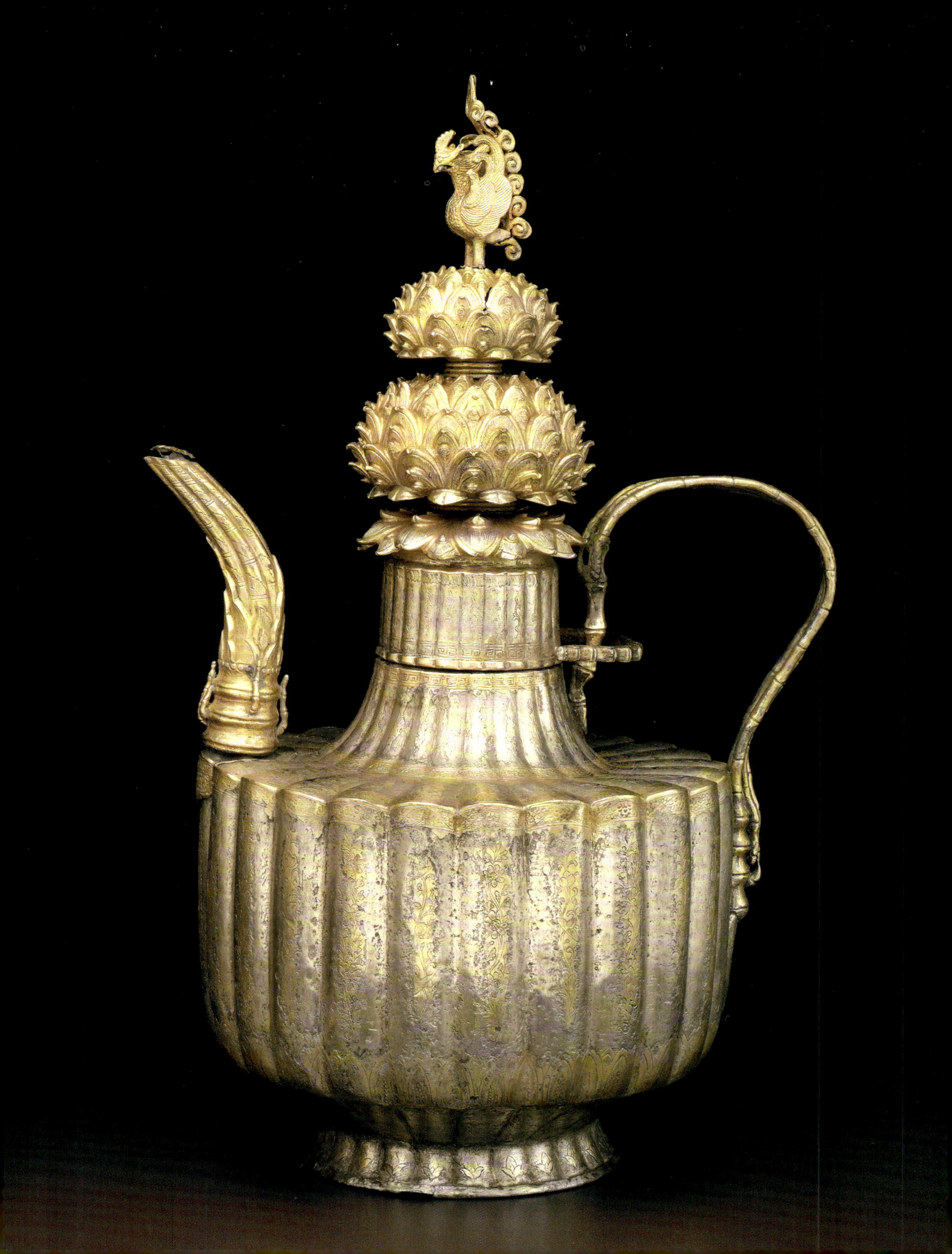

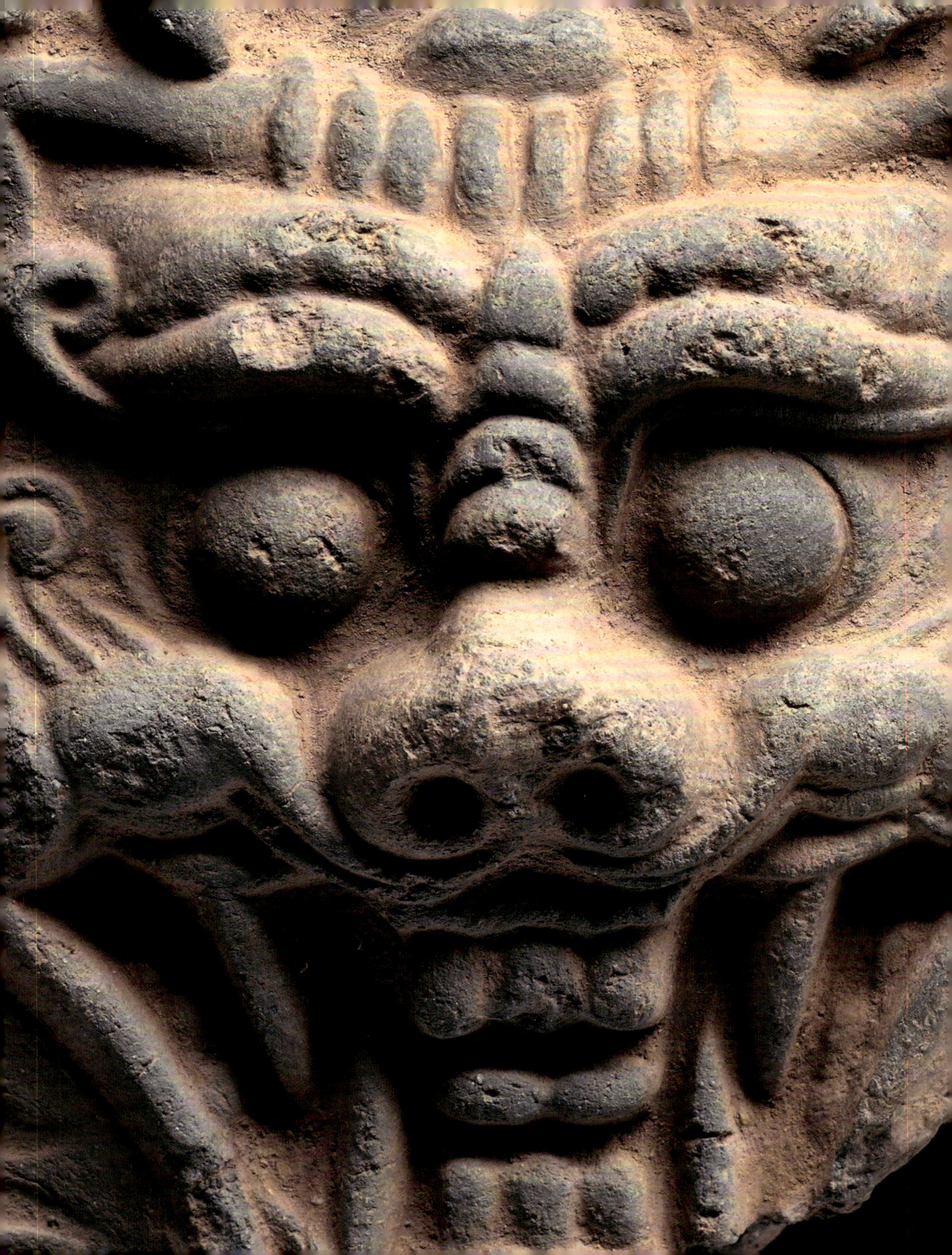

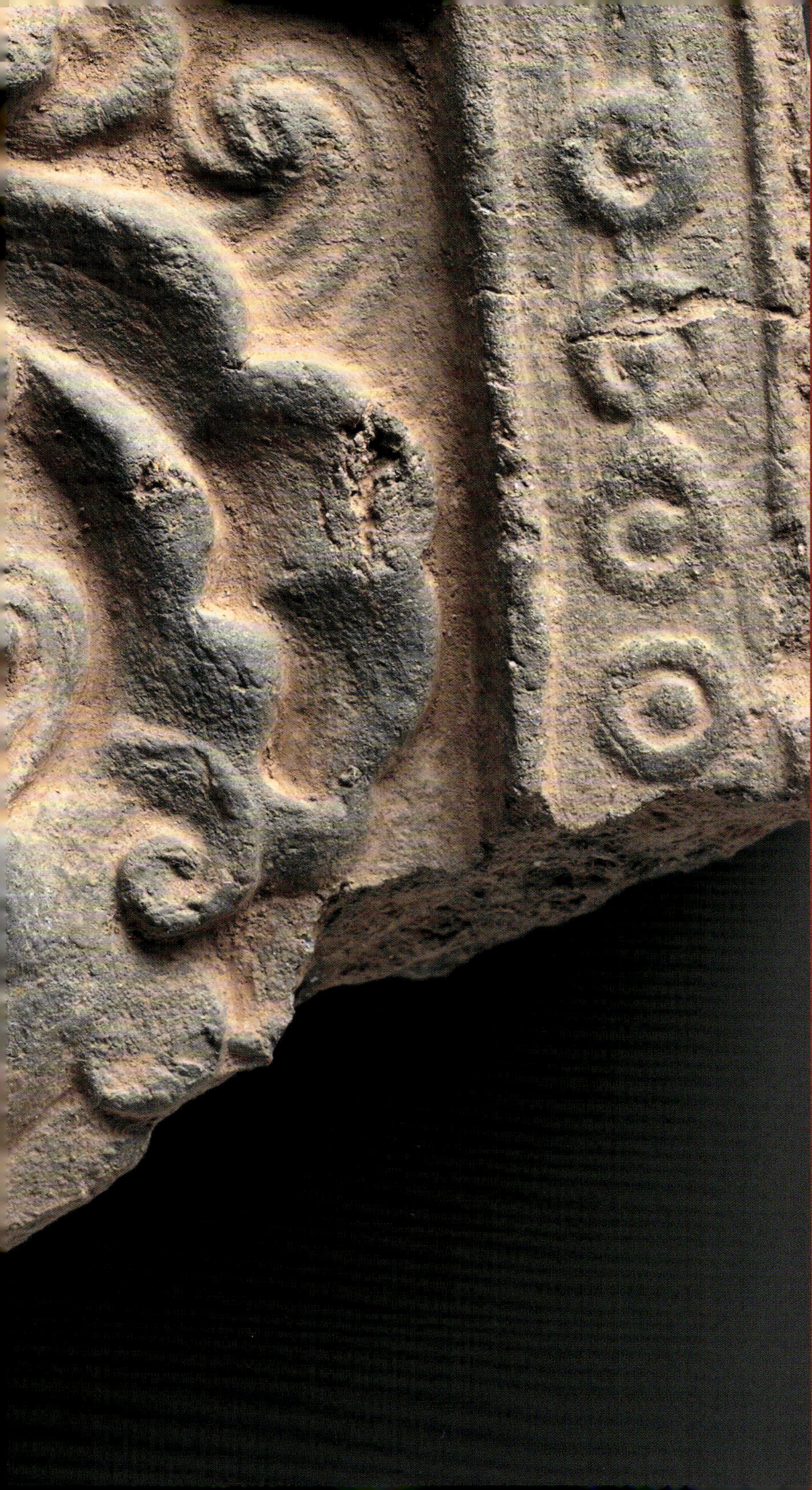

1 EARLY KOREA to the tenth century

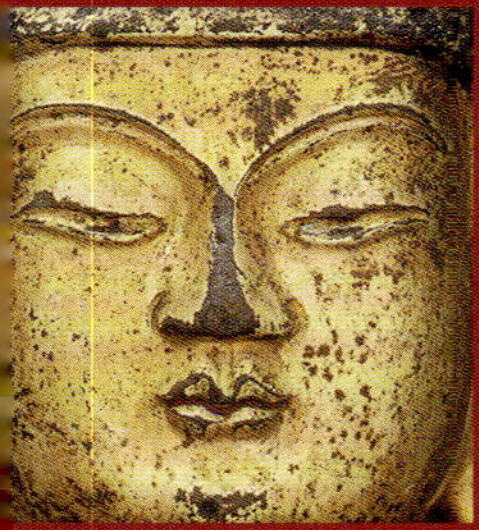
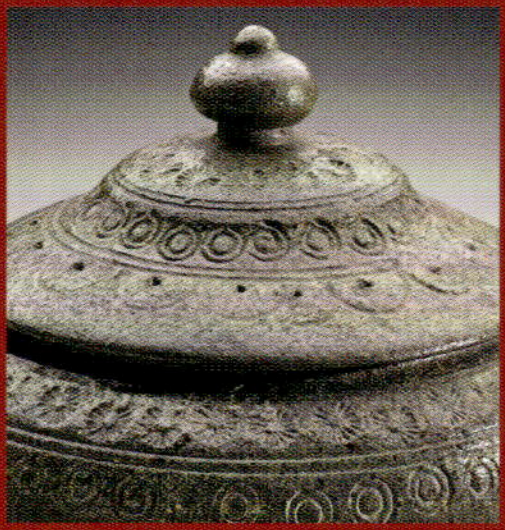
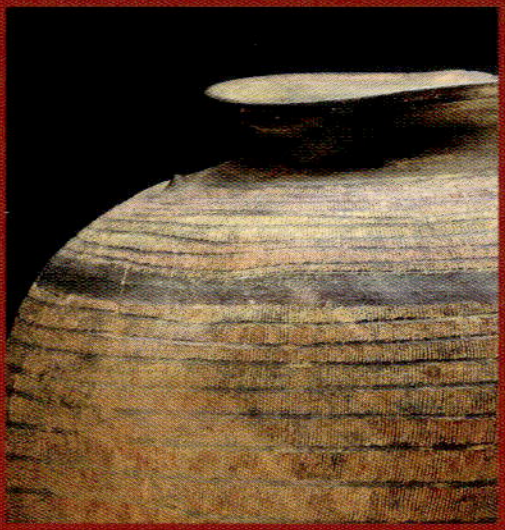
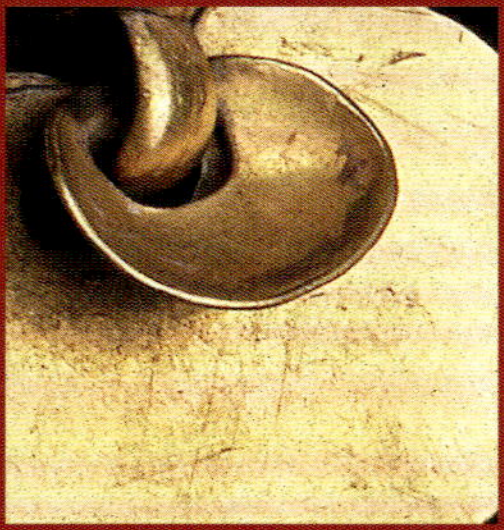
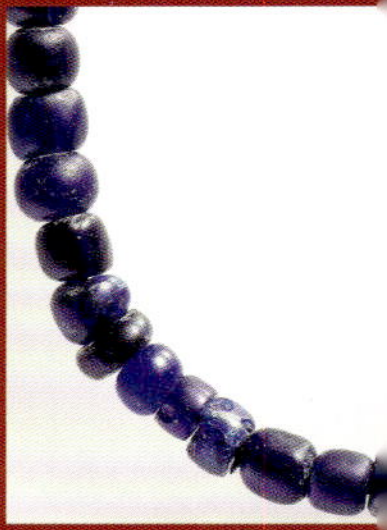

Early Korea to the Tenth Century

> What lies on the other side of China is unknown land. But high mountains rise up densely across from Kantu. These lie over in the land of Silla, which is rich in gold. Mohammedans who visit this country are often persuaded by its fine qualities to settle down there. Ghorraib, kino resin, aloe, camphor, nails, saddles, porcelain, atlas, cinnamon and galanga are exported from there.
>
> Ibn Khordhbeh, Arab trader, 9th century

Hundreds of archaeological sites dating to the Neolithic period indicate that the Korean peninsula sustained a thriving population of hunters, fishers, and gatherers from 6000 to 1000 B.C. The people used comb-patterned and other types of pottery, as well as shell, stone, and bone tools. During the Bronze Age, from 1000 to 300 B.C., a Tungusic people immigrated to the area from the north, bringing about a great change in the way of life. They developed fortified hillside dwellings, cultivated rice, and used bronze tools and undecorated burnished pottery. Elite members of this society were buried in cists (tombs lined with stone slabs), or sometimes underneath standing stones called dolmen.

Jar burials are characteristic of the period from 300 B.C. to A.D. 300, particularly in southern Korea. In the north, the rulers of China's Han dynasty set up five commanderies, the most famous and long lasting of which was Lelang (Nangnang in Korean). The Chinese also introduced iron technology to Korea at this time. Chinese lacquer, bronzes, and silks excavated from Han-style chamber tombs in the Pyongyang area tell us that there was active trade.

During the Three Kingdoms period (57 B.C.–A.D. 668), Korea's mountainous peninsula was divided into the large Goguryeo kingdom in the north and the Baekje and Silla kingdoms in the south, with Baekje to the west and Silla to the east. A south-central confederation of states called Gaya was eventually absorbed into Silla. The native shamanistic religion flourished during the Three Kindoms period, with Silla kings and queens interceding with the gods on behalf of their subjects. The production of sophisticated sheet-metal gold crowns and gold and silver jewelry led to Silla becoming known by Arab travelers as the land of gold. Silla craftsmen also used stoneware technology to manufacture large and dramatic funerary wares decorated with combed and pierced patterns.

After Buddhism was introduced into Silla from China in the sixth century, Koreans began to practice cremation, which required the production of smaller funerary urns. Many magnificent Buddhist temples were built, and uniquely Korean sculptures were produced in stone and bronze as Buddhism gradually replaced Shamanism. Sculptors, potters, and other artists from Silla and Baekje frequently visited Japan during this period and took their artistic traditions and technologies with them. Many Japanese sculptures, such as the famous seventh-century wooden Kudara Kannon in the Horyuji temple in Nara, show evidence of Korean craftsmanship.

After most of the Korean peninsula was brought under the Unified Silla (A.D. 668–935), the rulers modeled their splendid capital at Gyeongju on the Tang Chinese capital of Chang'an (present Xian), the biggest city in the world in the eighth century and the center of the overland Silk Road, which stretched from the Mediterranean Sea to Gyeongju and Nara, Japan. Great Korean sculptures produced in the eighth century, such as the huge Sakyamuni Buddha at Seokguram cave temple outside Gyeongju, show an international style influenced by many cultures along that trade route. The archaeological evidence strongly suggests that for much of the Three Kingdoms and Unified Silla periods, despite the movement of traders and settlers in both directions along the Silk Road, the main flow of artistic styles was from China and Korea to Japan. Korea acted as both a cultural bridge and an independent source of inspiration for Japanese art.

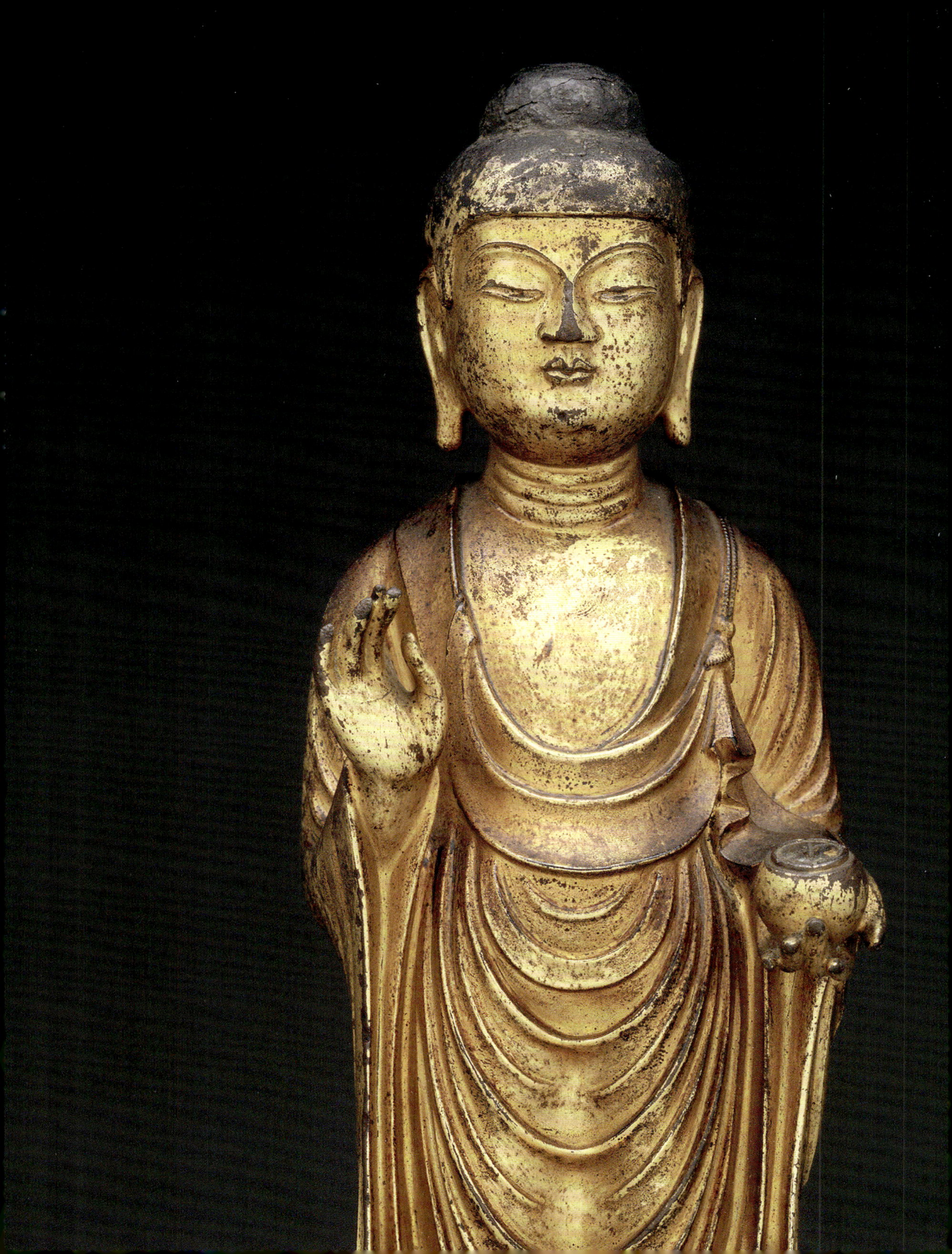

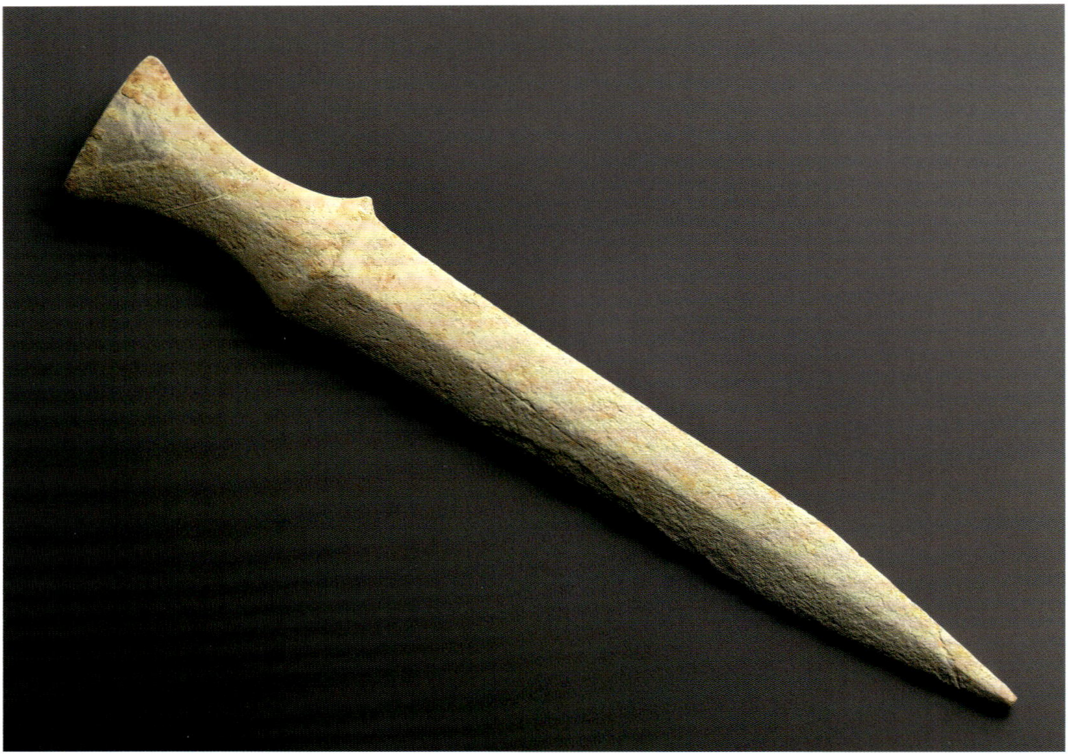

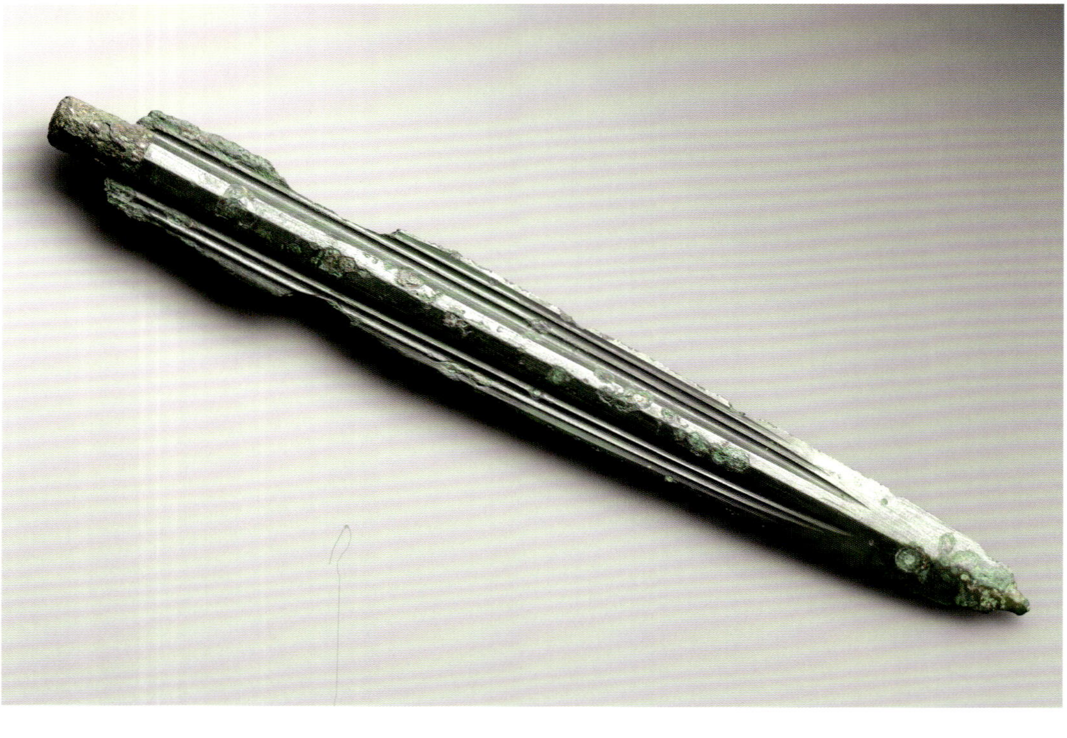

Dagger

Bronze Age, 10th–3rd century B.C.

Slate

L. 40 cm (15¾ in.)

Keith McLeod Fund 1977.480

Dagger

Bronze Age, 5th–3rd century B.C.

Bronze

L. 37.5 cm (14¾ in.)

Keith McLeod Fund 1977.482

Although both of these daggers were excavated from tombs, only the bronze one was originally used. The dagger made of fine polished stone was most likely a ceremonial instrument. Similar stone daggers have been excavated from Bronze Age dolmens and cists, where they were buried alongside thin-walled burnished-red or burnished-black pots, jade beads, bronze mirrors, and the remains of their owners, who were most likely members of an elite class. The slim profile of the bronze dagger is typically Korean, in contrast to the more curvaceous and mandolin-shaped daggers that were imported from Liaoning in northeast China until the fourth century B.C. Korean-style daggers were made with stone molds rather than the ceramic piece molds used to make bronzes in China.

Storage jar with cord marks

Three Kingdoms period, Gaya, 4th century

This large storage jar is made of coils of stoneware clay that were built up by hand and then beaten flat inside and out. The rows of vertical incisions around the belly were probably created with a wooden comb or roller, and then the completed body was decorated with a pinched lug on each shoulder. When the jar was fired at high temperatures in the kiln, the mixture of silicon and aluminum in the stoneware clay fused together, making the vessel watertight. This type of pottery therefore represents a great advance over porous earthenware.

Korean potters were producing stoneware pottery by the fourth century, making them second only to the Chinese. Potters who emigrated from the Gaya region in south-central Korea transferred the stoneware technique to Japan during this period. The Japanese call this type of pottery *sueki* ware.

This jar was fired at a temperature of 800–1000 degrees centigrade in a sloping kiln that climbed up a hillside, a design introduced from China. The jar's neck acquired its undulating form when it partially collapsed during firing. The reddish color is due to oxidization of the clay in the kiln, and the natural glaze is made by ash falling serendipitously from the kiln roof. Many stoneware jars like this one have been excavated from Gaya tombs in the area around present-day Gimhae, near Busan, giving rise to the Korean name, Gimhae ware.

Stoneware with ash glaze
H. 43.2 cm (17 in.), w. 40.6 cm (16 in.)
Museum purchase with funds from the Charles Bain Hoyt Fund and with funds donated by Hung Cheng, Jan Dorman, Kate Feldstein, Bill Clark, and Pat Pratt 2005.122

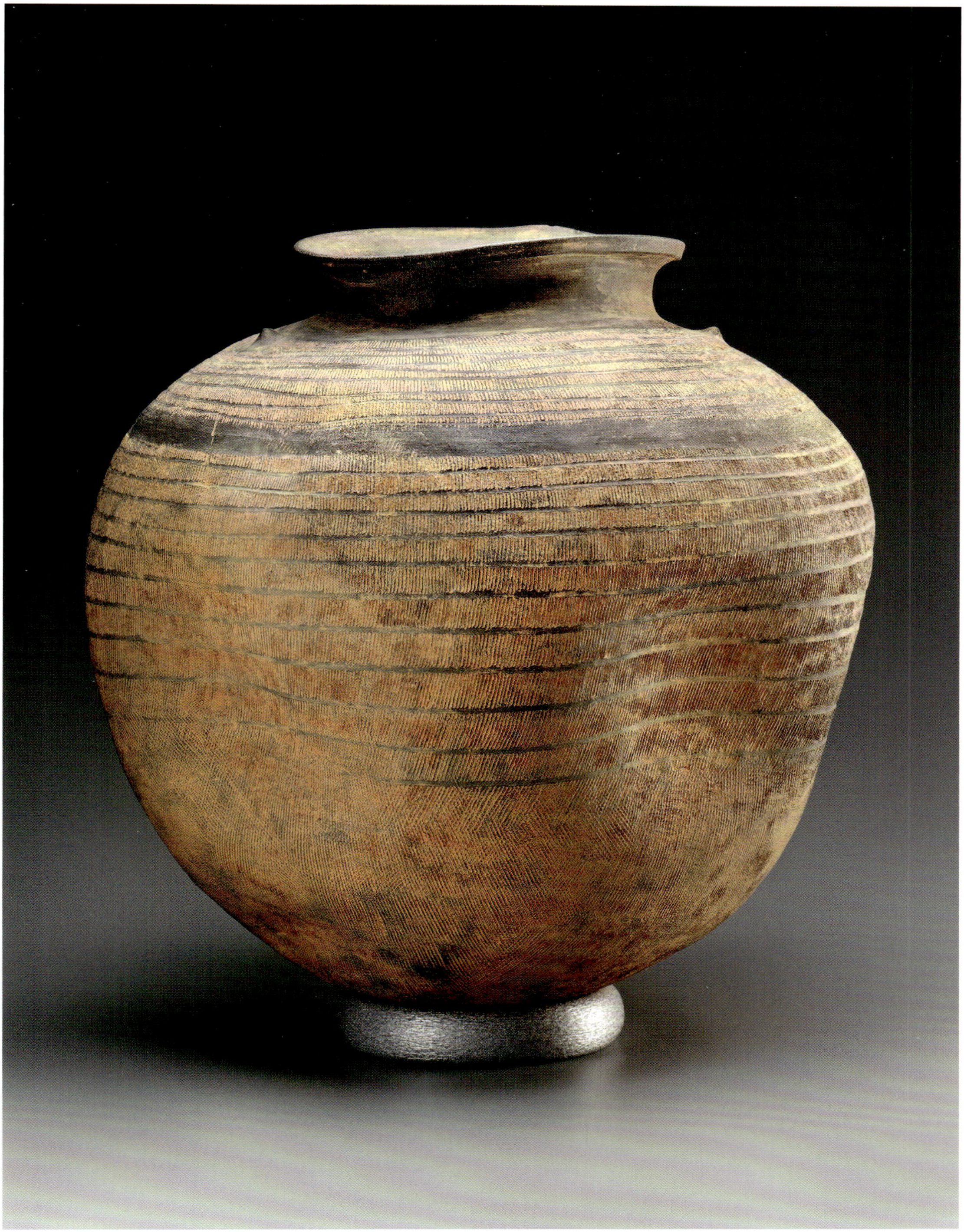

Long-necked jar and stand

Three Kingdoms period, Silla, 5th–6th century

Large vessels on stands were buried in great numbers in tombs of the Three Kingdoms period from about A.D. 300 to 600. They held ritual wine and food for shamanistic burial rites. The biggest were used outdoors, perhaps in state rituals. Jars of the long-necked variety, such as this one, were commonly buried in Silla tombs of this period.

This jar has a rounded base for fitting on its tall, dramatic stand, which was made separately. Other jars have a shorter integrated stand or foot ring. The stand acts as a support. Its pierced holes, here rectangular and aligned in alternating rows, on other examples are sometimes triangular and aligned directly beneath one another. Its zigzag comb patterns were used on pottery in Korea as early as 5000 B.C.

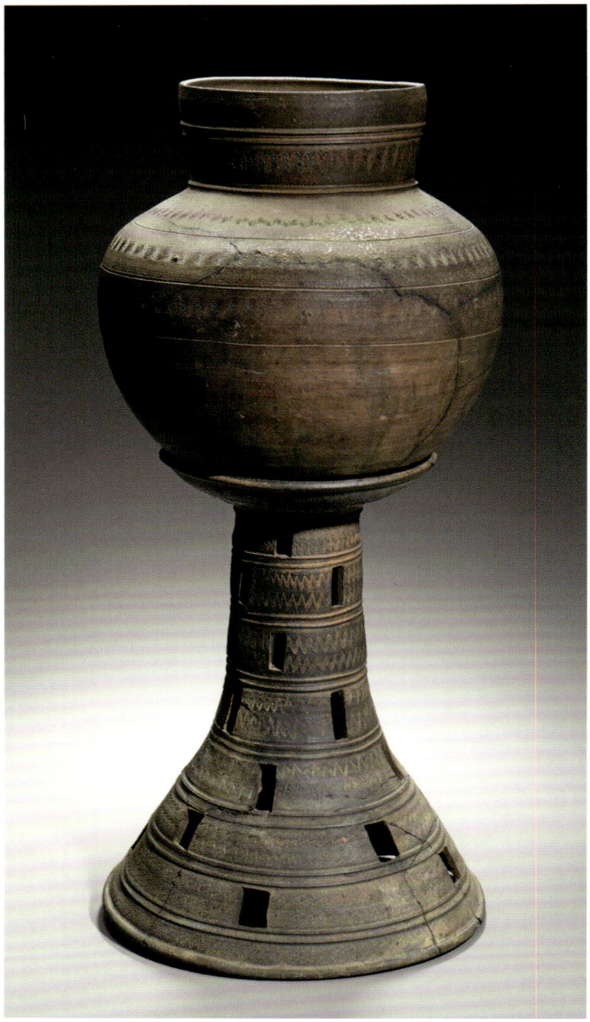

Stoneware with incised decoration and perforations
Jar: H. 30.2 cm (11 7/8 in.), diam. of rim: 17.8 cm (7 in.)
Stand: H. 34.4 cm (13 9/16 in.); diam. of rim: 20 cm (7 7/8 in.); diam. of foot: 27.8 cm (10 15/16 in.)
Edward Sylvester Morse Collection. Museum purchase with funds donated by contribution 92.2959a–b

Pottery lamp with three cups

Three Kingdoms period, Silla, 5th–6th century

This oil lamp is constructed with three small cups connected to a doughnut-shaped hollow base. The lamp can be filled through any one of the cups. This type may be a later form of a lamp with seven cups excavated from the Han Chinese commandery of Lelang near Pyongyang in North Korea. A number of three-cup lamps have been excavated from Three Kingdoms–period tombs in South Korea. Some, such as one excavated in 1924 from the royal Gold Bell Tomb in the Silla capital of Gyeongju, are more elaborately constructed and are decorated with hanging pottery leaves and stand on pierced foot rings. The cups of this lamp were probably formed by throwing on a wheel; the base was probably built by hand.

Stoneware with ash glaze
H. 10.4 cm (4 1/8 in.), w. 12.5 cm (4 15/16 in.)
Edward Sylvester Morse Collection 92.2964

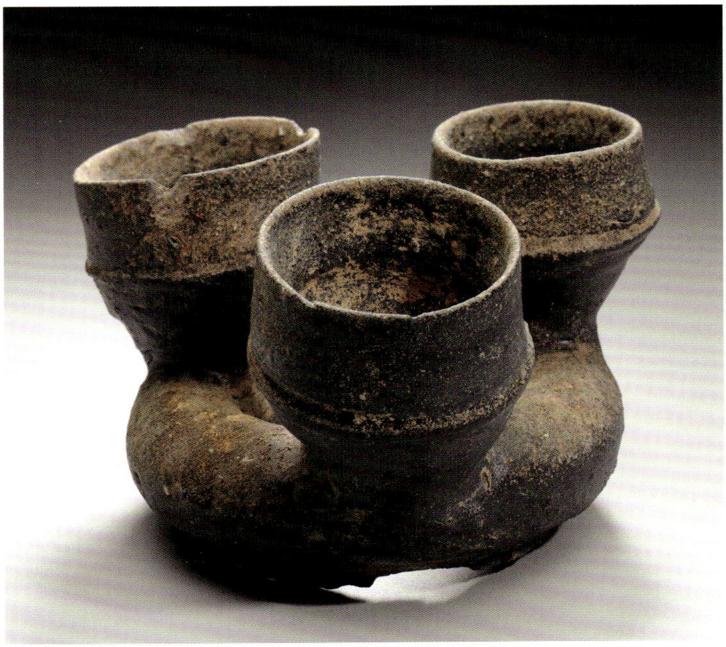

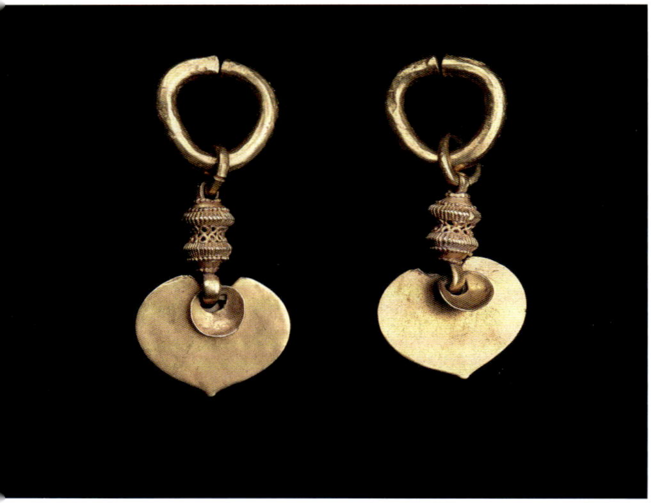

Pair of earrings

Three Kingdoms period, Silla, 6th century

Large numbers of gold earrings have been excavated from royal tombs in the area of Silla's capital, Gyeongju, together with smaller numbers of belts and crowns. The presence of many more earrings than other adornments suggests that they were worn by members of the upper echelons of Silla society, both male and female, rather than just buried as grave goods. The sophisticated metalworking techniques used to make gold earrings such as these may be evidence of contact between Silla craftsmen and northern nomadic peoples between Central Asia and China.

These examples are typical of Silla earrings, which usually consist of three parts: a main ring for placing in the pierced earlobe, a middle ornament, and a pendant. This pair has a main ring of solid gold, but in other examples it is made of a wider, hollow tube of sheet metal. The middle ornament here is a hollow hourglass shape with two rows of openwork rings in the center and notched ornaments above and below, with solid gold rings at top and bottom for joining the middle ornament to both the main ring and the pendant. The small beadlike decoration at the top and bottom may have been produced with a granulation technique by which molten droplets of gold are dribbled onto a bed of sand and then picked up individually with tweezers and soldered onto the earrings after they solidify. The pendant forms are heart-shaped leaves with extra, tiny round gold leaves attached in front and behind. Sometimes clusters of such small leaves are attached to the pendants.

Gold

L. 5.3 cm (2 1/16 in.)

Gift of Mrs. Albertine W. F. Valentine, residuary legatee under the will of Hervey E. Wetzel 19.699–700

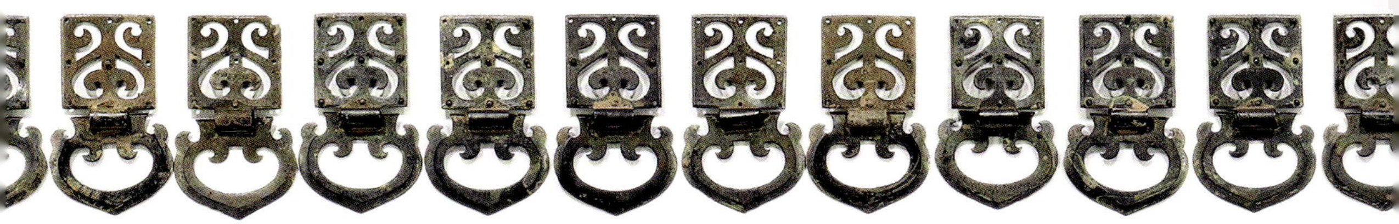

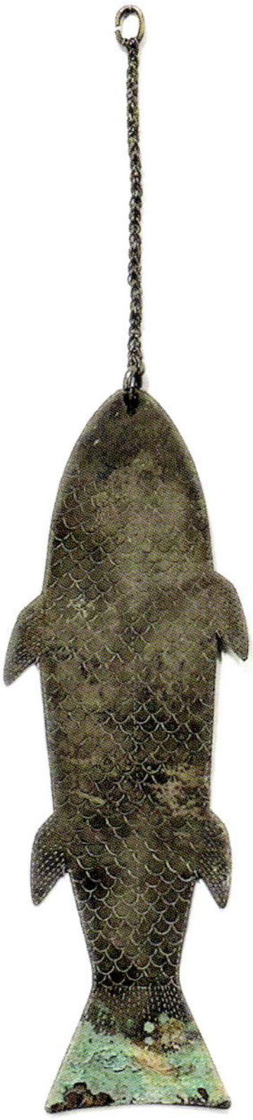

Belt with pendants

Three Kingdoms period, Silla, 5th–6th century

The plaques that make up this silver belt were originally sewn to a backing of fabric or leather. Each plaque is square with pierced, curved designs and hinged to a heart-shaped loop. There are three pendants on this belt. More elaborate belts with as many as thirteen pendants have been excavated from royal tombs near Gyeongju. One of the pendants on this belt consists of a series of ovoid plaques joined together with small squares, whereas the other two, a fish and an openwork cylindrical silver tassel, are suspended on small chains. Other belts have pendants in the shape of small knives, whetstones, purses, or curved jades.

The custom of wearing such belts is thought to have originated with northern nomads from Central Asia. People of the Han and Tang dynasties of China shared it as well. The pendants originally had a practical use that became symbolic over time. In the strictly stratified society of Silla, the wearing of each pendant symbol was codified and regulated in what was called the "bone rank" system. The highest ranks were the "sacred bone" or the "true bone."

Silver
Hook: L. 7.6 cm (3 in.)
Plaque: L. 6 cm (2⅜ in.)
Belt-end ornament: L. 12.5 cm (4⅞ in.)
Waist pendant: L. 68 cm (26¾ in.)
Keith McLeod Fund 68.45.1–35

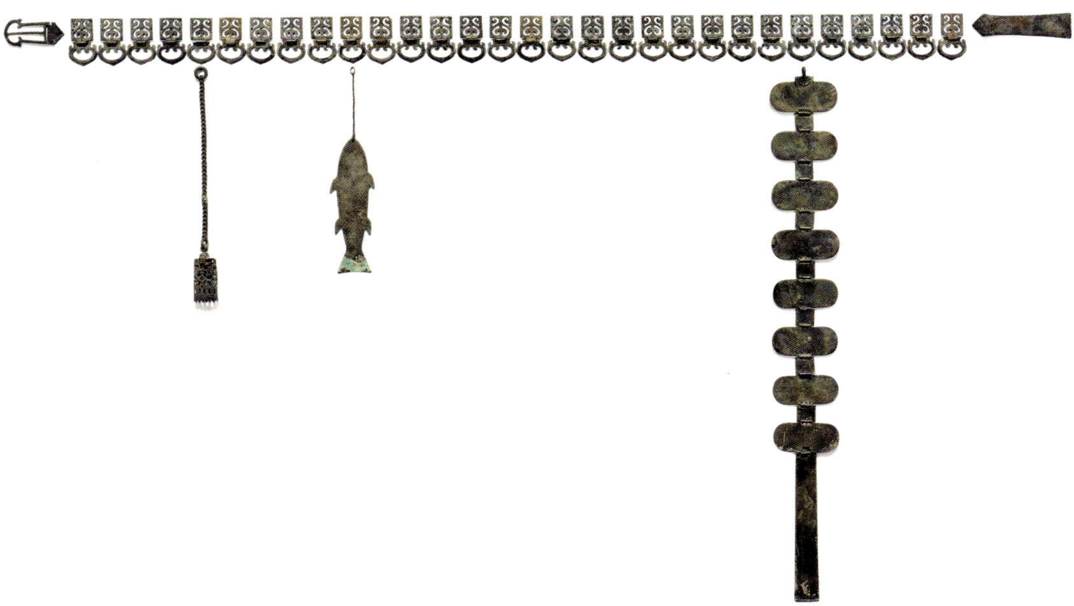

Necklace of blue beads

Three Kingdoms period, 5th–6th century

Glass beads and vessels excavated from tomb and temple sites of the Three Kingdoms period are evidence of Korean trade with Central and Western Asia as well as with China. By the fourth to sixth centuries, some glass beads were being made domestically, but many were imported from as far away as the territories of the Roman, Sassanian, and Syrian empires. Korean craftsmen began to make lead glass without barium about A.D. 400, and then developed it into lead-silica glass between the seventh and tenth centuries.

This necklace consists of fat, tubular blue glass beads. In other necklaces from the period, such beads are mixed with ones made of amber, crystal, or jade. Curved jade beads, which may represent embryos, teeth, or the crescent moon, have also been found on gold crowns and belts.

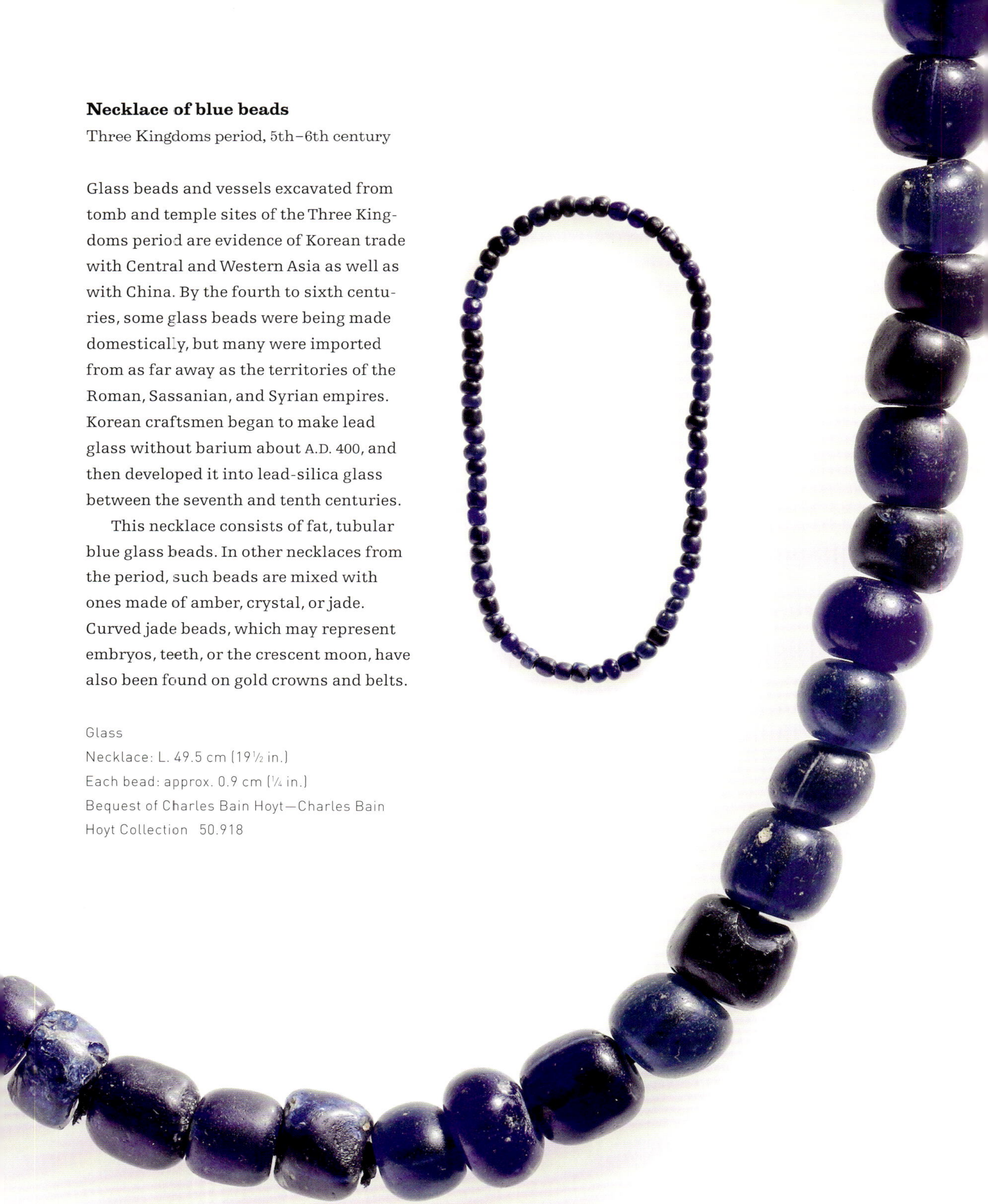

Glass
Necklace: L. 49.5 cm (19½ in.)
Each bead: approx. 0.9 cm (¼ in.)
Bequest of Charles Bain Hoyt—Charles Bain Hoyt Collection 50.918

Medicine Buddha

Unified Silla period, 8th century

This statue is one of the most important examples of early Korean Buddhist sculpture in a Western museum. It is carved in the classic eighth-century Unified Silla style, which originated in China during the Tang dynasty. Korean features here include the openwork octagonal base and the pedestal in the form of a double lotus in deep relief, as well as the figure's relatively large head and hands. The small size indicates that it was used as a personal votive image.

The figure represents the Buddha of Healing (Bhaisajyaguru in Sanskrit or Yaksayeorae in Korean), who may be identified by the medicine jar in his left hand. It may have come from a temple called Yujeomsa in the Diamond Mountains of North Korea. According to legend, Yujeomsa was founded when fifty-three Buddhist images reached Silla from India. Whether or not they originally came from there, fifty-three sculptures were dispersed from Yujeomsa during the Japanese occupation of Korea between 1910 and 1945. The temple itself was destroyed during the Korean War.

Gilt bronze
H. 36 cm (14 3/16 in.)
Gift of Edward Jackson Holmes in memory of his mother, Mrs. W. Scott Fitz 32.436

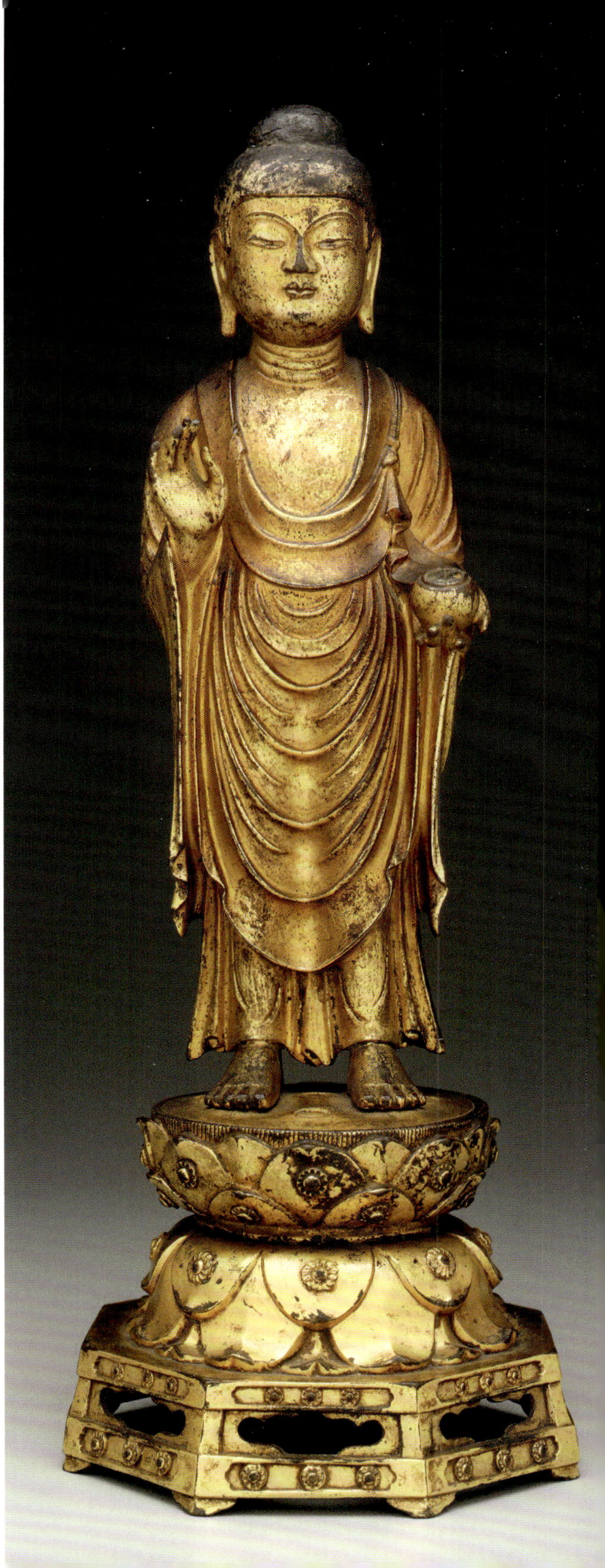

Burial urns with stamped decoration

Unified Silla period, 8th–9th century

Stoneware with natural ash glaze
H. 9.8 cm (3 7/8 in.); diam. of lid: 10 cm (3 15/16 in.);
diam. of foot 7.1 cm (2 13/16 in.)
Bequest of Charles Bain Hoyt—Charles Bain Hoyt Collection
50.959a–b

Stoneware
H. 27 cm (10 5/8 in.); diam. of lid: 22.7 cm (8 15/16 in.);
diam. of foot 17.8 cm (7 in.)
Edward Sylvester Morse Memorial Fund 1992.476a–b

With Korea's adoption of Buddhism came the practice of cremation and the production of burial urns. The smaller of these two urns may have been contained in an outer urn like the bigger one, but they are not a matched set. Each one probably contained a different high-ranking monk's or aristocrat's ashes. The shape of the smaller urn is modeled after gold and silver vessels. It has a lotus-shaped knob, the lotus being a Buddhist symbol of purity. The small stamped spirals and flower designs are arranged in regular rows and may also have been inspired by punched designs on metalwork. The natural ash glaze on the body and lid occurred when kiln ash accidentally fell on the urn during firing. The larger urn has dense, stamped designs of jewels and clouds and perhaps flames in regular rows. Its lug handles have holes pierced in them so the lid could be securely fastened to the body with cords.

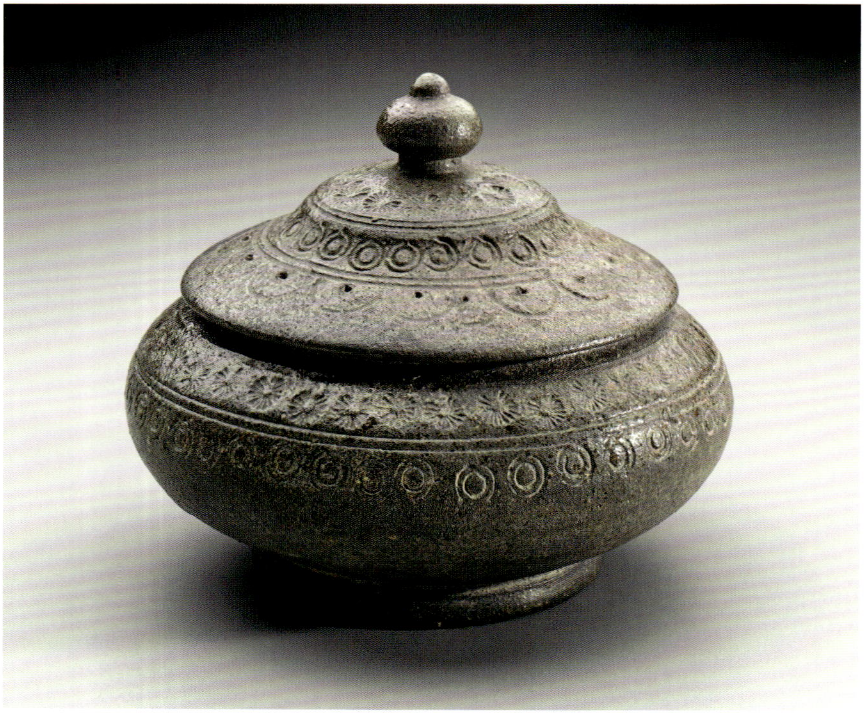

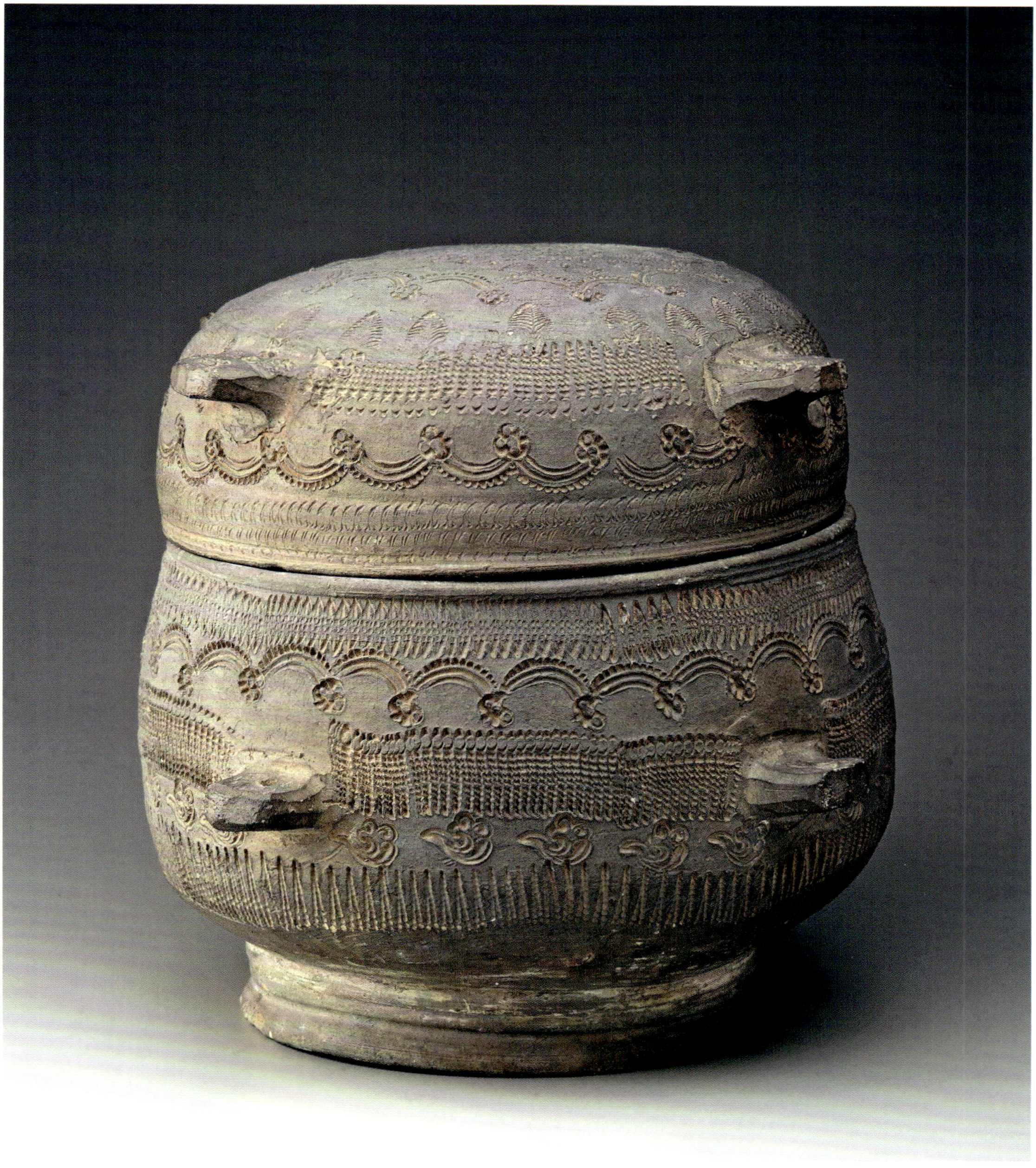

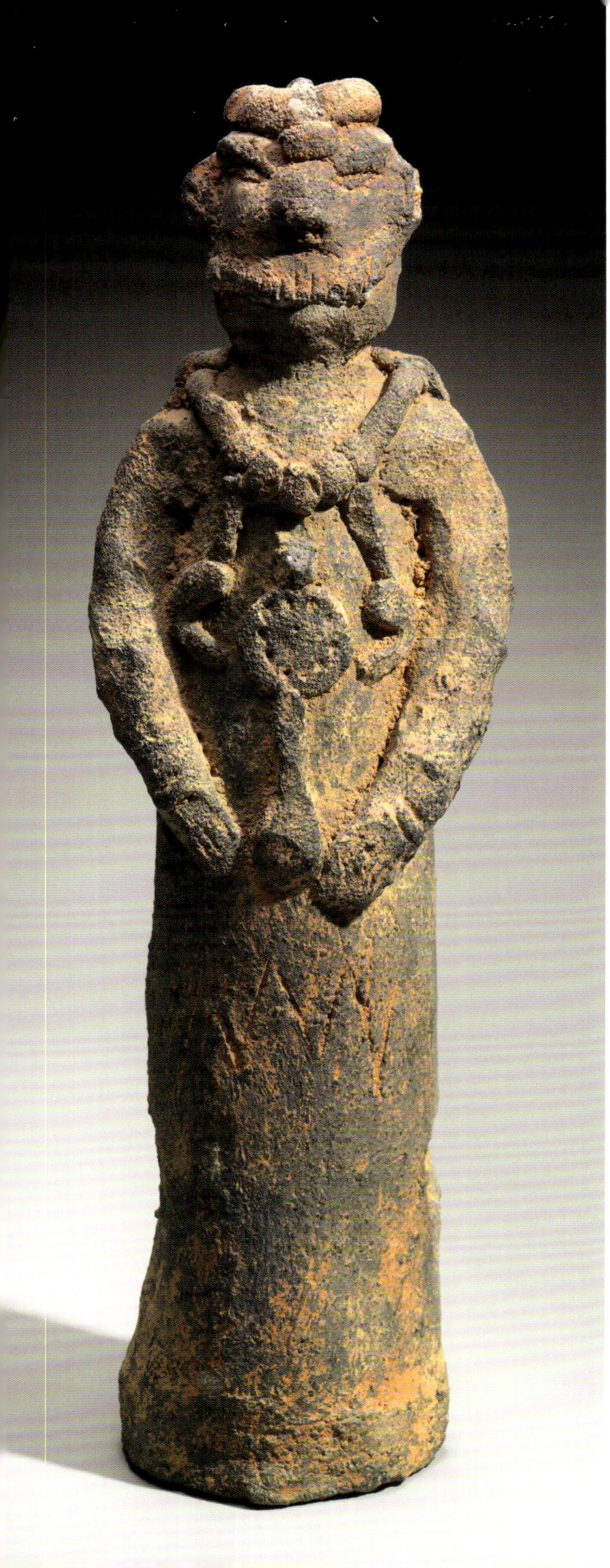

Human figure

Unified Silla period, 8th–9th century

Although small and simply modeled human and animal figures were made in Silla during the Three Kingdoms period for attaching to the outsides of pottery jars, freestanding figures of men and women, horses, oxen, dancers, officials, foreigners, zodiac figures, soldiers, and servants were made only in the Unified Silla period. They were placed in tombs to accompany high-ranking persons in the afterlife, probably in place of the living family members and slaves who were buried alive in earlier times.

This male figure's beard and prominent nose suggest that he may be a foreigner from Central Asia, perhaps from as far west as Iran. He is wearing a carefully modeled necklace decorated with comma-shaped jade pendants and shells. Figures like this one reflect the Unified Silla elite classes' wealthy lifestyle and their connections to the Korean capital at Gyeongju, as well as to Tang-dynasty China and beyond.

Stoneware with applied decoration
H. 26.2 cm (10 5/16 in.), w. 8 cm (3 1/8 in.)
Bequest of Charles Bain Hoyt—Charles Bain Hoyt Collection
50.950

Roof tile with a demon face

Unified Silla period, 8th–9th century

This roof tile is similar to ones excavated from Anapji, an artificial lake in Gyeongju on the grounds of a detached palace once used for state banquets, receptions, and boat trips for foreign embassies. It attests to the magnificence of the Unified Silla capital. Based on the Tang-dynasty Chinese capital of Chang'an (Xian), the largest city in the world in the eighth century, Gyeongju was laid out on a north-south-east-west grid of streets. According to the *Samgukyusa*, the Memorabilia of the Three Kingdoms, "When Silla reached the height of her prosperity, the capital, Gyeongju, consisted of 178,936 houses, 1,360 sections, 55 streets, and 35 mansions. There was a villa and pleasure ground for each of the four seasons, to which aristocrats resorted. . . . During the reign of King Heongang [reigned A.D. 875–886], houses with tiled roofs stood in rows in the capital and not a thatched roof was to be seen."

This tile's ferocious face indicates that it once stood on the end of a roof's top ridge to ward off evil. Opinions vary as to whether the face is that of a monster or a dragon. The building it covered may have been a house, a palace, or one of the many splendid Buddhist temples erected in Gyeongju during this period, when Buddhism enjoyed royal patronage. Tiles at this time were made of low-fired earthenware, produced in molds. Occasionally tiles were glazed with a green lead glaze.

Earthenware with impressed decoration
L. 22.5 cm (8⅞ in.), w. 20 cm (7⅞ in.)
Gift of Colonel John R. Fox 63.1379

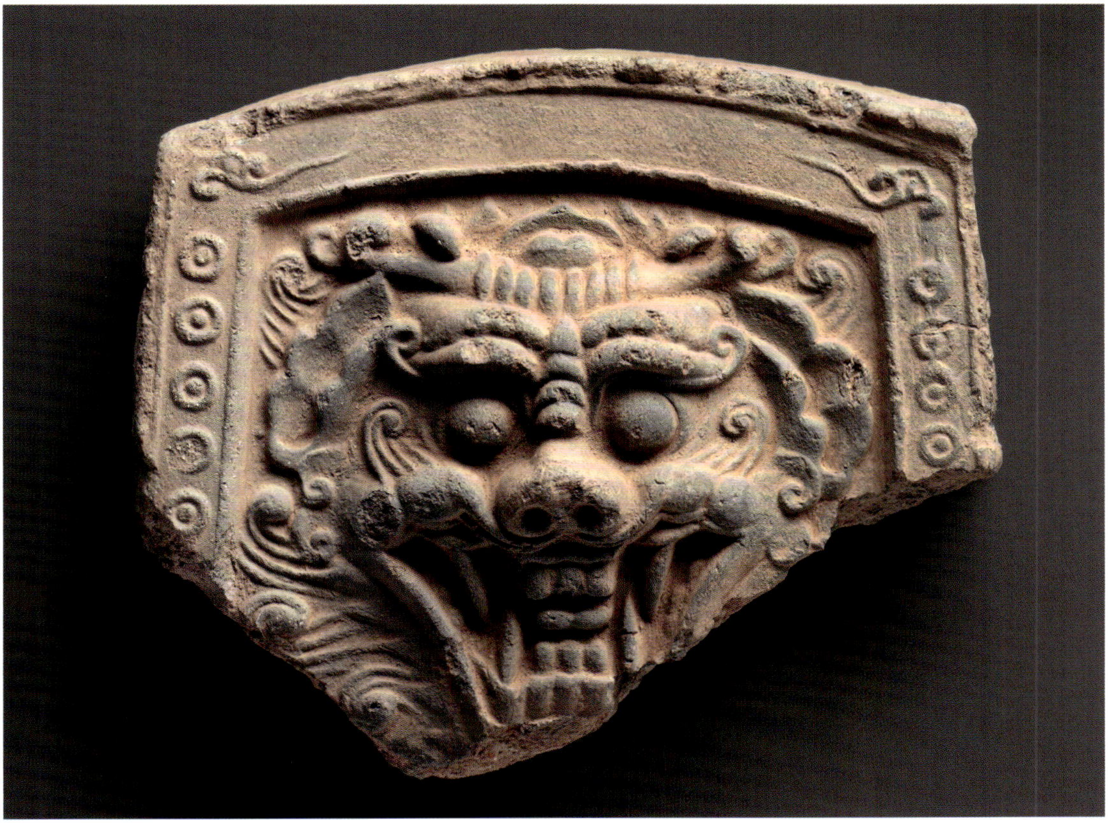

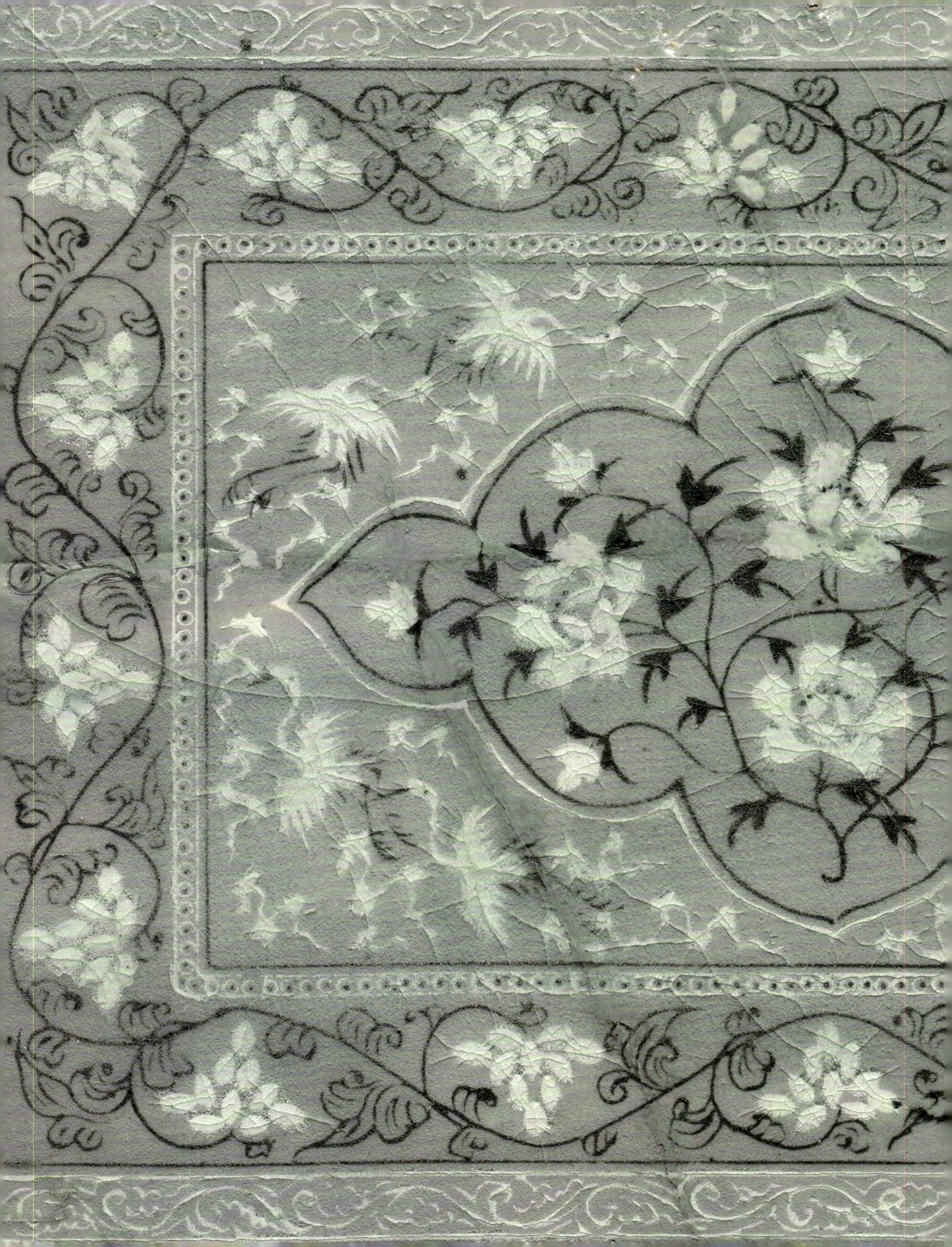

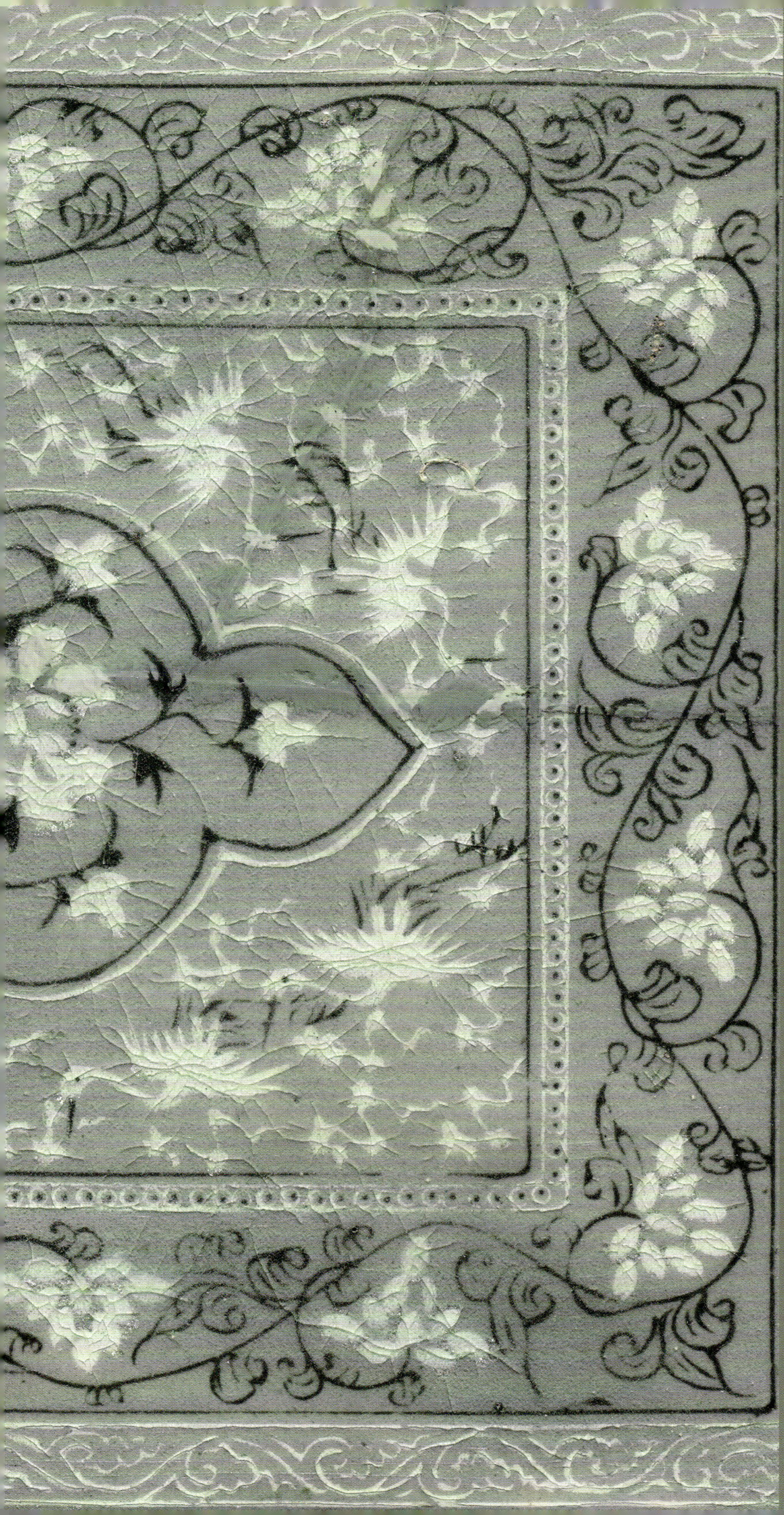

2 GORYEO PERIOD

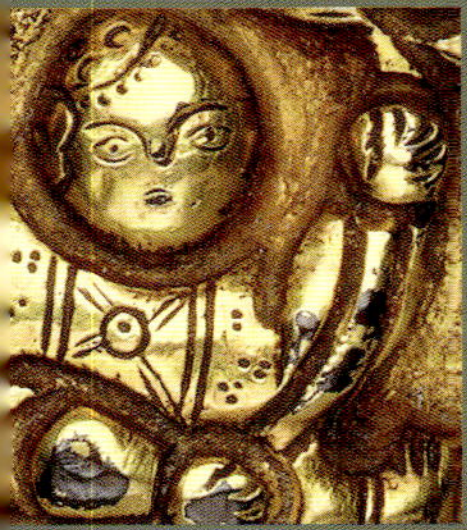
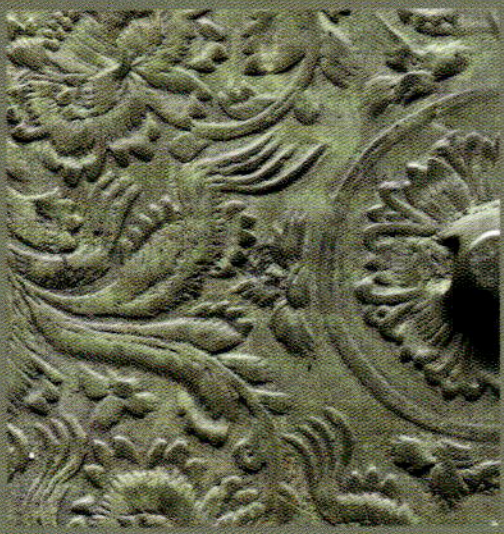
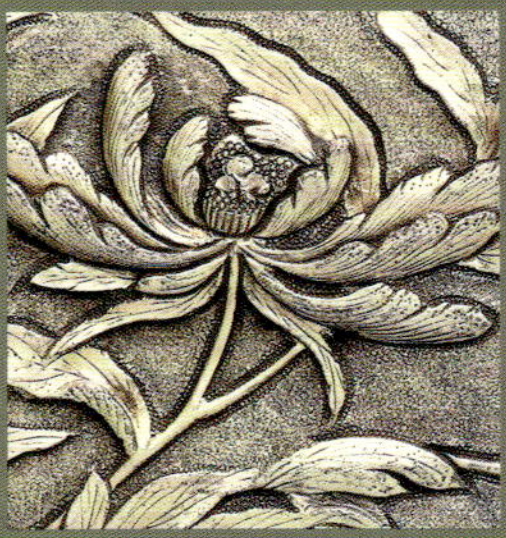
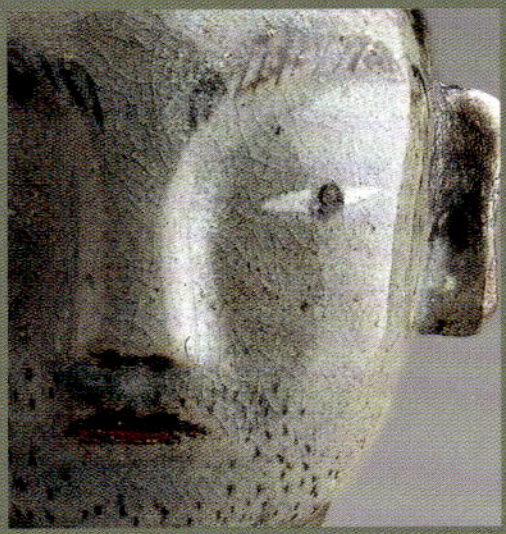
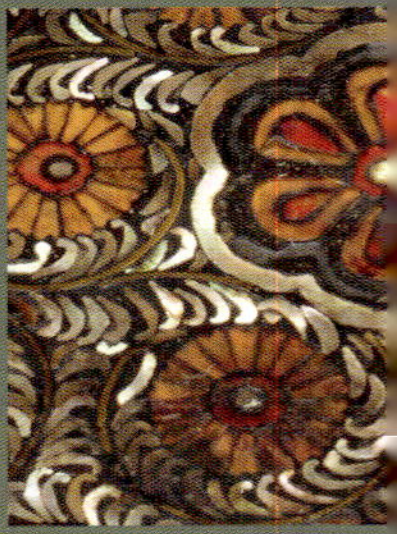

Goryeo Period (918–1392)

> The pottery wares are green in color and are called kingfisher colored by the people of Gaoli. In recent years they have been made more skillfully and their color and luster have become finer. There are wine pots of gourd shape with small covers in the form of a duck amongst lotus flowers.
>
> Xu Jing, Chinese envoy to Goryeo, 1123

The long Goryeo period was an era of great cultural development. The capital moved to a new location at Songdo (present-day Kaesong in North Korea), and during the early Goryeo there was peaceful economic and cultural exchange with Song China. Arab ships recorded having arrived at Songdo's port, evidence of trade between Goryeo and the Middle East. King Uijong's reign (1147–70) is usually regarded as the highpoint of this early period. He is infamous for ordering celadon roof tiles for one of his royal pavilions, an act that was seen by later historians as the epitome of decadent luxury. Invasions from the Khitans and the Mongols led the court to eventually move the capital to Ganghwa Island in 1232. There followed an age of much Mongol influence on Korea and of intermarriage between Korean kings and Mongol princesses.

Buddhism flourished and influenced all aspects of life in the Goryeo period. Temples and religious festivals proliferated, families sent sons to become monks, and artists produced illuminated manuscripts of Buddhist sutras and paintings of Buddhist deities. Commissioning works of art was seen as a way of not only glorifying the church but also accumulating spiritual merit. Reproducing the image or words of the Buddha could have a positive affect on a person's subsequent rebirth. The principal Buddhist deities in the Goryeo period were the historical Buddha Sakyamuni; Amitabha Buddha, who ruled over the Western Paradise of the Pure Land sect; and bodhisattvas such as Ksitigarbha and Avalokitesvara. Bodhisattvas were beings who stayed in the world to help mortals achieve nirvana. Buddhist temple complexes that centered on the worship of these deities always included at least one stone or wood pagoda. The Goryeo buildings that have survived, such as the Hall of Eternal Life at Buseok temple in Andong, show evidence of developed woodworking techniques.

Two of the Goryeo's greatest achievements were the carving of the entire Buddhist scriptures twice on over eighty thousand woodblocks, and the invention of metal movable type, the earliest in the world. The former was done as a kind of prayer in the face of invasion from the Mongols in the thirteenth century. The set of blocks is now stored in Haein temple in South Korea and is thought to be the finest extant version of the Buddhist scriptures. Korea also developed paper making to a fine art during the Goryeo, exporting much to China, especially for printing Buddhist scriptures. Made from pith of the paper mulberry shrub, it was tough enough to withstand the pressure of metal type.

Craftsmen of the Goryeo period produced some of the most exquisite celadons—green-glazed, high-fired stonewares—the world has ever known. Korean celadons were held in great esteem in China from as early as the Song dynasty (960–1279), when they were called "first under heaven" and compared with such high-quality Chinese items as inkstones from Duan, teas from Jianzhou, and peonies from Luoyang. Most Japanese and Western collectors did not become familiar with Korean celadons until they started to be excavated from Goryeo tombs in the twentieth century during the Japanese Occupation. Chinese celadons, however, had been known since the seventeenth century in Europe and had gained their name in reference to the color of the green ribbons on the costume of a character called Céladon in a French play by Honoré D'Urfé. Of particular value to connoisseurs and collectors are the jadelike blue-green glaze, the deliberate fine crackle, and the quiet subtlety of Korean celadons when compared to Chinese ones.

The technique of making celadons was introduced from China to Korea probably during the ninth and tenth centuries, and they became very popular for use at court and in temples. Made mainly in the southwest of Korea in controlled communities of workers, celadon wares were transported by boat up the west coast to the capital. Excavations of shipwrecks have provided fascinating evidence of the size and shape of the boats and the large scale of the cargo. Some of the celadon vessels were even labeled with what they contained. Smaller numbers of white porcelains as well as unglazed gray stonewares for everyday use were also produced in some of the 270 kilns recorded during the Goryeo.

Although Goryeo celadons were at first very similar to Chinese ones, Korean craftsmen developed a pronounced preference for vessel shapes echoing natural forms, such as fruits, flowers, and vegetables, and for the use of openwork (pierced) decoration. One innovation of which Koreans are justifiably proud is the invention of *sanggam* slip inlay. This technique involves incising a pattern in the leather-hard body of the vessel, filling the incisions with colored slip (clay mixed with water), wiping off the excess slip, and then glazing. Painting with red pigment derived from copper under a celadon glaze was also a Korean innovation. It was used successfully in the twelfth century in Korea but it remained very difficult to control the process and ensure a good color.

Beautiful examples of metalwork and lacquer were also produced during the Goryeo period for use in Buddhist temples and at table at court. There is even a record of a tower at Heungwang temple being made in 1067 of about 563 pounds of silver and 190 pounds of gold. The most important cast bronze objects were enormous Buddhist temple bells, for which Korea was famous in Asia beginning in the Silla period. The practice of bell casting was a burden on the people, as they had to donate used bronzeware for new bells. The technique of silver inlay, which also came down from the Silla period, was used to decorate bronze vessels and may have influenced the development of the sanggam inlay technique on celadons. Secular metalwares include tablewares such as silver ewers and cupstands, bronze bowls, chopsticks, and spoons, as well as cosmetic and sewing items. Some of the tablewares used the beaten bronze technique rather than casting. Decorative techniques include *repoussé*, where a pattern is pressed and hammered out from the reverse side; chasing, where the metal is indented with a hammer and tools without a cutting edge; and gilding.

Although there are not many extant examples of Goryeo lacquerware, their quality is very high. Many of them are Buddhist sutra boxes or boxes for incense or rosaries. Nearly all the extant Goryeo lacquer pieces are decorated with inlaid mother-of-pearl and sometimes with tortoiseshell, in intricate and geometric designs of stylized chrysanthemums and lotus scrolls. In general the pieces of shell are smaller and thinner than those used later in the Joseon period. There is only one known example of Goryeo lacquer inlaid with a pictorial scene.

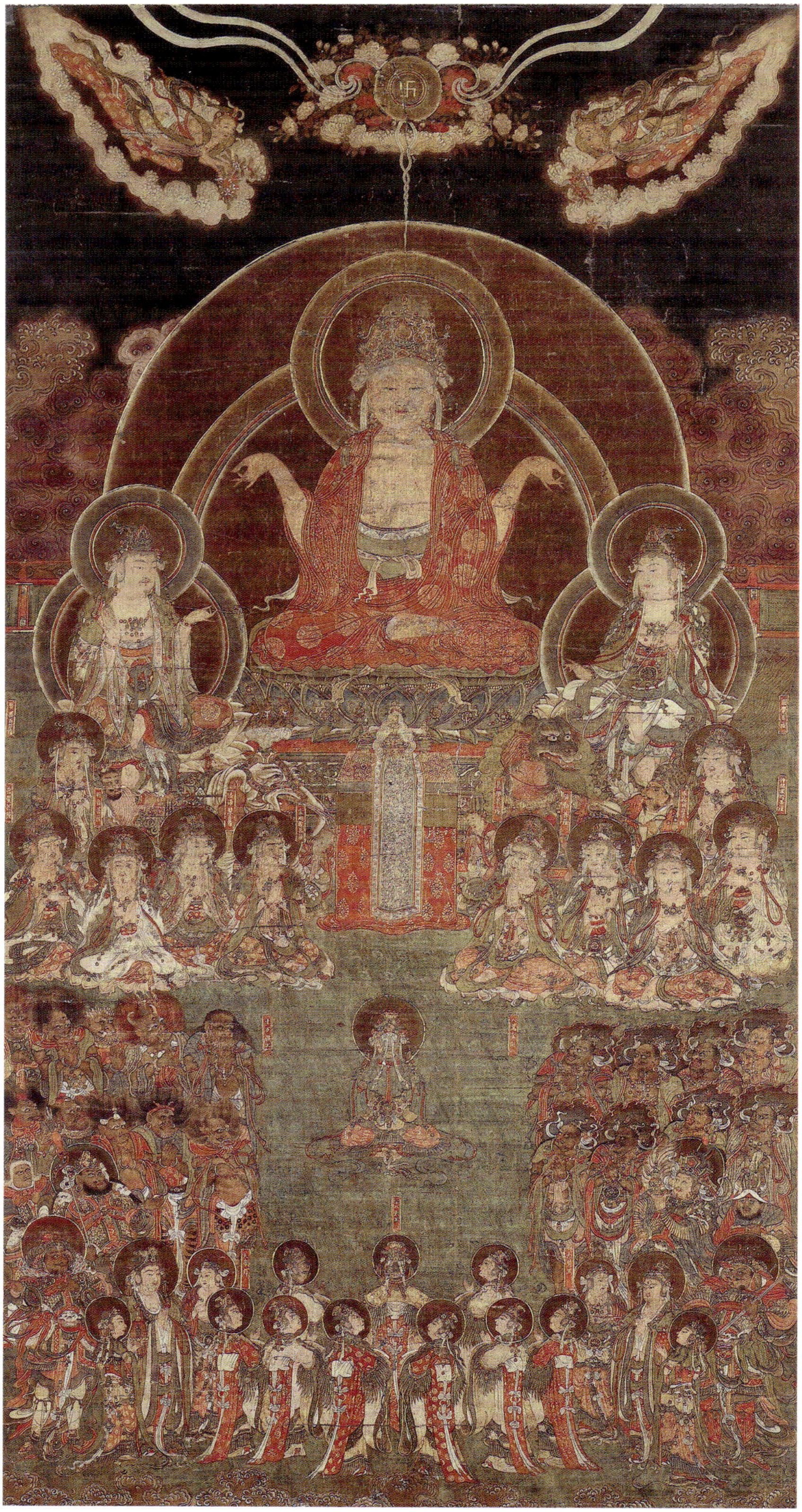

Perfect Enlightenment Sutra Illumination

Goryeo period, 14th century

This painting illustrates the *Sutra of Perfect Enlightenment*, in which the Vairocana Buddha teaches twelve bodhisattvas how to attain a pure state of perfect enlightenment. Vairocana formed the center of a teaching based on the *Flower Garland Sutra*, a popular text in the Goryeo period that absorbs all other Buddhist systems into one all-encompassing world centered on Vairocana. It also presents a vision of the Buddhist cosmology as a universe of mutually penetrating phenomena. In this painting the Vairocana Buddha has his hands outstretched to show that he is preaching. The twelve bodhisattvas seated around him include Manjusri on his lion to the Buddha's left and Samantabhadra on his elephant to the right. These two bodhisattvas often appear together and are associated respectively with wisdom and action.

Beneath the larger figures are smaller depictions of the Heavenly Kings and other Buddhist followers, most labeled with Chinese characters in red cartouches. The bulging eyes and fearsome expressions of the Heavenly Kings contrast with the benign and gentle expressions of the bodhisattvas. One lone bodhisattva kneels below the Buddha to receive the teaching, and two flying heavenly beings guard the Buddha above stylized swirling clouds that suggest a heavenly atmosphere. The gold stylized floral roundels on the Buddha's rich red robe and the lozenge shapes on the red altar cloth are typical Goryeo features, as are the beautifully painted transparent draperies and rich jewels.

The depiction of Vairocana with Manjusri and Samantabhadra is unusual. These bodhisattvas more usually form a triad with the historical Buddha Sakyamuni. Many Goryeo Buddhist paintings depict deities from the Pure Land sect, such as the Amitabha Buddha or the bodhisattvas Ksitigarbha and Avalokitesvara.

Hanging scroll; ink and colors on silk
165.5 x 85.5 cm (65 3/16 x 33 11/16 in.)
William Sturgis Bigelow Collection 11.6142

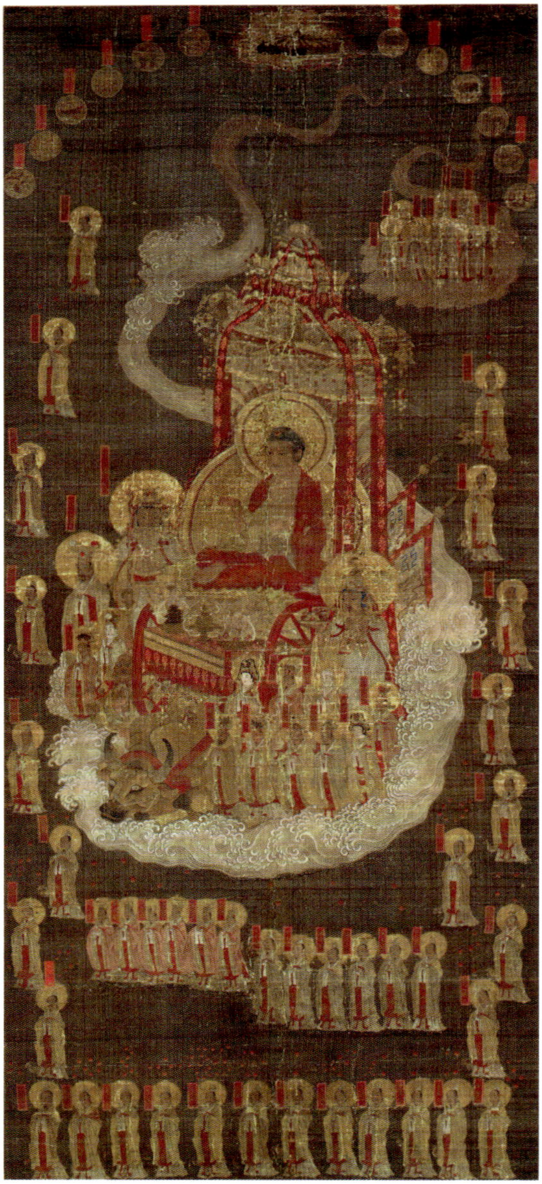

The Descent of Tejaprabha Buddha

Goryeo period, late 14th century

Tejaprabha Buddha, the Buddha of the Blazing Lights and a symbol for the North Star, is an unusual subject for a Goryeo painting. Because the subject can also be seen in paintings from Dunhuang, the cave temple site in northwestern China along the Silk Road, this painting is evidence of Chinese influence on the Korean painters of the Goryeo period. As in Dunhuang images, the Buddha is surrounded by numerous attendants and seated on a two-wheeled canopied and bejeweled carriage. On the carriage's platform are precious Buddhist accoutrements such as an incense burner, a piece of coral, and a miniature pagoda.

The three-quarter view and standing posture of the surrounding figures here is unusual; this feature supports the idea that the ox, with eyes staring forward and horns decorated with gold rings, is straining on his yoke as he pulls the carriage down through swirling clouds. The carriage's movement symbolizes the endless cycle of birth, death, and rebirth.

The Buddhist deities that embody the nine planets, which include the seven stars of the Great Bear constellation, appear in a group at the upper right. The deities representing the twelve symbols of the zodiac occupy the center, and those that symbolize twenty-eight other constellations stand along the edges. The twelve signs representing twelve months can be seen in diagram form in the sky. The representation of planets as figures probably derives from Chinese sutras that gave specific descriptions of the planets' human forms. Chinese sutras were most likely influenced by Indian scriptures, which in turn may reflect influences from Greece.

Hanging scroll; ink, colors, and gold on silk
124.4 x 54.8 cm (49 x 21 9/16 in.)
Fenollosa-Weld Collection 11.4001

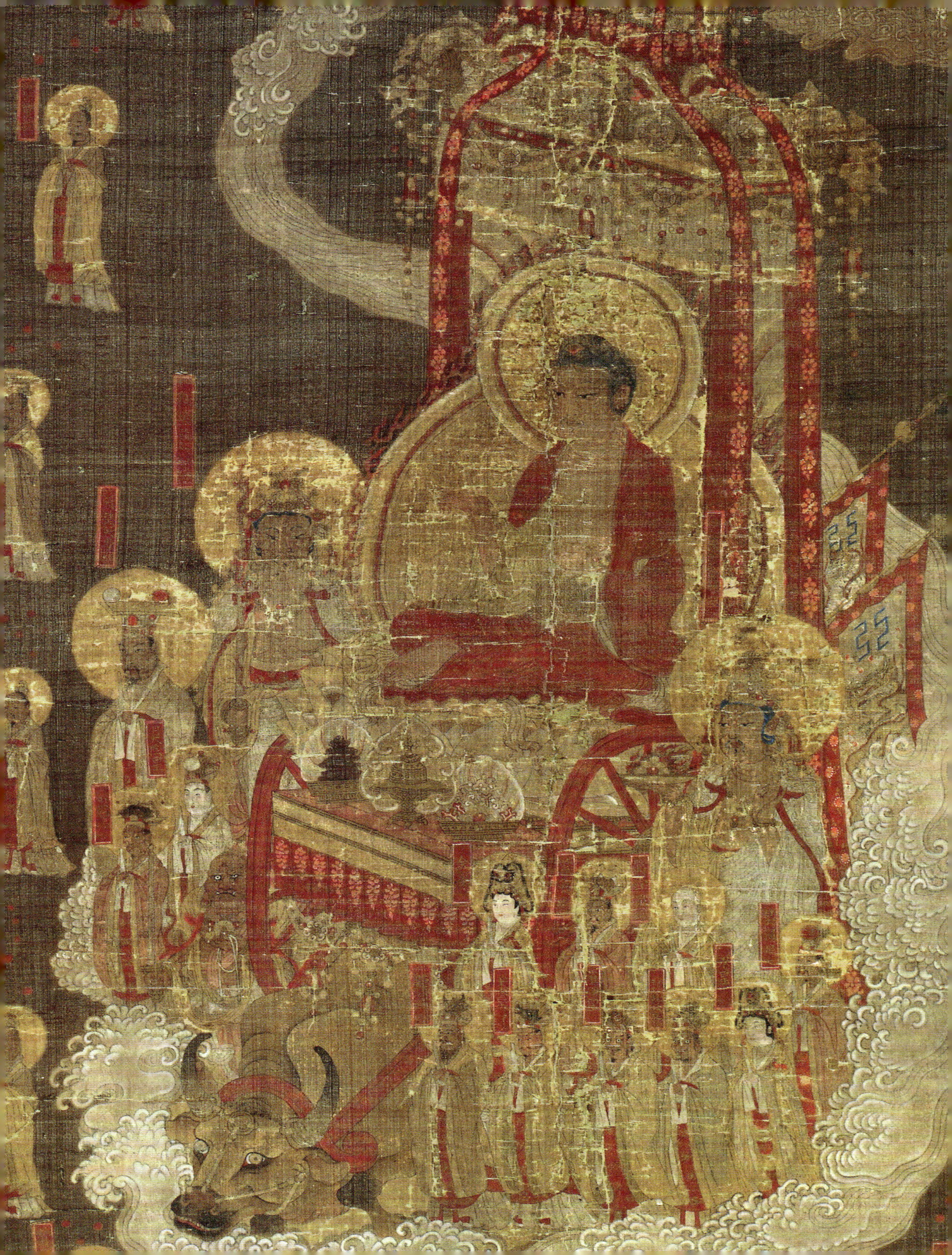

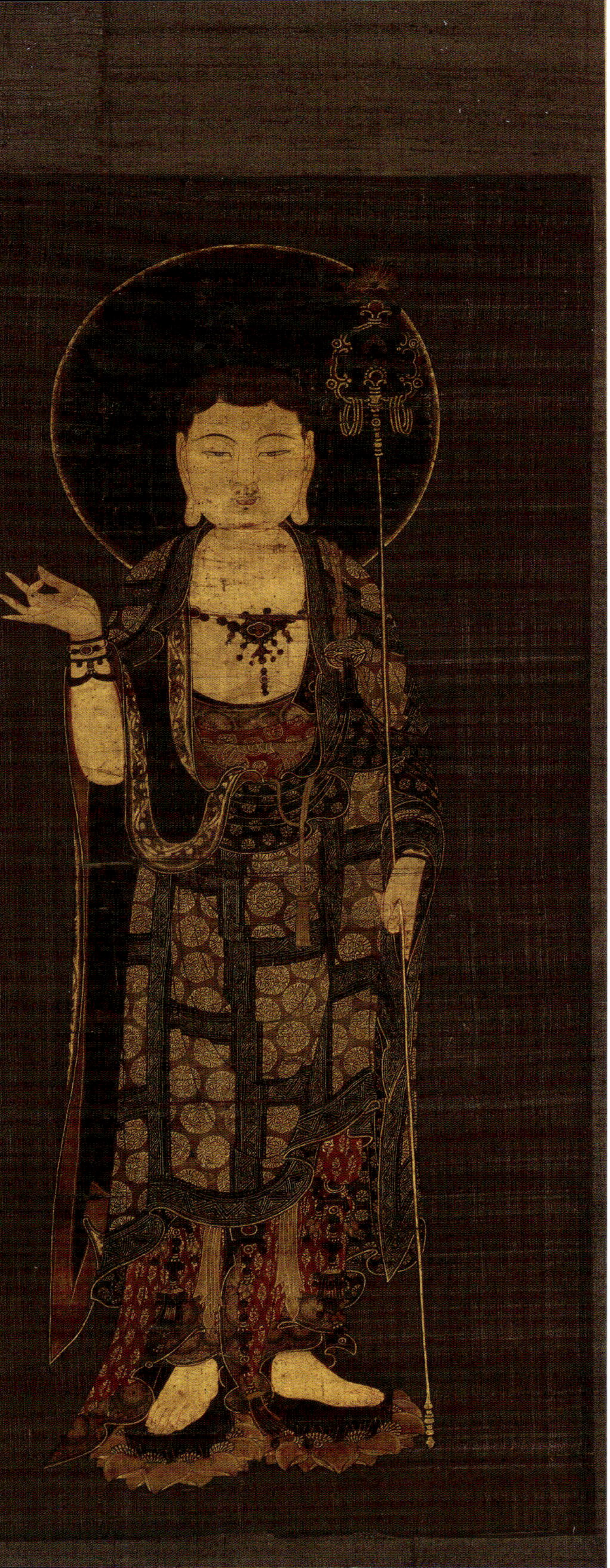

The Bodhisattva Ksitigarbha

Goryeo period, late 14th century

Ksitigarbha became popular during the late Goryeo period as the bodhisattva who saved souls suffering in hell. He was believed to be able to intercede after the Ten Kings of Hell determined how a person's soul might be reborn based on his or her past deeds. For this reason, images of Ksitigarbha are often combined with images of the Kings of Hell in Goryeo Buddhist paintings. In this painting, however, Ksitigarbha is shown alone, as a monk standing on two lotus flowers. He holds in his left hand a monk's staff and in his right hand a magic jewel that was thought to be able to answer prayers and bring wisdom. Compared to early Goryeo-period depictions of Ksitigarbha, here the bodhisattva wears no bandana or hood on his head and the decoration of his robes is less ornate and less refined. These characteristics indicate a late Goryeo date.

Panel; ink and colors on silk

92 x 40 cm (36¼ x 15¾ in.)

William Sturgis Bigelow Collection 11.6139

Sutra case

Goryeo period, 12th–13th century

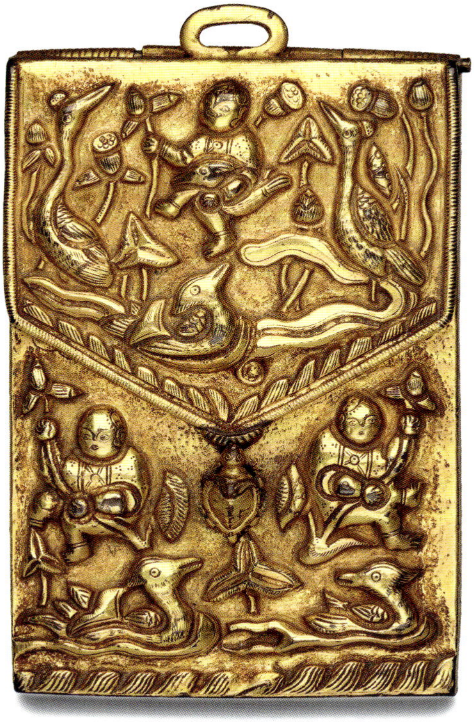

This small gilt bronze container is a delicate example of Goryeo metalworkers' artistry. Produced as a carrying case for small sutras used for personal devotion, it has a hinged flap secured with a clasp in the shape of a turtle and a loop on top, presumably for hanging on a belt or around the neck. Its entire surface is decorated with repoussé in high relief and features three boys carrying lotus branches, one with a duck under his arm. Two cranes or herons flank the boy in the center of the lid, and many-seeded lotus pods surround them. Mandarin ducks swim on stylized waves along the bottom of the case and the flap. These auspicious motifs are also common on Korean and Chinese ceramics of this period. Children suggest fertility, ducks convey marital harmony and fidelity, and cranes symbolize long life. The case is decorated under the flap with six incised Sanskrit characters representing a prayer or mantra, and on the long thin sides with scrolls and waves.

Gilt bronze
L. 9 cm (3 9/16 in.), w. 6.1 cm (2 3/8 in.), d. 2.1 cm (7/16 in.)
Charles Bain Hoyt Fund 67.1

Buddhist temple bell

Goryeo period, 12th century

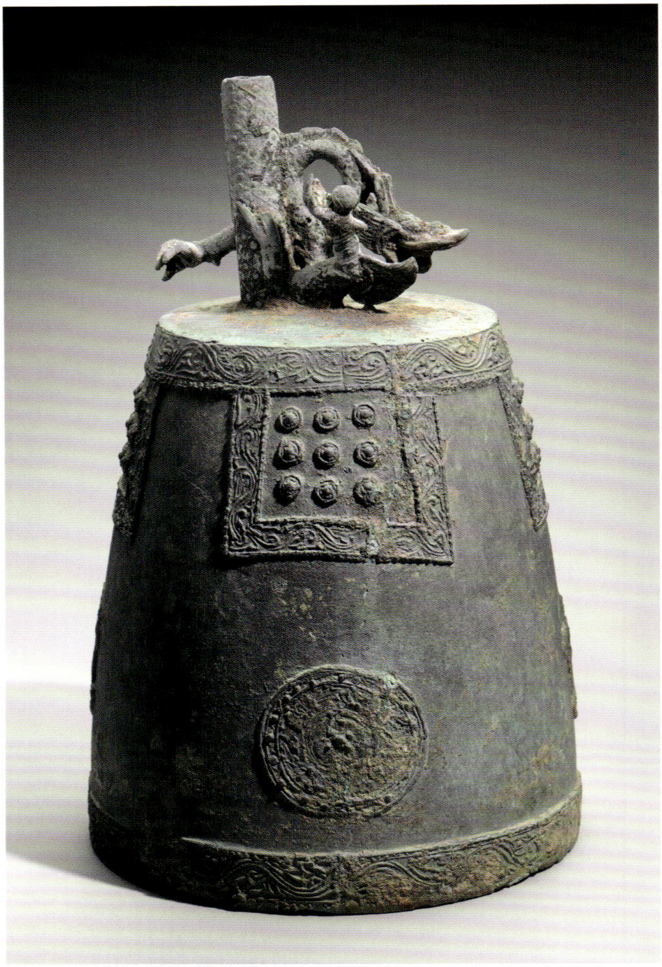

This bronze bell has the dragon-shaped loop handle and the tubular pipe at the top common to all Korean bells. The pipe was a Korean invention to improve on the sound of Chinese models. Bronze bells were used in Buddhist temples to sound the times of day and to summon monks to services. They were struck on the outside with a wooden mallet and do not have the hanging clapper of Western bells. The circular floral designs on either side, perhaps stylized lotuses, served as striking points; they are interspersed with two bodhisattvas standing on clouds. On some bells these figures are flying heavenly beings, but the figures on this bell can be identified as bodhisattvas on the basis of the halos (*mandorlas*) around their heads. There are bands of stylized lotus scrolls decorating the shoulder and the bottom of the bell, and four square decorative panels around the shoulder, each square containing nine nipple-like protrusions representing lotus buds. The shoulder itself is flat, which indicates that this bell dates to the twelfth century. Bells dating to the thirteenth century have shoulders decorated with a row of triangular spikes.

Bronze
H. 39.2 cm (15 7/16 in.),
diam. of rim: 24.1 cm (9 1/2 in.)
Keith McLeod Fund 1972.388

Buddhist reliquary

Goryeo period, 14th century

Buddhist reliquaries preserve relics of the Buddha and important Buddhist monks. The relics can be real, such as the hair, teeth, or bones of the religious figures, but they can also be symbolic, as they are in this reliquary. Small beads of glass and bronze stand for the remains of the Seon (Chan in Chinese or Zen in Japanese) monks Naong (1320–1376) and Jigong (died 1363). The beads are held in two of five small octagonal containers in the shape of miniature stupas (Buddhist monuments). The pedestal, pagoda body, roof, and three-tiered finial of each one suggests the architectural form from which they are derived. These mini-stupas are held in turn inside the main reliquary, which has the shape of a Tibetan-style stupa on a base decorated with three layers of upturned lotus petals made of thin gilt silver. The design of the outer reliquary reflects Mongol influence on Yuan-dynasty China (1271–1368) and by extension on Goryeo-period Korea. The lotus is a symbol of purity for Buddhists because just as the beautiful lotus flower emerges from the mud of the pond, so does the pure and unsullied Buddha from the dirty world.

Each of the five mini-stupas has an inscription in Chinese on its base. Two of the inscriptions refer to the monks Naong and Jigong, and the other three refer to past Buddhas. The references to past Buddhas in the same reliquary testify to the importance of the two monks. Jigong came from India to Korea via China, arriving in 1326. He is thought to have brought the *Patra Leaf Sutra* with him and to have housed it in the Hwajangsa temple in present-day Kaesong, North Korea. He was the teacher of Naong, who was associated with the Hoeamsa temple near Seoul.

Silver and parcel gilt with repoussé decoration
Stupa: H. 22.2 cm (8¾ in.), w. of base: 12.1 cm (4¾ in.)
Miniature stupas: H. 5 cm (1 15/16 in.), w. of base: 3 cm (1 3/16 in.)
Charles Goddard Weld Collection, by exchange 39.591a–f

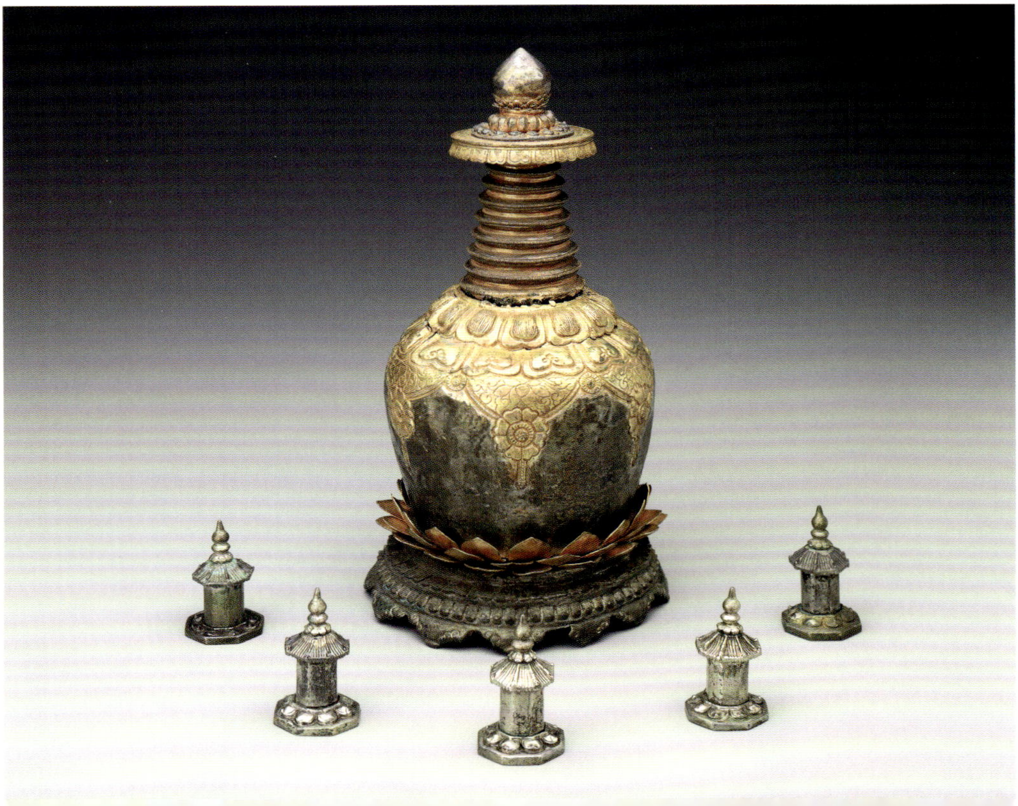

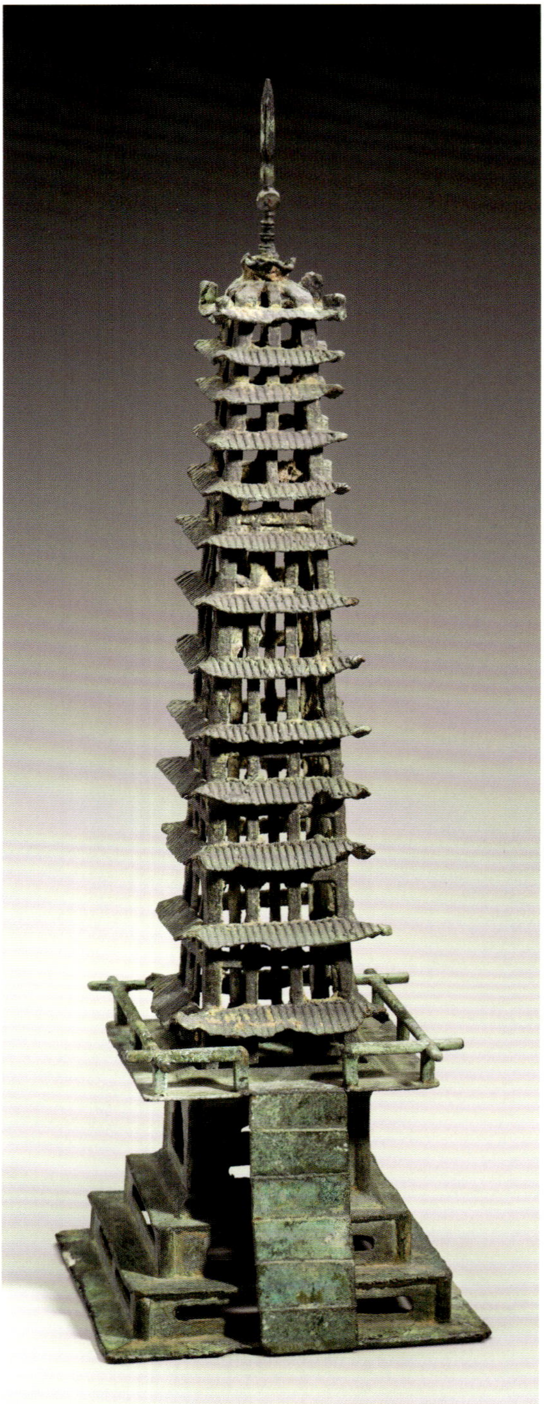

Miniature pagoda

Goryeo period, 12th–13th century

Small bronze pagodas may have been placed on Buddhist temple altars or used as reliquaries. Sometimes they are cast in a single piece, but this one is made of three parts. The three-tiered base has railings and a staircase. The main body has thirteen stories, each with a tiled roof, decreasing in size at each level, with the remains of dragon heads at the corners of the uppermost roof. The finial, which was once decorated with various ornaments, emerges out of the remains of a lotus-shaped bowl that symbolizes purity.

Miniature pagodas were produced in large numbers during the Goryeo period. They reflect mostly lost wooden architecture built with bracket systems and earthenware-tiled roofs. Pagodas were an East Asian architectural development from the Indian stupa. Each of the many Buddhist temples in the Goryeo period had at least one wooden or stone pagoda for storing precious scriptures or reliquaries within its precincts.

Bronze
H. 39.2 cm (15 7/16 in.)
Marshall H. Gould Fund 1970.344

Ewer and basin

Goryeo period, 12th century

This ewer and basin set is a unique example of the highest quality of Goryeo metalworking, surely a royal piece used at the Gaeseong court. The set was probably used to serve wine, with the lotus-shaped basin filled with hot water to keep the wine in the ewer warm. The body of the ewer is fashioned in the shape of twenty-four bundled bamboo stalks, and the handle and spout are made in the shape of bamboo shoots, following the Korean predilection for vessels that represent vegetables, flowers, and fruits. Made as a separate piece that fits into the neck of the ewer on two metal prongs, the lid is decorated with two lotus flowers in high relief surmounted by a phoenix. Engraved floral designs and arabesque patterns decorate the gilt parts of the ewer. There are similar ceramic examples of this ewer and basin combination in Chinese Song-dynasty Qingbai wares, as well as in Korean celadons.

Very few Goryeo silver vessels survive, and this ewer and basin are the most elaborate examples known. Analysis of the metal content revealed that the ewer is made from many different pieces of silver of 90–95 percent purity; the other metals present, in varying amounts, are mainly copper, lead, and gold. The surface of the object was once gilt, and significant traces of gold remain. The bottom of the ewer appears to be a replacement. The basin has a different silver alloy composition, with up to 40 percent copper present in some places.

Parcel gilt silver with engraved decoration
Ewer: H. 34.3 cm (13½ in.); diam. of base: 9.5 cm (3¾ in.)
Basin: H. 16.8 cm (6⅝ in.); diam. of mouth: 18.8 cm (7⅜ in.); diam. of base: 14.5 cm (5 11/16 in.)
George Nixon Black Fund 35.646a–b

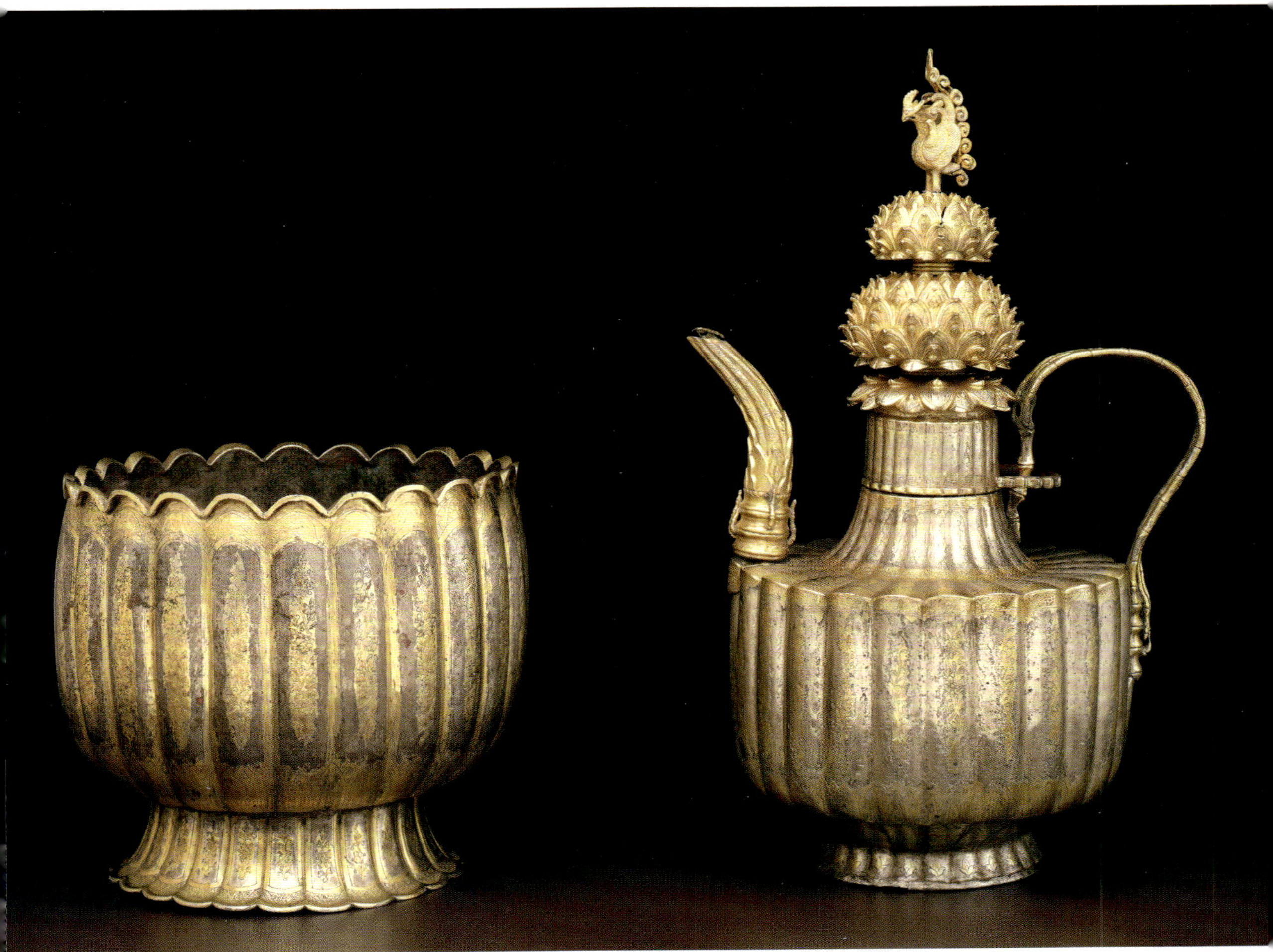

Belt ornament with chrysanthemum design

Goryeo period, 12th–13th century
Gilt silver with repoussé decoration
L 6.2 cm (2 7/16 in.), w. 23 cm (9 1/16 in.), d. 0.5 cm (3/16 in.)
Gift of Robert T. Paine, Jr. 60.1321

Sheath with slit and loop handle

Goryeo period, 12th–13th century
Gilt silver with repoussé decoration
L. 23.5 cm (9 1/4 in.), diam. 1.9 cm (3/4 in.)
Gift of Yamanaka & Company, Boston 39.607

Needle container

Goryeo period, 12th–13th century
Silver with engraved decoration
L. 9 cm (3 9/16 in.), w. 1.1 cm (7/16 in.)
Keith McLeod Fund 1977.390

Each of these three items shows a different silver decoration technique used by skilled Goryeo metalworkers. The rare belt ornament or buckle is decorated with chrysanthemums on one side made by *tachul*, which is a Korean term for repoussé that means "beat and impress." The relief flowers on the other half were attached to the buckle after having been fashioned separately.

The small knife sheath is gilded and also elaborately decorated in high-relief repoussé with lotuses in beaded circles, a design influenced by Chinese Tang-dynasty metalwork, which was in turn influenced by Sassanian metalwork. It also has a background made by ring punching, a technique in which small rings are punched all over the surface of the metal. A slit at the top and side would accommodate a knife blade so its ornamental handle could sit on top. A loop handle in the shape of a flower allowed the owner to attach the sheath to a belt with a cord. This knife may have belonged to a woman; knives were symbols of chastity, and women were supposed to commit suicide with a knife if violated or widowed.

The beautifully decorated cylindrical needle container is evidence of the important role sewing played in aristocratic women's lives at this time and the value placed on needles. Similar examples have been excavated from tombs, together with women's celadon cosmetic sets. Such containers usually held small spools of thread as well as needles, rather like a portable sewing kit. The grapevine decoration is chased, with ring punching filling the background. Grapevines, probably introduced to Korea as a decorative motif by Silk Road traders, became popular in paintings and decorative arts from the Goryeo through the Joseon period.

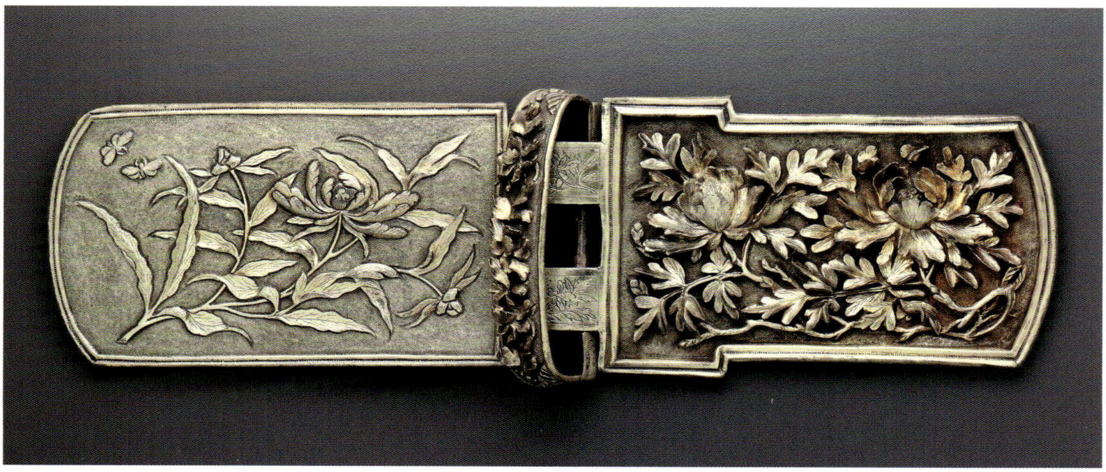

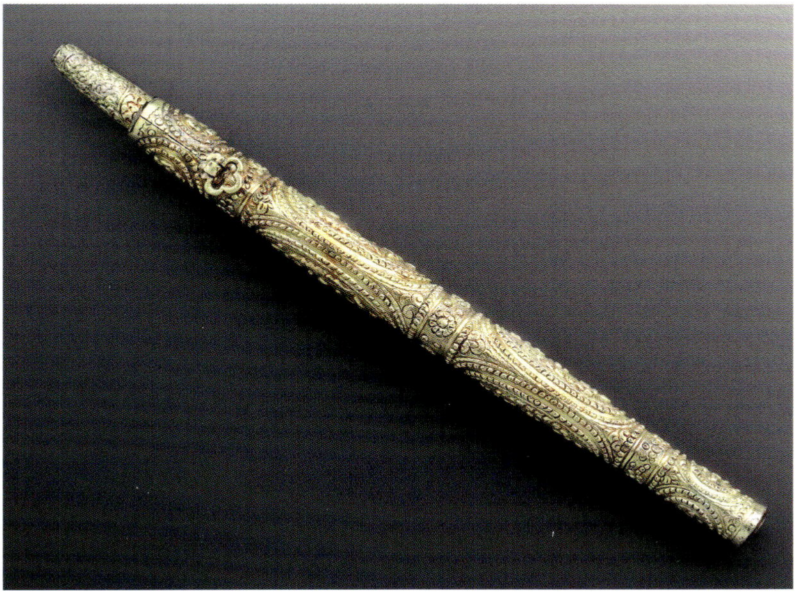

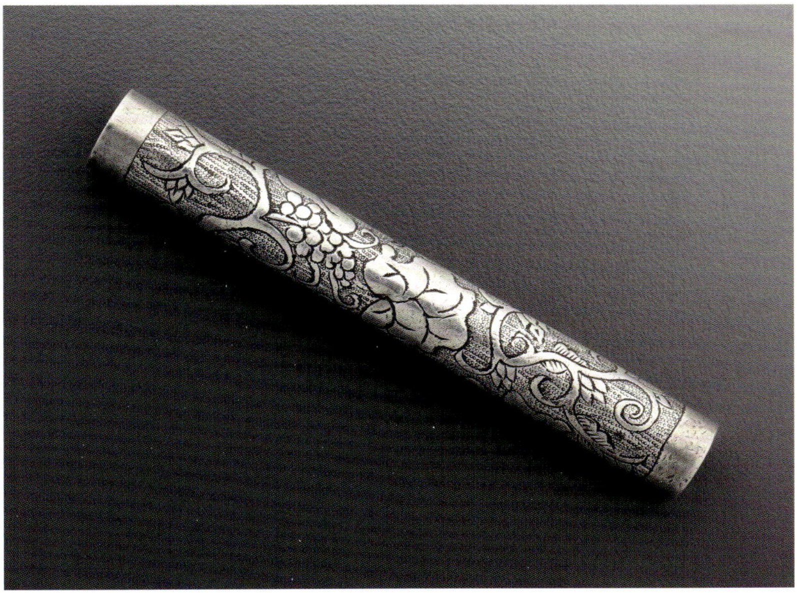

Flower-shaped mirror with knob and raised border

Goryeo period, 12th–13th century

Cast bronze mirrors were used in the Goryeo period for cosmetic purposes as well as for burial in tombs to represent the status of the incumbent. The mirrors have a shiny, reflective plain side backed by a side decorated in relief and a loop in the center by which to thread a cord so they could be hung up or held in the hand. Large numbers of extant bronze mirrors from the Goryeo period are evidence of the high level of metal production during this time.

Most mirrors were circular in shape but some were square or shaped like flowers or peaches. Some had small handles instead of a central loop. This flower-shaped mirror has eight petals and a central knob or loop surrounded by a flower-shaped base within a raised border. Beyond the center are five beautifully cast sprays of peonies, their feathery leaves forming an S-shape. The whole ensemble makes a continuous undulating circular pattern.

Bronze
Diam. 21.5 cm (8 7/16 in.)
Bequest of Charles Bain Hoyt—Charles Bain Hoyt Collection
50.903

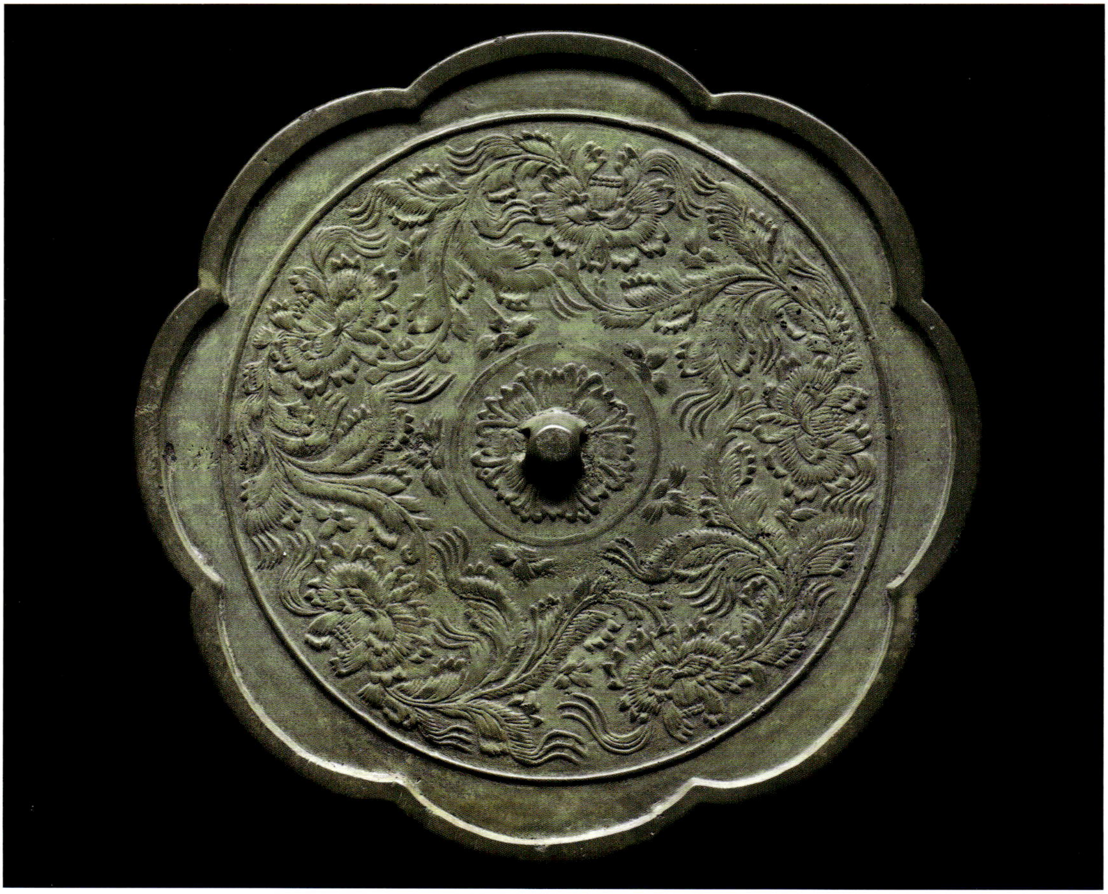

Hairpins

Goryeo period, 12th–13th century

Silver with gilt head
L. 4.3 cm (1 11/16 in.), w. 0.8 cm (5/16 in.)
Keith McLeod Fund 1977.404

Bronze
L. 7.2 cm (2 13/16 in.), w. 1.4 cm (9/16 in.)
Keith McLeod Fund 1977.399

Bronze
L. 11.7 cm (4 5/8 in.), w. 1.1 cm (7/16 in.)
Anonymous gift RES.51.66

Tweezer set and nail cleaners or ear picks

Goryeo Period, 12th–13th century
Copper alloy (tweezer set) and silver (nail cleaners)
L. of each: 13.6 cm (5 3/8 in.)
Keith McLeod Fund 1977.439; 1977.441.1–2

Paintings of the Joseon period show that Korean women traditionally put their long black hair up in a bun at the nape of the neck using metal hairpins. Many such hairpins made of bronze and silver have been excavated from the Goryeo-period tombs of aristocratic ladies. The smallest hairpin shown here is made of silver with a gilt, half-egg-shaped head and upper part. The gold gave it a higher value and represented greater status for its wearer. One of the bronze hairpins has a similarly shaped half-egg head decorated in repoussé with round knobs, which resemble the way a Buddha's hair is usually represented in sculpture and painting. By comparison the longer bronze hairpin is simple and undecorated, and the thin prongs are more pointed at the ends, making it functional rather than decorative.

The tweezers and nail cleaners or ear picks form a handy set that folds compactly into one vertical unit, with an elegant handle and faceted finial. Tweezing the eyebrows into an arch was an important element of the female toilette at this time in East Asia. The other two tools could have been used for cleaning the nails or removing wax from the ears. Decoration of these small metal utensils was often intricate, executed with techniques such as ring punching, chasing, and engraving.

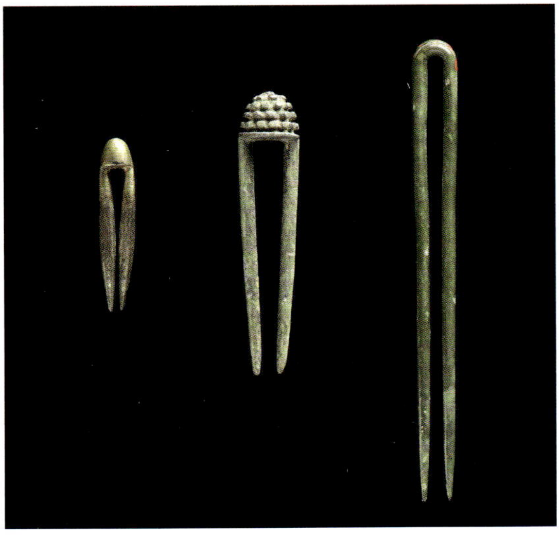

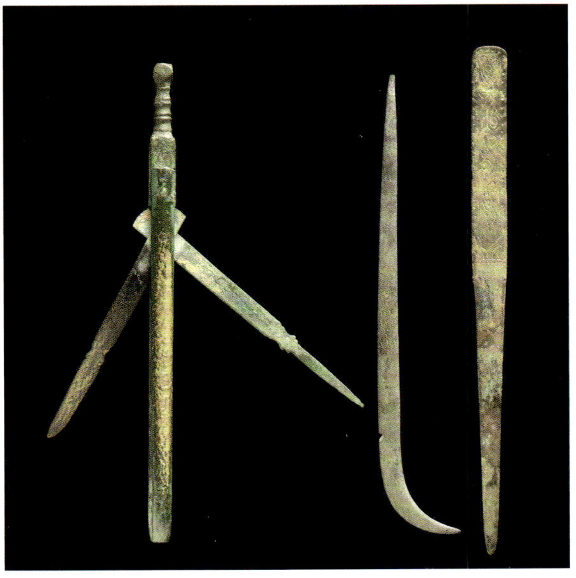

Bowl with lid

Goryeo period, 12th–13th century

Bronze with lacquer

Overall: H. 17 cm (6 11/16 in.); diam. of lid: 16.7 cm (6 9/16 in.); diam. of foot: 10.2 cm (4 in.)

Bequest of Charles Bain Hoyt—Charles Bain Hoyt Collection

50.914a–b

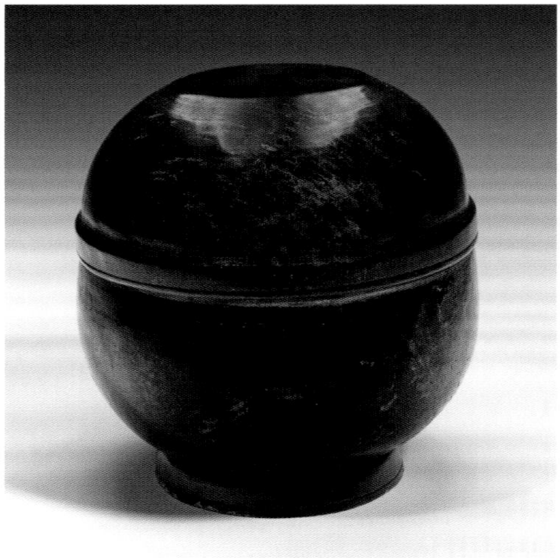

Chopsticks

Goryeo period, 12th–13th century

Bronze

L. 25.4 cm (10 in.)

Denman Waldo Ross Collection 17.830a–b

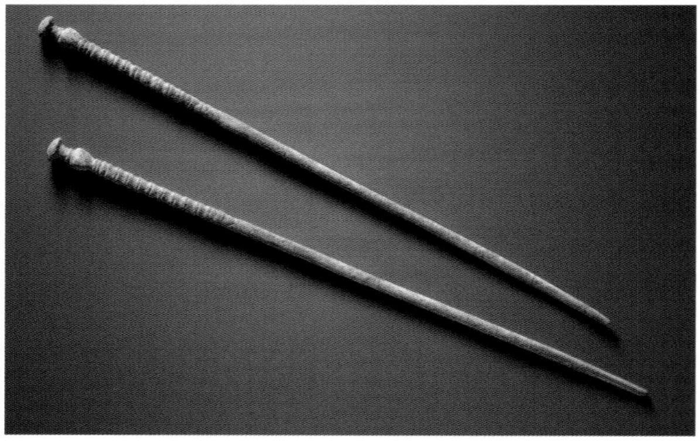

Spoon

Goryeo period, 12th–13th century

Bronze

L. 25 cm (9 13/16 in.)

Gift of Mrs. George C. Shattuck in memory of Langdon Warner

56.880

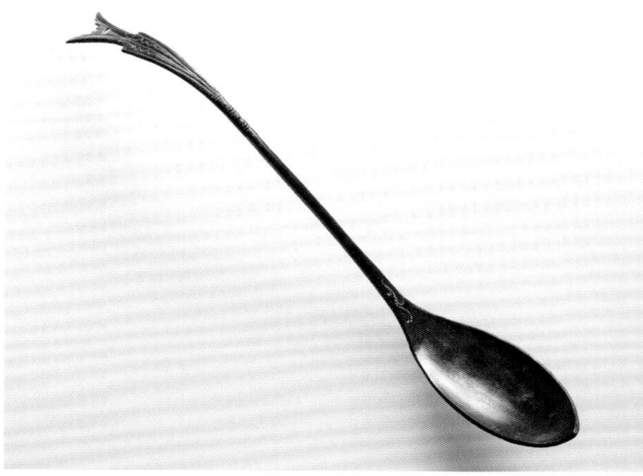

Bronze utensils are widely used at table throughout Korea. Lidded bowls hold rice or other food. This one has a close-fitting lid with a ridged lip, making it convenient and easy to lift the lid off the bowl. The bowl was not cast but was made by the beaten bronze technique, in which thin sheets of bronze are hammered into shape; the foot has been joined to the bowl with nails.

Koreans have been using bronze chopsticks from at least the seventh century. They still prefer metal chopsticks to wood, ivory, jade, or lacquer ones. This sophisticated pair is tapered at the end that was brought to the mouth, and has a series of beadlike ridges at the end held with the hand, terminating in a spherical ornament sometimes called a *boju* or "magic gem."

Spoons were and still are used for eating rice in Korea, more than in other East Asian countries. A pair of chopsticks and a spoon often form a set. This spoon has a dramatic and typically Goryeo S-shaped profile. The handle is decorated with an incised wave pattern and dotted lines. The long pointed bowl and the elegant pierced handle shaped like a swallow's tail are particularly fine examples of Goryeo design.

Flower-shaped box with stylized chrysanthemums

Goryeo period, 13th–14th century

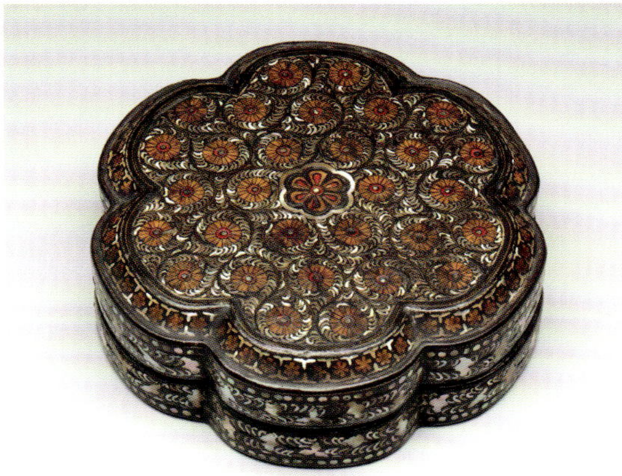

This rare floral box may have once contained a rosary of Buddhist prayer beads, or perhaps incense or cosmetics. It is the only known Goryeo lacquer box made in the shape of a six-petal flower, most likely a chrysanthemum. The lid features a large stylized six-petal chrysanthemum inlaid with painted tortoiseshell at the center and surrounded by smaller flowers, each of which is encircled with small C-shaped pieces of mother-of-pearl. The slanting edge of the lid is decorated with smaller six-petal flowers, and the vertical sides of the lid and box have rows of inlaid trefoil-shaped leaves and C-shaped pieces of shell. The small circular dots of inlaid shell on the sides make this box a precursor of Joseon period inlay, which featured larger dots. This design suggests that the box dates to the late Goryeo, or late 13th–14th century.

The unusual combination of mother-of-pearl and tortoiseshell makes the box especially rare and beautiful. The tortoiseshell pieces are painted on the back in red and yellow, a technique that originated in Tang-dynasty China. The painting makes the flowers stand out from the white iridescent mother-of-pearl and creates a dazzling effect—remarked upon in an important account by the Chinese envoy Xu Jing of his visit to Korea in 1123.

Lacquered wood inlaid with mother-of-pearl and painted tortoiseshell

H. 4.4 cm (1¾ in.), diam. 11.5 cm (4½ in.)

Gift of Charles Bain Hoyt—Charles Bain Hoyt Collection

34.69a–b

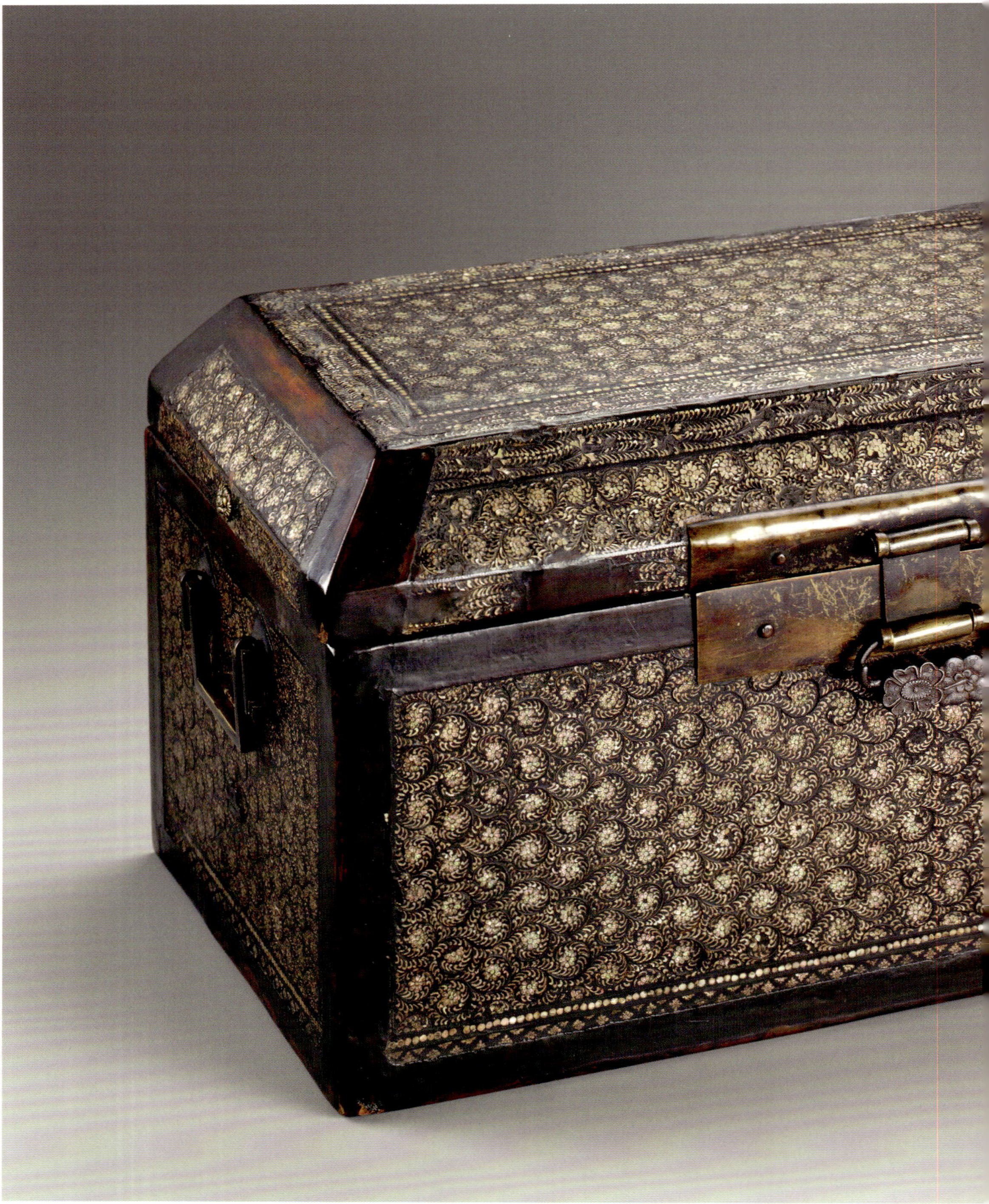

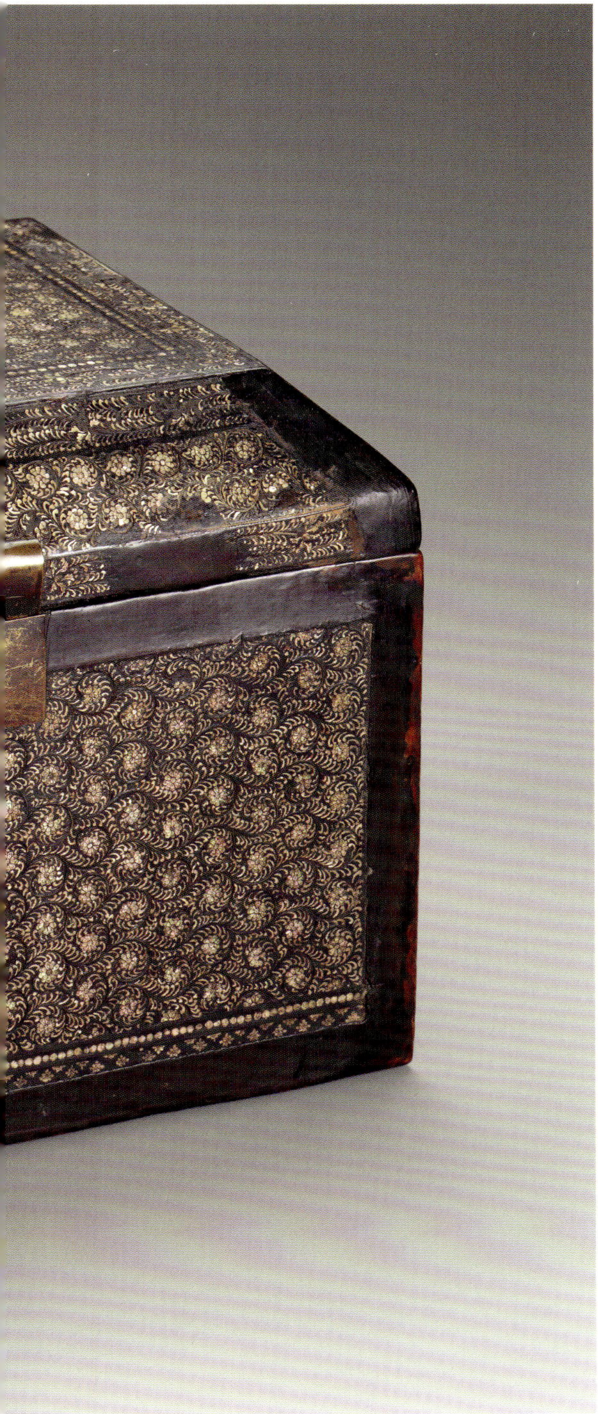

Sutra box

Goryeo period, 13th century

Lacquer was used for decorative purposes in Korea since at least the Three Kingdoms period, when a government bureau was made responsible for the care of lacquer trees and for extracting the sap. In 1272, another government agency was established to manufacture lacquer cases for a set of the *Tripitaka Koreana*, the entire Buddhist scriptures. This box may have been part of that set. Today seven others like it are known; they are dispersed among museums and private collections around the globe. One of them has an inscription on the lid describing which sutra it contained. This group of sutra boxes forms the majority of the fifteen remaining Goryeo inlaid lacquer objects known in the world.

The inlaid decoration on this sutra box consists of rows of chrysanthemums encircled with rings of C-shaped pieces, all in mother-of-pearl (abalone shell). Twisted copper wire forms the branches, stems, and borders. Sometimes silver was also used for this purpose, as can be seen on other examples. The density of decoration on this box is similar to that of inlaid celadon of the same period. The accurately cut and mass-produced pieces of mother-of-pearl testify to the organization and high skill level of late-Goryeo lacquer workers.

Lacquered wood inlaid with mother-of-pearl
L. 25.8 cm (10 3/16 in.), w. 47.2 cm (18 9/16 in.), h. 24.8 cm (9 3/4 in.)
William Sturgis Bigelow Collection 11.10556

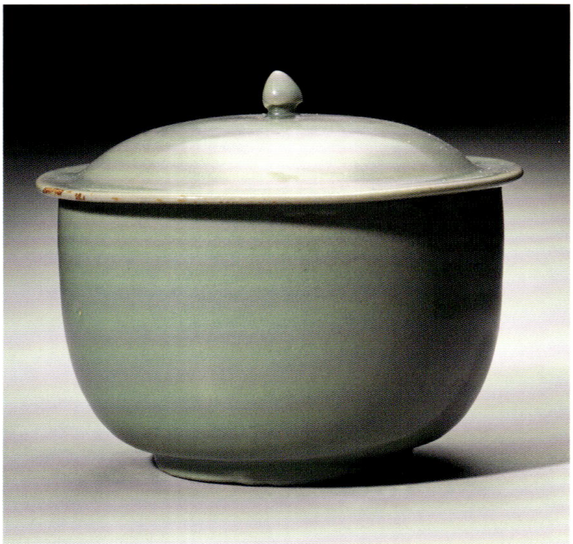

Lidded cup with lotus-bud-shaped knob

Goryeo period, first half of 12th century

Plain, undecorated celadons dominated Korean ceramic production during the first half of the twelfth century. Potters took a great deal of trouble to perfect the shape of the vessel and quality of its glaze rather than the surface decoration. For example, the lid of this cup is cleverly made with a ledge inside so that it may rest securely on the cup. The deep blue-green glaze is particularly subtle.

Cups with covers were produced under the influence of Chinese wares from the Northern Song–period kilns of Ding, Cizhou, and Ru. However, the knobs of the Chinese cups usually have different shapes. Lotus-bud knobs may have been a uniquely Korean feature. The lotus bud is a Buddhist symbol of purity, which suggests that the users of this simple but refined cup were Buddhist. This lidded cup was probably made at the Sadang-ri kilns in southwest Korea and it is similar in shape and size to one excavated from the tomb of King Injong, who reigned from 1122 to 1146.

Stoneware w th celadon glaze
Overall: H. 9.3 cm (3⅞ in.)
Cup: H. 7 cm (2¾ in.); diam. of rim: 10.4 cm (4⅛ in.);
diam. of foot: 6.1 cm (2⅜ in.)
Special Korean Pottery Fund 11.1817a–b

Tea bowl with carved lotus leaves

Goryeo period, 12th century

The custom of drinking tea became very fashionable by the Goryeo period. Originally associated with Buddhist monks, tea drinking was eventually practiced by aristocrats and courtiers, with considerable ceremony attached to its brewing, pouring, and consumption. At this time tea was made not with tea leaves steeped in a pot but with powdered tea whisked with water in a bowl. Celadon bowls were thought to be perfect for tea, because their pale blue-green glaze, similar to jade, enhanced the liquid's color.

This bowl is plain inside and simply decorated on the outside with carved overlapping lotus petals. Its form and decoration are very similar to those of Chinese celadon wares made at the Yue kilns in southeastern China. It has been suggested therefore that Chinese potters brought the celadon technique from these kilns to southwest Korea in the tenth century. However, there is no proof that this happened, and it is more likely that celadon manufacture developed gradually in Korea in the context of long and lively trade between the two regions.

Stoneware with celadon glaze
H. 11 cm (4 5/16 in.); diam. of rim: 21.3 cm (8⅜ in.);
diam. of foot: 8.2 cm (3¼ in.)
Special Korean Pottery Fund 11.1834

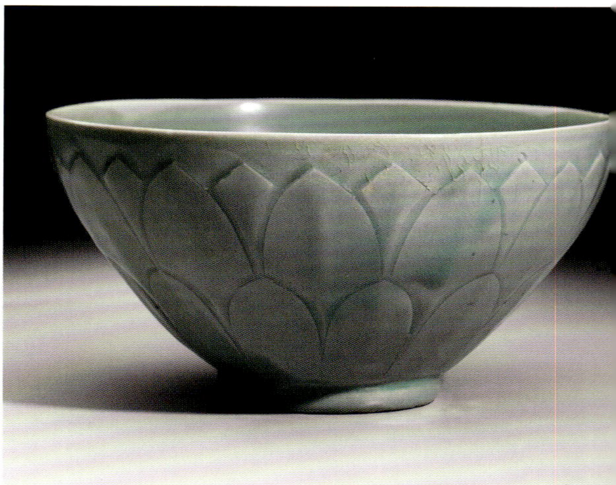

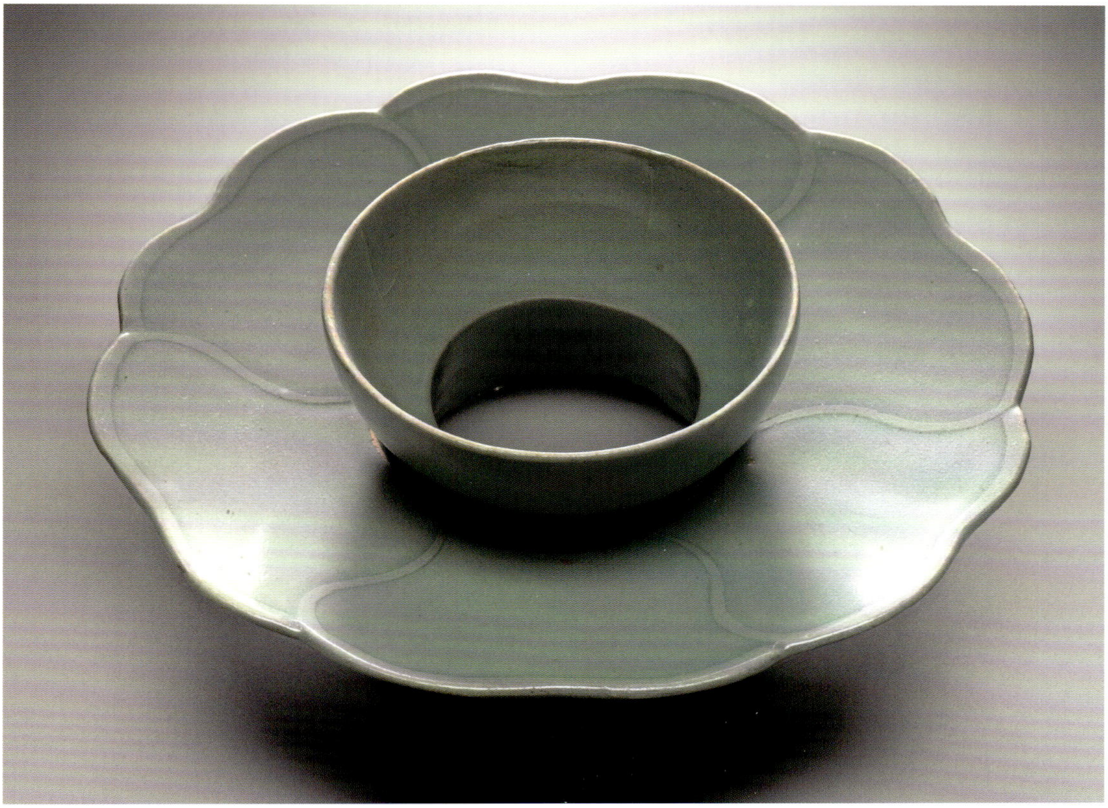

Flower-shaped cup stand

Goryeo period, 12th century

Nearly all Goryeo cup stands were made in floral shapes. The small cups they held were probably for drinking wine but possibly for tea. This stand has a deep hole in the center and an integrated cup-shaped holder. It is beautifully modeled in the shape of a six-petal mallow flower, reminiscent of rare Chinese Ru ware. Each incised petal overlaps the next one. The glaze is perfect, pale and subtle. The base of the high, flared foot is unglazed and has marks from the spurs used for firing.

Stoneware with celadon glaze

H. 5.6 cm (2 3/16 in.); diam. of cup holder: 8.6 cm (3 3/8 in.); diam. of foot: 6.9 cm (2 11/16 in.)

Special Korean Pottery Fund 11.1826

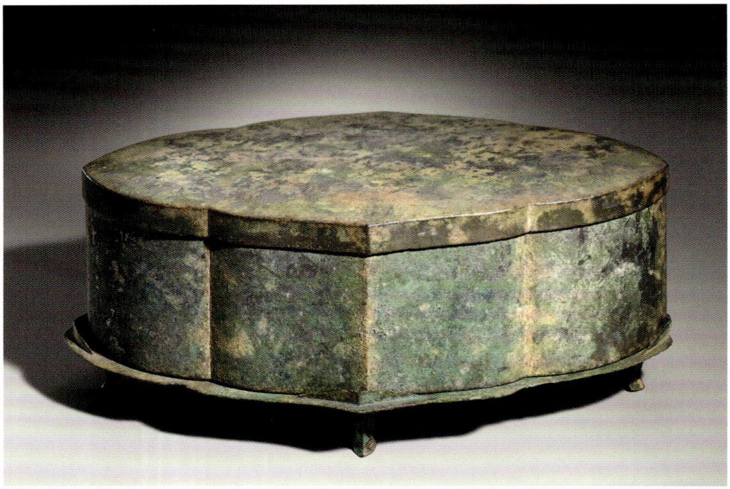

Casket with stand

Goryeo period, first half of the 12th century

The elegant and understated shape of this bronze casket transforms it from an ordinary box into a work of art. The shape, which was also used for lacquer boxes during the Joseon period, imitates that of a water chestnut flower called *neunghwa*. The box's thin bronze was not cast but hammered into shape, and then each component was beautifully welded together. The close-fitting flat lid is the same shape as the casket, as is the separate stand, which is slightly larger and has a rim and four small cabriole legs.

Although other flower-shaped boxes of lacquer and ceramic were used in the Goryeo period for cosmetics, this rare casket may have been a royal burial urn, as it is similar in shape and size to a casket excavated with a larger stone outer container from the tomb of King Injong.

Bronze
Case: H. 15.4 cm (6 1/16 in.)
Stand: L. 33 cm (13 in.), w. 18.8 cm (7 3/8 in.)
Bequest of Charles Bain Hoyt—Charles Bain Hoyt Collection
50.913a–c

Melon-shaped vase with flower-shaped mouth

Goryeo period, first half of the 12th century

With its simple glaze and balanced shape, this vase is a fine example of the sophisticated undecorated celadons perfected in the early Goryeo period under royal patronage. The mouth has the shape of a flower with eight petals, the body has the form of an eight-lobed melon, and the foot is carved in a series of overlapping pleats, like a skirt. The vase was clearly influenced by Song-dynasty Chinese wares, both Qingbai porcelains and celadons manufactured at the Yaozhou kilns. Such Chinese vases have been excavated from the Gaeseong area of Korea. A vase similar to this one was excavated from the tomb of King Injong. This example was most likely manufactured at Sadang-ri in southwest Korea.

Stoneware with celadon glaze and incised decoration
H. 23.2 cm (9 1/8 in.); diam. of mouth: 9.7 cm (3 13/16 in.); diam. of foot: 7.5 cm (2 15/16 in.)
Gift of Mr. and Mrs. John Dolliver MacDonald 59.308

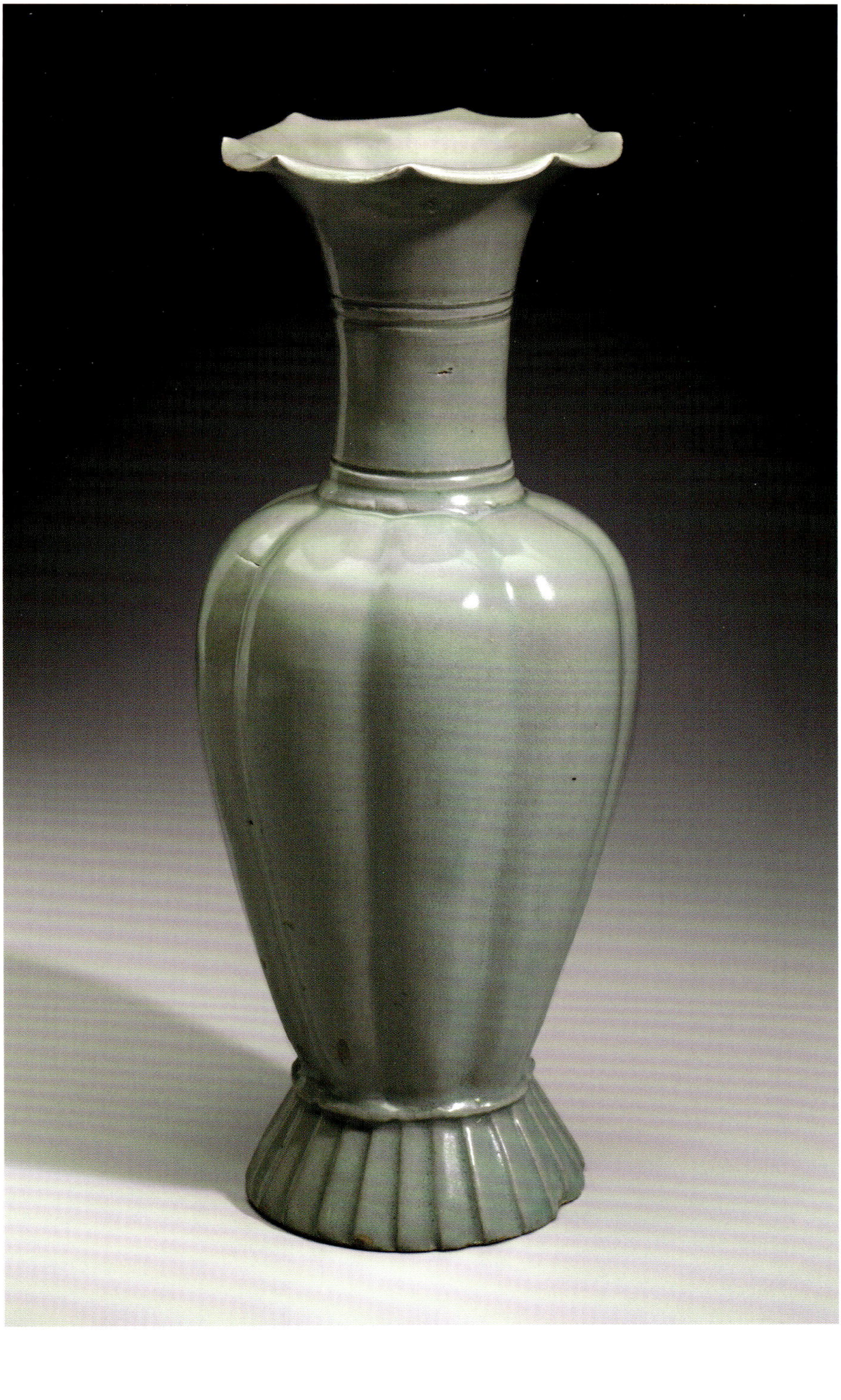

Pear-shaped bottles with trumpet-shaped mouths

Goryeo period, 12th century

Stoneware with celadon glaze and incised decoration
H. 34.8 cm (13 11/16 in.); diam. of mouth: 9 cm (3 9/16 in.); diam. of foot: 11.9 cm (4 11/16 in.)
Special Korean Pottery Fund 11.1819

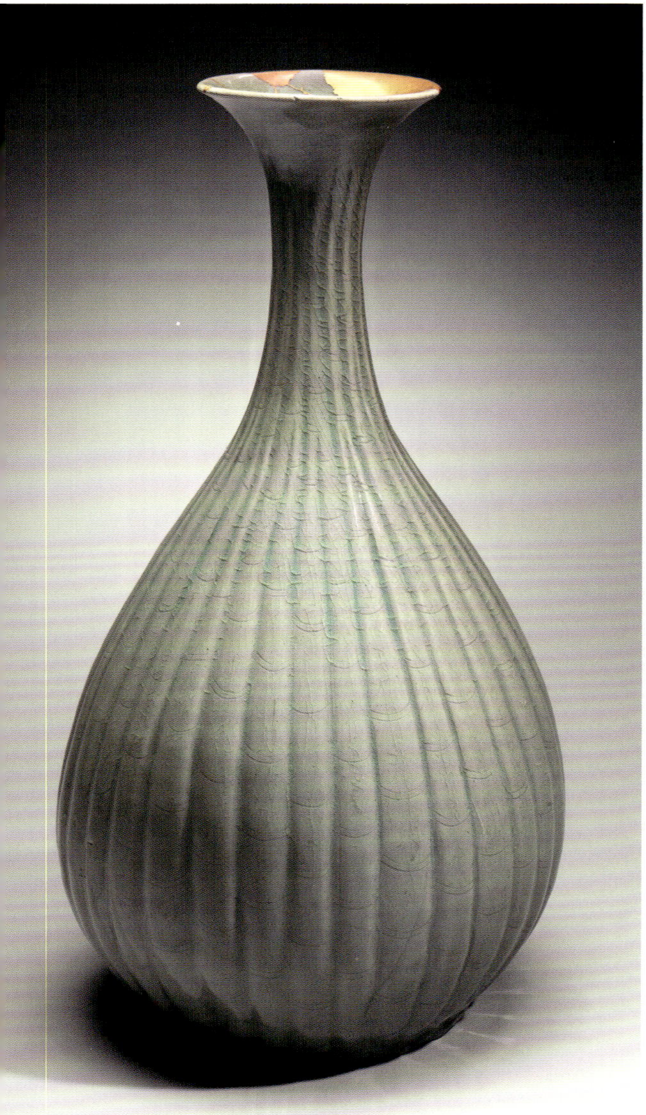

Bronze
H. 30.3 cm (11 15/16 in.); diam. of rim: 8.5 cm (3 3/8 in.); diam. of foot: 9.1 cm (3 9/16 in.)
Bequest of Desmond FitzGerald 27.198

These two bottles were probably used for wine. The celadon one, with its vertical ribs incised with horizontal joints to make them look like strips of bamboo, is a uniquely Korean creation. The entire vessel appears to be made of woven bamboo instead of clay.

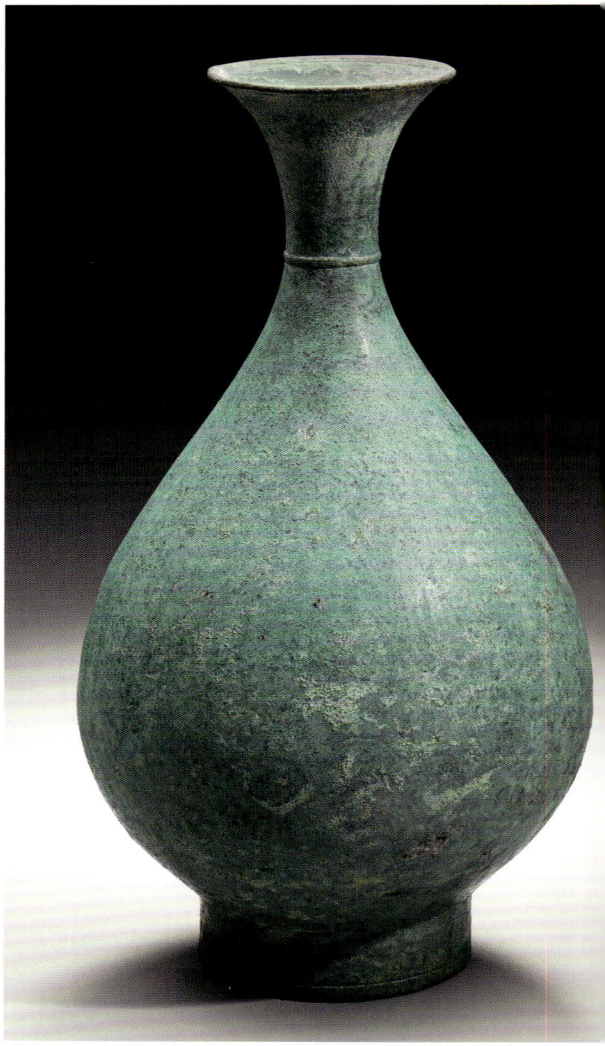

The base is unglazed and has spur marks. The mouth has been repaired in Japan with gold lacquer, which suggests that it was collected and highly prized there.

Pear-shaped bottles with round bodies and slender necks widening to a trumpet-shaped mouth such as these derive their shapes from Chinese wares. Their contours became exaggerated in Korea. Although a fundamentally ceramic shape in China, in Korea it was also made in beaten bronze. There is a close correlation between ceramic and bronze vessel shapes in the Goryeo period, and it has been suggested that bronze vessels were used in the winter and ceramic in the summer.

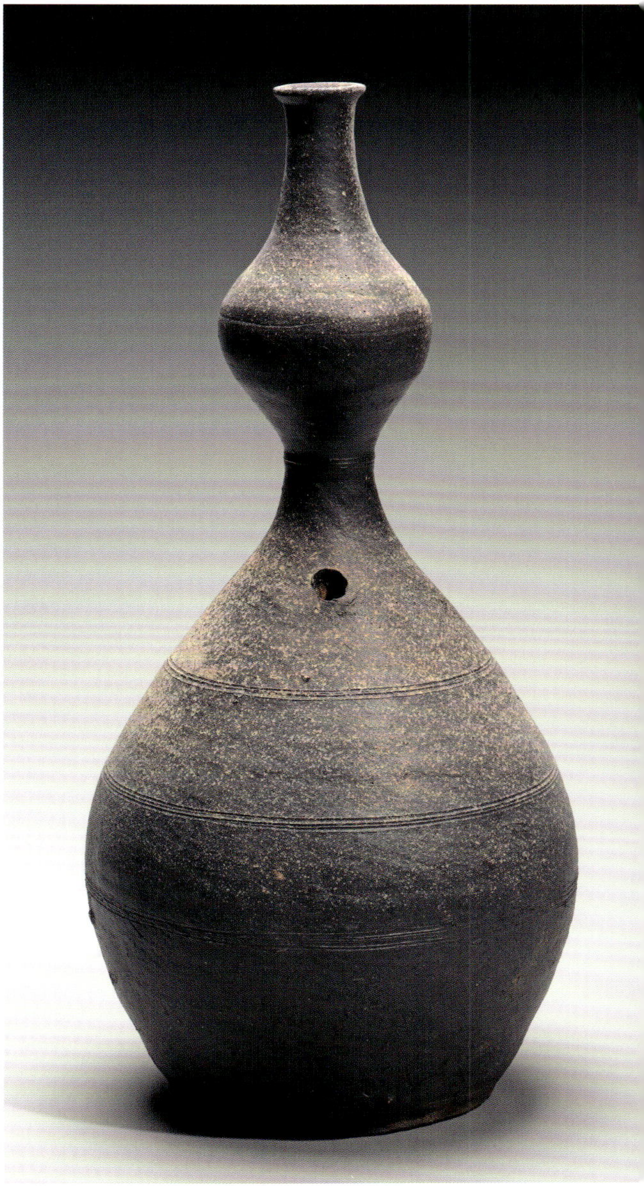

Bottle in the form of a double gourd

Goryeo period, 12th century

This graceful bottle has the shape of an elongated double gourd. Although unglazed, it shares its form with some celadon wares of the period. Aristocrats used the bottle at table for wine. The small hole in the shoulder of the lower body was for pouring, or possibly for the insertion of a spout.

Concentric lines are incised in three places on the lower body and around the pinched waist, forming a simple decorative scheme. Traces of natural glaze on the largely unglazed surface were caused by ash falling onto the vessel during firing. The gray stoneware clay was fired at a temperature of about 1000 degrees centigrade in a dragon kiln that climbed up the slope of a hill. It was probably one of the same kilns in southwest Korea used for celadons.

Stoneware with natural ash glaze
H. 41.6 (16 5/16 in.); diam. of base: 13 cm (5 1/8 in.)
Promised gift of John C. Weber L–R 276.2011

Jar with four handles

Goryeo period, 12th century

This jar may have been used to hold the placenta and umbilical cord from a royal birth. Umbilical cords of noble and royal babies were preserved in such jars and buried or secreted in a chamber, accompanied by prayers for the child's well-being. Sometimes they were enclosed within larger lidded jars. The same type of vessel was also used to hold cremated remains for royal burials.

This jar has a short rim and wide shoulders; the four loops at the shoulder were attached with applied clay flowers. The broken loop was repaired in Japan with gold lacquer. Carved around the mouth is a decorative band of mushrooms, thought to be auspicious because their name means "as you wish." Around the body of the jar are alternating hollyhock sprays and lotus scrolls. The jar originally had a lid with a central crossed loop handle. One could fix the lid on tightly by weaving a cord or string between the four handles on the shoulder and the handle on the lid. The thick glaze is dark grayish green with no crackle, and the bottom of the jar is covered with glaze except for the foot rim, which has eight spur marks.

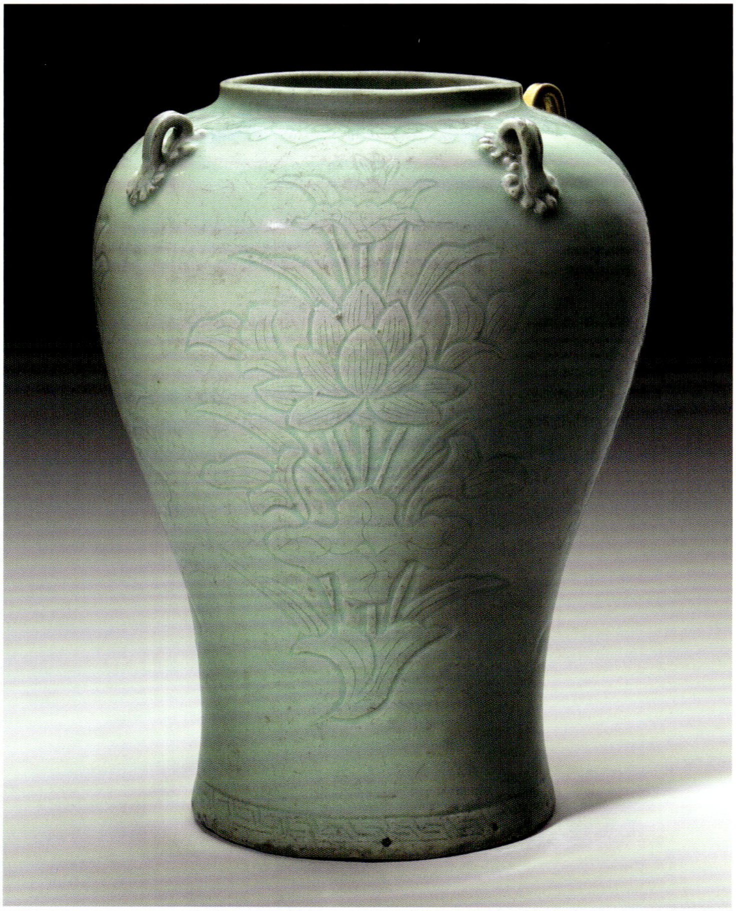

Stoneware with celadon glaze
H. 25.6 cm (10 1/16 in.); diam. of mouth: 10.4 cm (4 1/8 in.); diam. of foot: 12.2 cm (4 13/16 in.)
Gift of Miss Theodora Lyman—John Pickering Lyman Collection 19.927

Ewer in the shape of a bamboo shoot

Goryeo period, 12th century

This ewer resembles a bamboo shoot, another example of the Goryeo potters' inventiveness with natural forms. Its plump shape and exquisitely realistic modeling make it one of the finest examples known from the period. The different layers of the shoot are carved in overlapping fashion, and the striations on each layer are finely incised. The pointed tips of the outer layers appear to fold down realistically, while the inner tips point up toward the apex of the lid. The handle and the spout copy the form of bamboo stems; a twig-shaped loop at the top of the handle once accommodated a cord to attach the lid. The gray-green glaze is even and has hardly any crackle. The foot rim has eight spur marks. Both the base of the ewer and the interior of the lid are glazed. This ewer was made at the Sadang-ri kilns in Gangjin, in southwest Korea, and used for serving wine at a royal or aristocratic table, probably in the capital at Gaeseong.

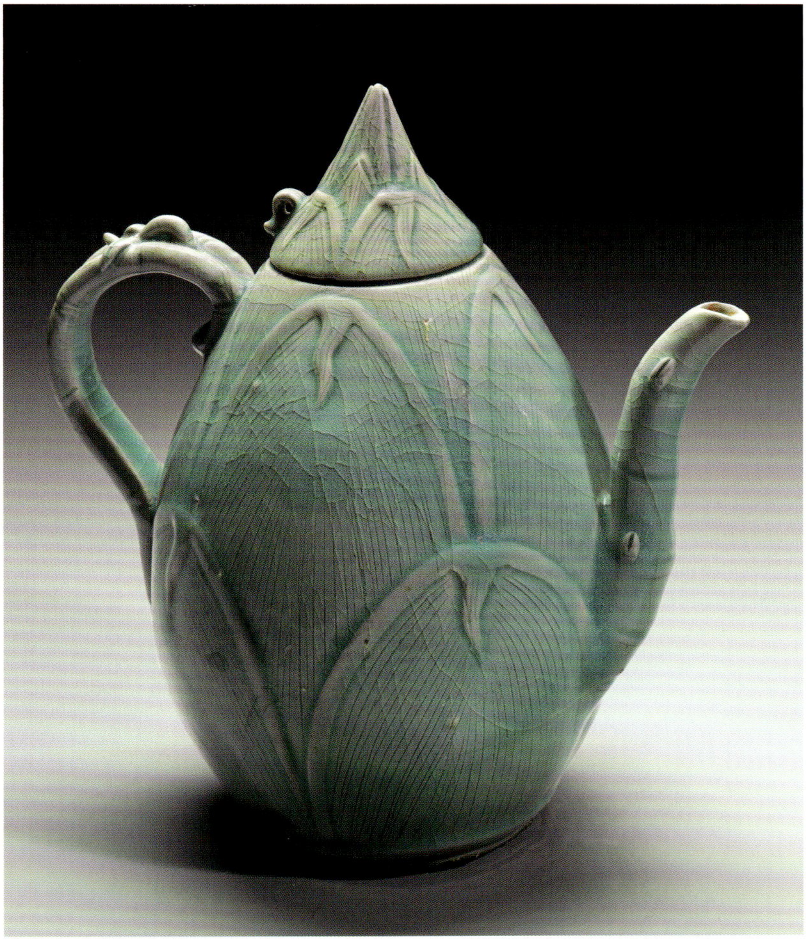

Stoneware with celadon glaze and carved and incised decoration
H. 24.9 cm (9 13/16 in.), diam. of foot: 9 cm (3 9/16 in.)
Bequest of Charles Bain Hoyt—Charles Bain Hoyt Collection
50.966a–b

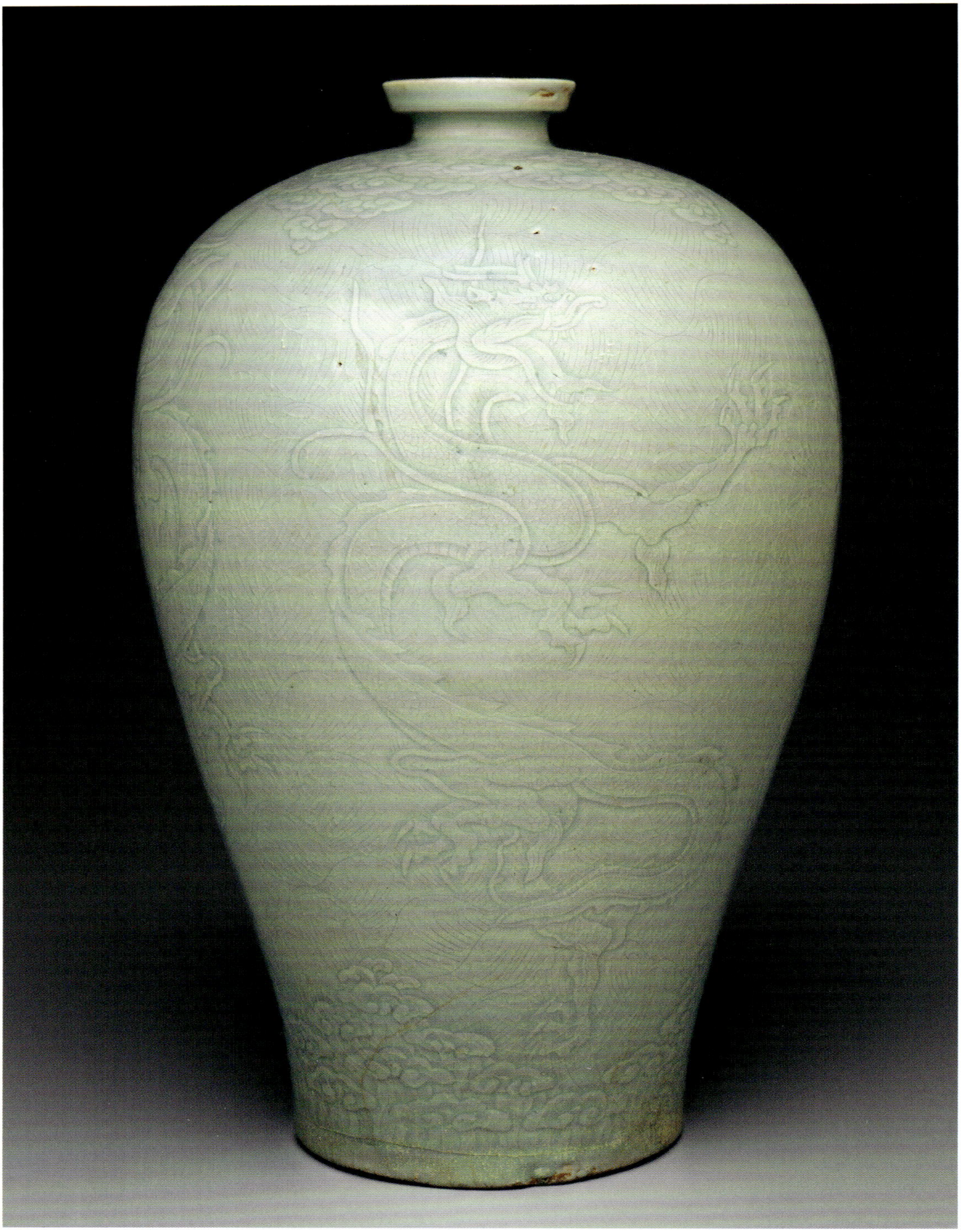

Prunus vase with carved dragon

Goryeo period, 12th century

Vessels of this type are traditionally thought to have contained wine. Called *maebyeong* or "plum blossom vase" in Korean, the type later came to be used to hold a single plum blossom, or prunus, branch. Excavations of ancient ships wrecked off the southwest coast of Korea have revealed a maebyeong labeled as a container for honey.

The shape of the vessel comes from Song-dynasty China. This early Goryeo example, with its straight sides, remains closer to its Chinese precedents than vases of the later Goryeo period, which have more exaggerated contours, bulbous shoulders, and slender waists that curve out toward the bottom. Carved lotus leaves decorate the shoulders and a carved design of a dragon emerging from waves covers the rest of the body. The wave designs and the face and scales of the dragon are particularly intricate and sophisticated among known vases of this type. The potter created shallow relief effects and smoother, softer lines by slanting the carving knife. This slanted-knife technique originated in the Yaozhou and Ding kilns in China during the Northern Song period (960–1127).

Stoneware with celadon glaze with incised decoration
H. 35.5 cm (14 in.); diam. of mouth: 6.2 cm (2 7/16 in.); diam. of foot: 12.5 cm (4 15/16 in.)
Special Korean Pottery Fund 11.1821

Duck-shaped water dropper

Goryeo period, 12th century

Aristocrats and scholars kept water droppers on their desks to moisten powdered ink, ground from an ink cake on an ink stone. The mixture of the water and ink powder was gently stirred with a brush and used to write. This delightful bird-shaped vessel dripped the water through a small opening next to its beak. The vessel may be filled through an opening on the bird's back, which probably once had a stopper in the shape of a lotus bud to complete the lotus flower petals modeled around the aperture. The duck's wing and tail feathers are finely carved and incised, and its eyes are dotted in iron black.

Several duck-shaped celadon water droppers have survived from the Goryeo period. Ducks were symbols of marital fidelity and happiness in both Korea and China and may also have been associated with examination success. This realistically modeled water dropper was produced at the Sadang-ri kilns in southwest Korea and shipped up the coast to the capital.

Stoneware with celadon glaze and underglaze iron-brown decoration
H. 6.1 cm (2 3/8 in.), l. 10.7 cm (4 3/16 in.), w. 5.8 cm (2 5/16 in.)
Bequest of Charles Bain Hoyt—Charles Bain Hoyt Collection 50.964

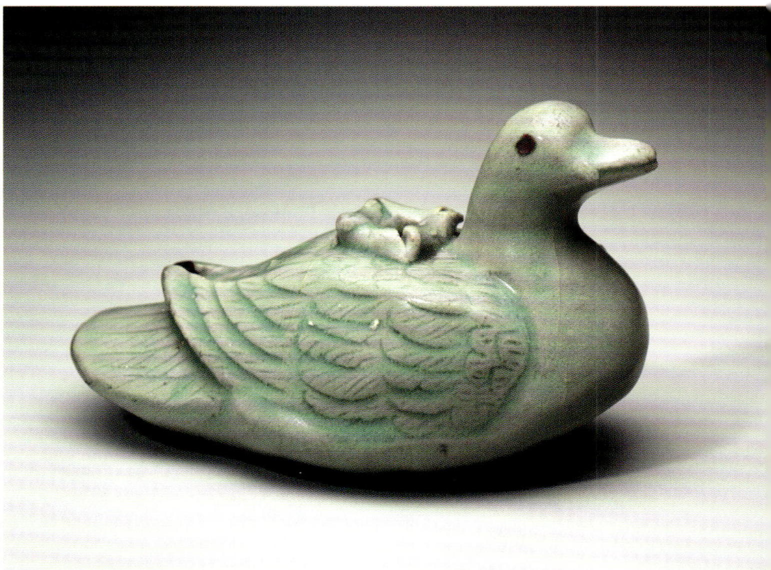

Lion-shaped pillow

Goryeo period, 12th century

Ceramic pillows or headrests were made in several shapes during the Goryeo period. Some were boxlike whereas others, such as this one, had animal-shaped bases. The latter were not as common and were most likely used by aristocrats at court. Decoration could be openwork, carved or incised, or inlaid, and sometimes included auspicious symbols, such as cranes for long life, peonies for marital bliss, or seeded fruit for many children. Pillows were also made of bamboo, and both the ceramic and bamboo types would have been comfortable for use in the hot summer.

The craftsman of this pillow concentrated on the naturalistic rendering of the lions and the balance of the slightly curved headrest held aloft by the two beasts. The lions—whose eyes, accentuated with iron-brown dots, make their expressions remarkably lively—sit back to back on an oblong base incised with a band of lotus petals. Their splendid bushy tails meet in the center of the pillow under the sloping headrest. Incised clouds and scrolls cover the area on top. The glaze of the entire pillow is even and thick, and there are six small spur marks on the bottom.

Stoneware with celadon glaze and underglaze iron-brown decoration
Overall: H. 11 cm ($4\frac{5}{16}$ in.); base: L. 16.5 cm ($6\frac{1}{2}$ in.); top: L. 19.5 cm ($7\frac{11}{16}$ in.)
Museum purchase with funds donated by Mrs. Charles Gaston Smith's Group 50.3592

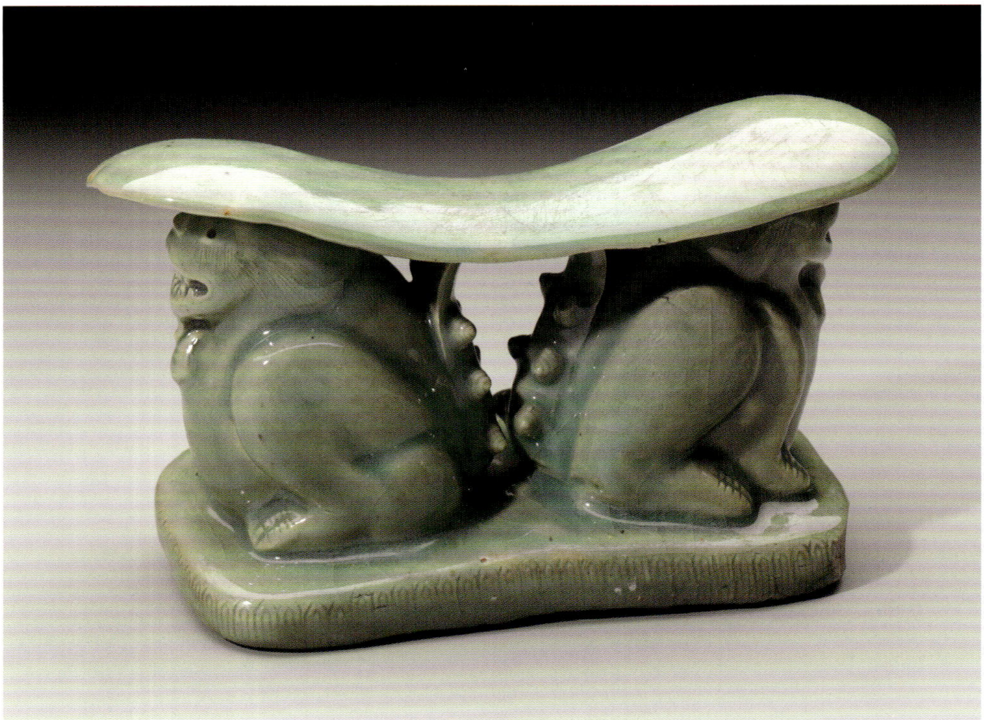

Rectangular incense burner

Goryeo period, early 12th century

Rectangular Korean incense burners are based on Song-dynasty Chinese archaistic bronzes, which were modeled after ancient ritual vessels. The later Chinese bronzes were smaller than the originals and came to be used as incense burners or as planters. Ceramic copies of the archaistic bronzes were also made in Song China and these no doubt influenced production of the form in Korean celadon. Xu Jing, the envoy from Song China who wrote an account of his visit in 1123, remarked on the fine celadon incense burners he noticed in Korea.

This vessel may have been used as an incense burner or as a planter, perhaps for narcissus bulbs or a miniature tree. The decoration was made in a mold, a technique also introduced from China. The lotuses and swimming ducks on the sides are in typical Song style, with tall stems supporting lotus flowers and leaves rising high out of the water. There are also auspicious fungus motifs around the bottom and chrysanthemums around the top of each side panel. The legs of the vessel are beautifully made in the shape of clouds; they resemble woodcarving but perhaps copy the legs of bronzes. The entire base of the vessel is glazed.

Stoneware with celadon glaze and impressed decoration
L. 16 cm (6 5/16 in.), w. 10.8 cm (4 1/4 in.), h. 14 cm (5 1/2 in.)
Gift of Mrs. Albertine W. F. Valentine, residuary legatee under the will of Hervey E. Wetzel 19.678

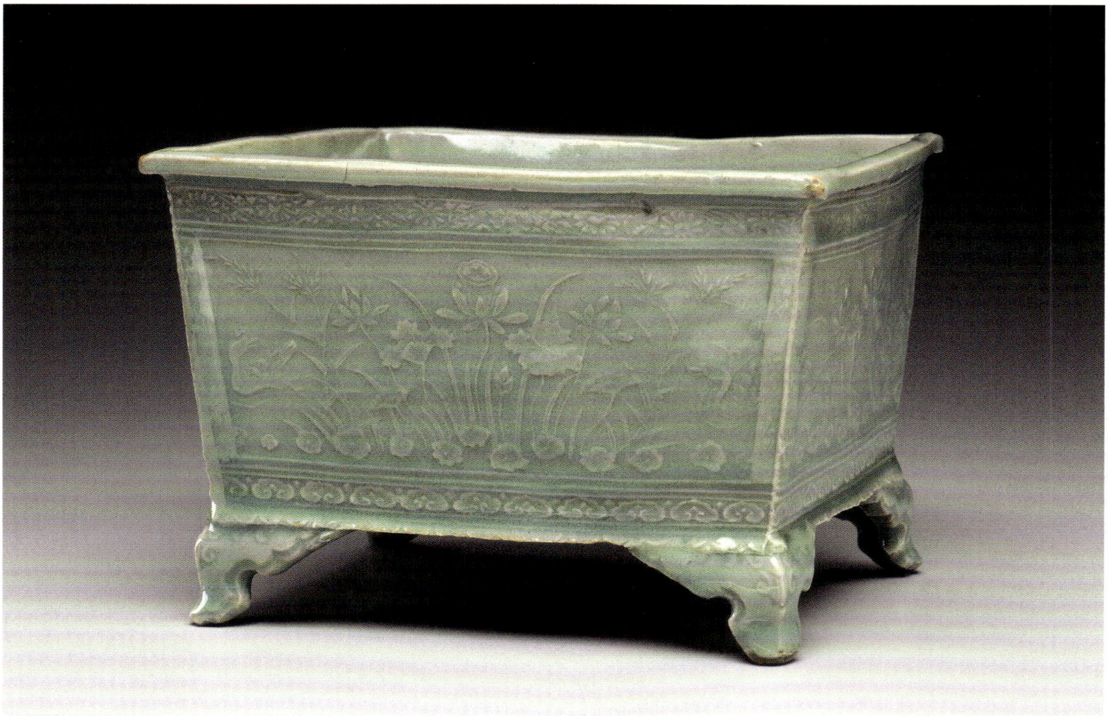

Dish with incised cloud and bird design

Goryeo Period, 12th century

Celadon wares were used at household tables and in the many Buddhist temples of the Goryeo period, so it is difficult to know what this shallow dish once contained. Although low in profile, it has an elegant contour. The precisely incised decoration of the interior consists of two lines at the top and bottom of the inner wall with delicate clouds between them. The center of the dish features two long-tailed birds, which seem to be chasing each other as they fly around the dish. This motif, usually identified as a pair of parrots, was popular on Goryeo celadon wares as well as metalwork. However, some scholars believe that the parrots are a variant of paired phoenixes. Phoenixes were symbols of good fortune, as they were thought to appear only in times of peace and prosperity. Pairs of phoenixes frequently decorated Chinese Yue-ware dishes, which had great influence on Goryeo celadons. The Goryeo potters' attempts at depicting the mythical, unseen phoenix may have resulted in the parrot, a bird they might have actually seen. This dish has a good blue-green glaze with slight crackle and the usual three spur marks on the base. The color is due to the low quantities of iron oxide in the glaze.

Stoneware with celadon glaze
H. 4.4 cm (1¾ in.), diam. of rim: 17.7 cm (6 15/16 in.)
Morse Collection. Museum purchase with funds donated by contribution. 92.3003

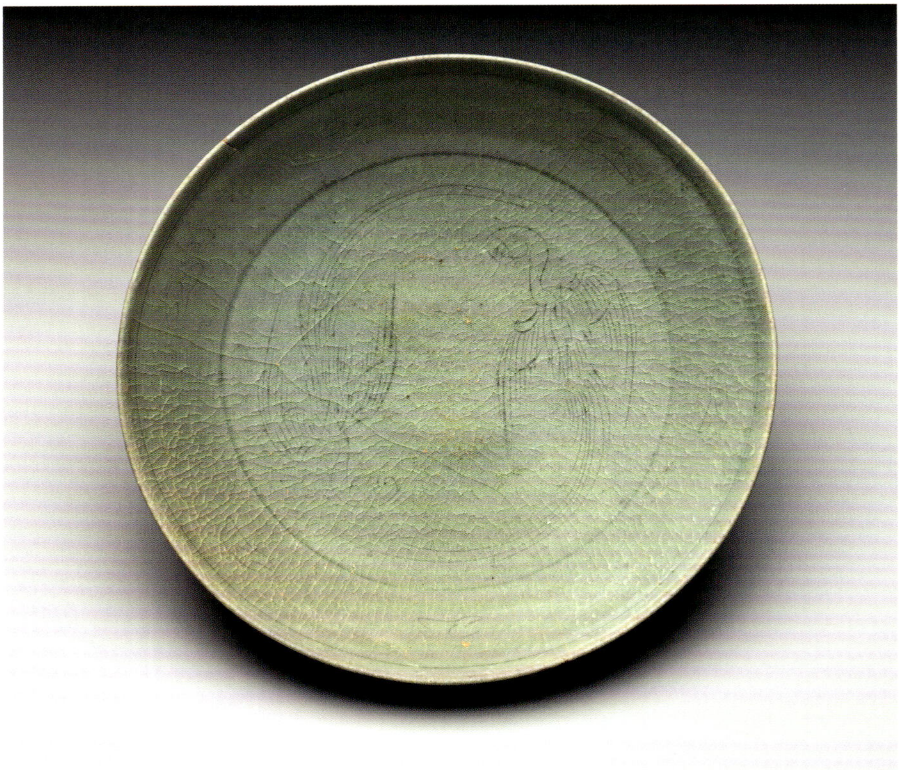

Spouted bowls

Goryeo period, 12th century

Bronze
H. 7.1 cm (2 13/16 in.); diam. of rim: 16.6 cm (6 9/16 in.);
diam. of foot: 9.7 cm (3 13/16 in.)
Bequest of Charles Bain Hoyt—Charles Bain Hoyt Collection
50.1410

Stoneware with celadon glaze
H. 5.6 cm (2 3/16 in.), diam. of rim: 17.2 cm (6 3/4 in.)
Bequest of Charles Bain Hoyt—Charles Bain Hoyt Collection
50.980

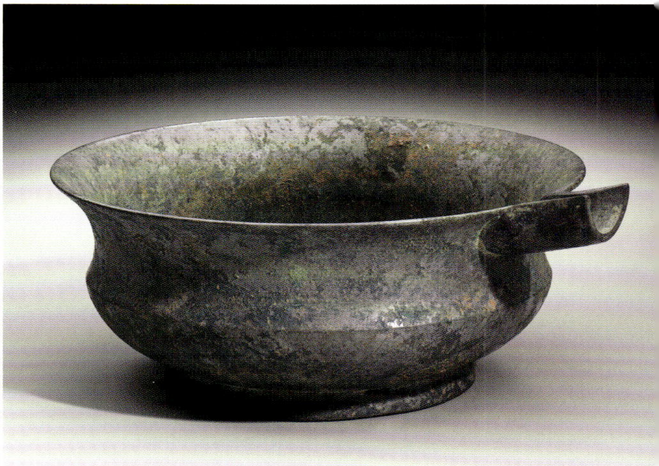

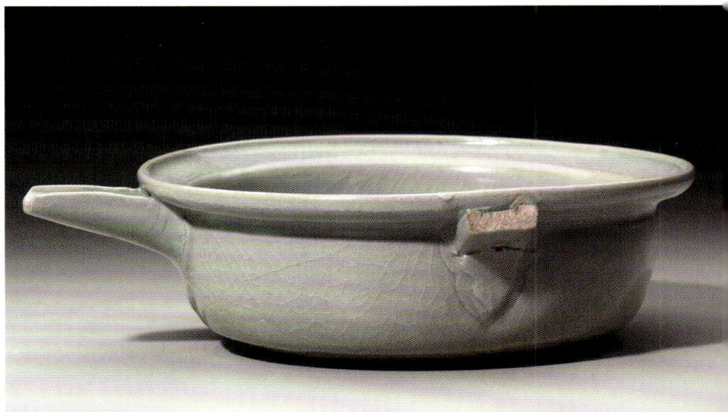

The same vessel shapes were often produced in ceramic and in metal during the Goryeo period. Some scholars surmise that the bronze vessels were used in winter and the ceramic ones in summer. It is difficult to know with certainty what purpose this spouted vessel type served. It may have held water or wine for pouring at table or in rituals, perhaps ablutions.

The plain bronze bowl has a dramatically curvaceous profile in typical Goryeo style, with a flared lip and a separately made, attached spout and foot. The celadon bowl has a straighter profile and a spout that was added after the body was thrown. The handle at the side has broken off. The interior of the bowl is decorated with incised scrolls around the everted lip and a fine pale green glaze over the whole. The glaze on the exterior is a yellowish color in places from oxidization in the kiln. The finest pale green celadon glaze is produced in a reducing atmosphere, which causes the iron oxide in the glaze to lose its oxygen and turn green in the process. If oxygen is inadvertently allowed to enter the kiln during the firing process, perhaps because someone opens the kiln door, a yellow color is the result, as in this piece.

Long-necked bottle with lid

Goryeo period, 12th century

This long-necked bottle type originated in the Yue kilns of southeastern China. Such bottles in Korea may have had a ritual use, perhaps as containers for pure water or wine. They all once had flat lids or stoppers. This bottle has retained its lid with a lotus-shaped knob. The knob and the decoration of incised lotus designs—petals around the bottom of the neck and base, and floral sprays on the body—suggest an originally Buddhist context. The neck features scattered cloud designs. There is a shallow circular foot ring with five spur marks.

Very few bottles like this one remain, especially with their lids intact. Korean potters elongated the neck and produced a much more elegant and graceful shape than the Chinese models on which their vessels are based. Some Korean versions are also octagonal or beveled and some are a plain cylindrical shape. Other examples are decorated with inlay. Korean celadon long-necked bottles were popular in Japan, where they are known as "crane-necked" bottles or "gun barrel" bottles.

Stoneware with celadon glaze and incised decoration
H. 37.1 cm (14 5/8 in.); diam. of mouth: 2.4 cm (15/16 in.); diam. of foot: 10 cm (3 15/16 in.)
Julia Bradford Huntington James Fund and Gift of Mrs. Frank Gair Macomber 13.1559a–b

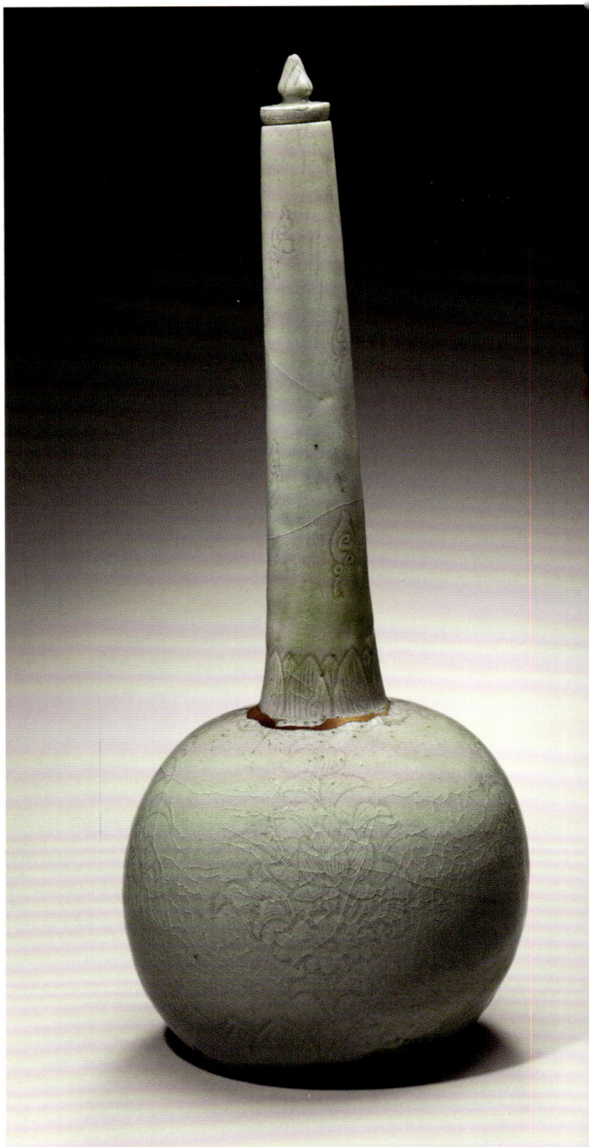

Kundika with inlaid peonies

Goryeo period, late 12th–13th century

The shape of this vessel, called a *kundika*, is based on bronze versions that originated in India and spread to Southeast Asia and China during the Tang dynasty. Monks probably first used kundikas as personal water containers. Eventually the practice developed of using kundikas in Buddhist ceremonies to purify the ground by sprinkling it with water. The kundika may be filled by pouring water in through the short spout at the side and emptied by pouring it out through the tall spout at the top. The Korean name for such vessels is *jeong-byeong*, which means "pure water bottle."

A well-balanced clay vessel in this shape, with rounded shoulders and a gently tapering body, is not easy to make. Ceramic kundikas from Korea usually have tall faceted spouts, as in this example. The inlaid peony design is also typically Korean—the stylized flowers are arranged as roundels, similar in fashion to designs on silk costumes worn by deities in Goryeo Buddhist paintings. This kundika has lost the small round lid that once covered the short spout at the side and has suffered from some oxidization during firing, which turned the top of the tall spout yellow-brown.

Stoneware with celadon glaze
H. 35.5 cm (14 in.), diam. of foot: 9.8 cm (3 3/8 in.)
Helen and Alice Colburn Fund 27.328

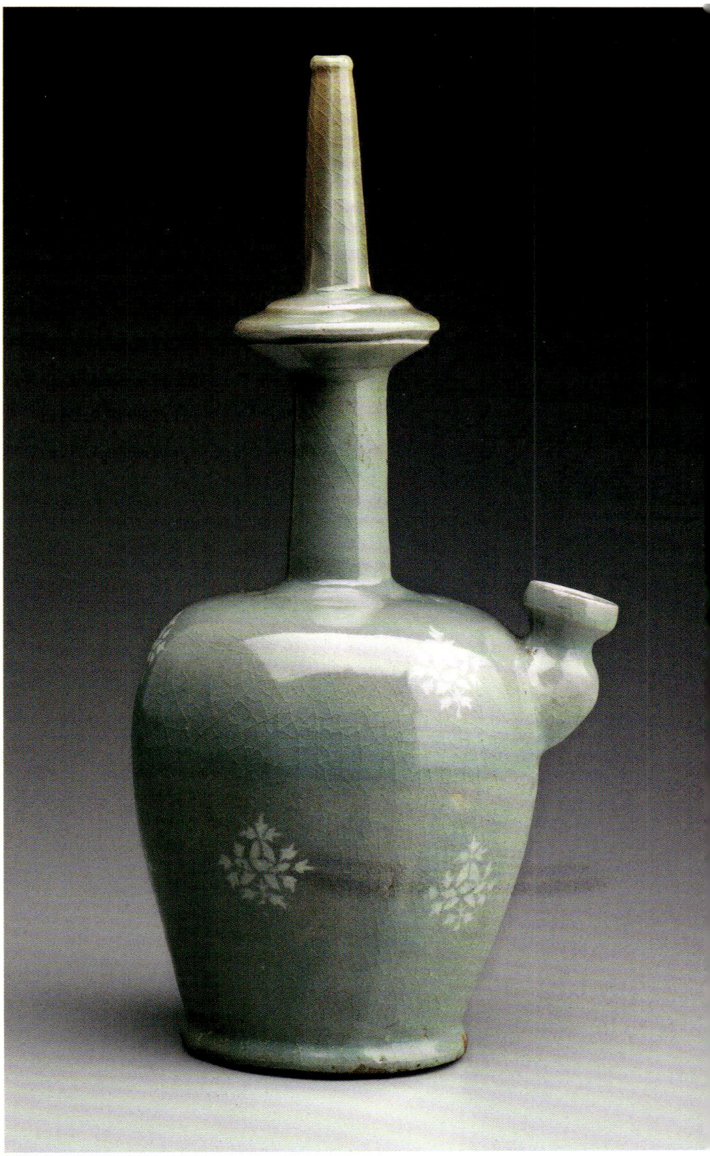

Prunus vase with inlaid bamboo and cranes

Goryeo period, early 13th century

This vase was originally made as a wine bottle with a lid in the shape of an inverted flat-bottomed cup, now missing. The masterfully executed sanggam inlay of bamboo and birds on this piece is unique among celadon maebyeong vases. The decorative scheme is unusual because there are no horizontal decorative bands at top or bottom and the entire vessel surface is used as if it were a painting. The design is reminiscent of bird and flower paintings of Song-dynasty China. A bird sits in a bamboo branch on one side, and a group of three cranes fly away on the other. The birds are inlaid in white slip, with the details of their feathers, beaks, and eyes, as well as the bamboo branch, picked out in black.

Stoneware with celadon glaze
H. 30.8 cm (12 1/8 in.); diam. of mouth: 5.3 cm (2 1/16 in.); diam. of foot: 10.8 cm (4 1/4 in.)
Bequest of Charles Bain Hoyt—Charles Bain Hoyt Collection 50.989

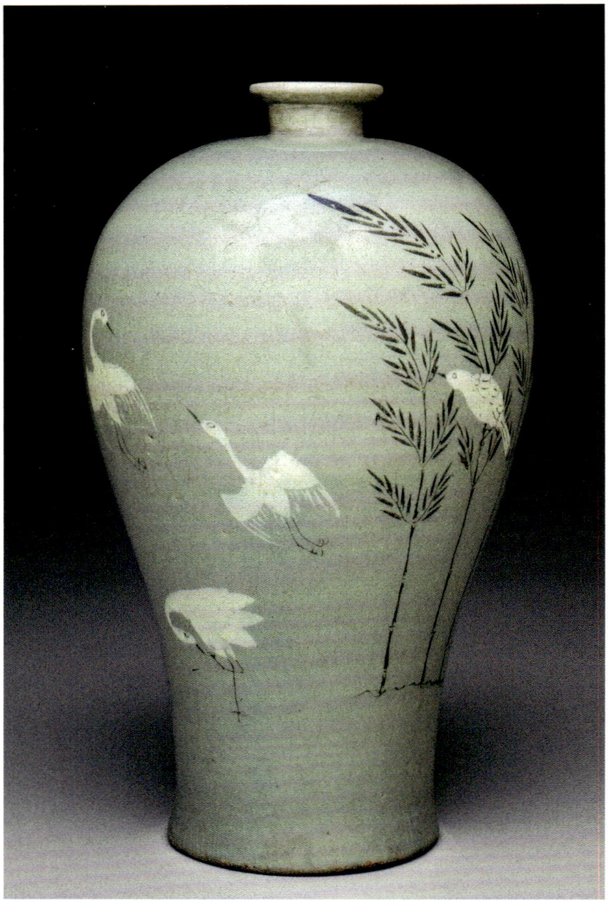

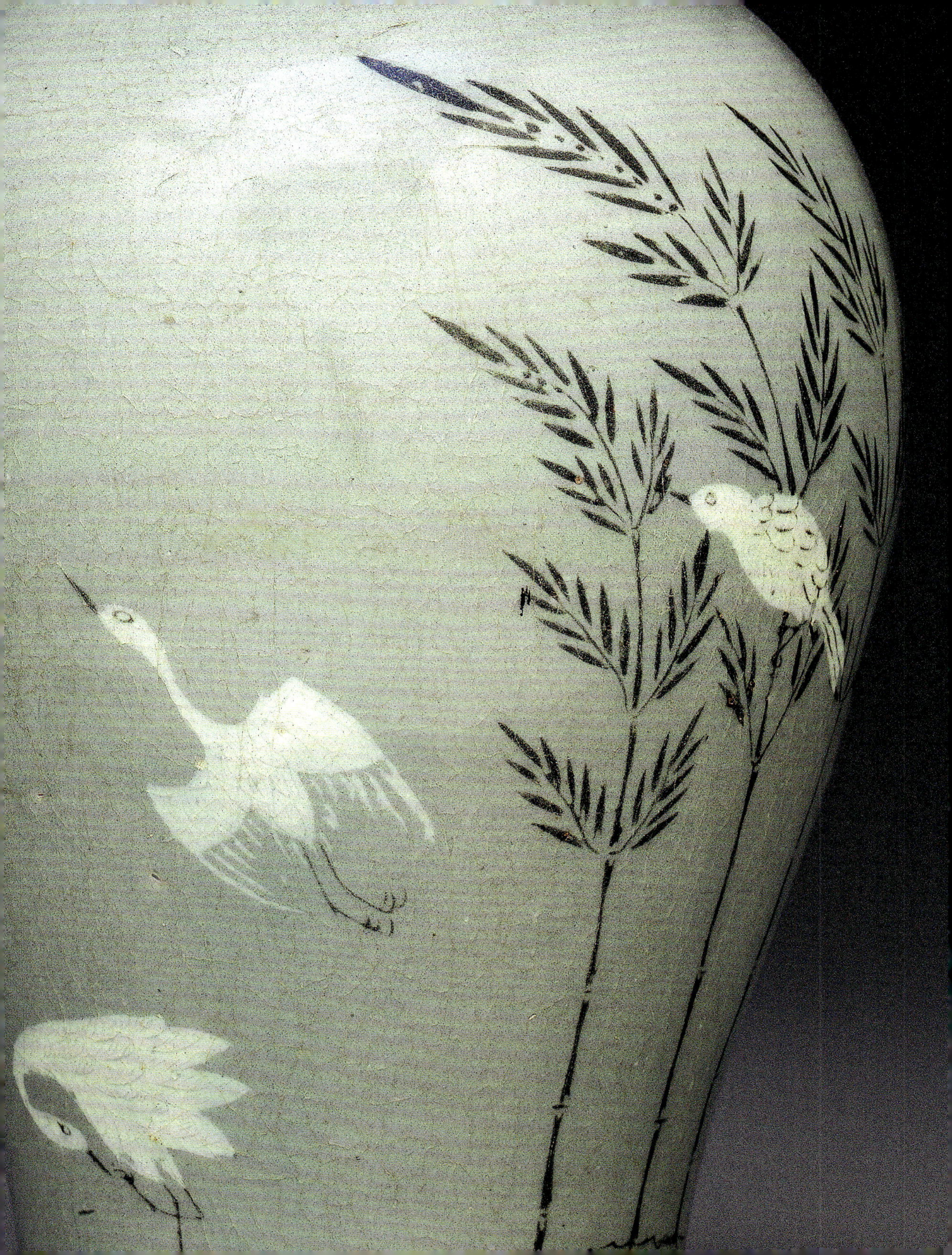

Luohan figure

Goryeo period, 13th century

This figure is very rare. It portrays either a Buddhist monk or a disciple of Buddha called a *luohan (nahan* in Korean), sometimes also called an *arhat*. It may have been part of a set of sixteen or eighteen luohan. Such sets often adorned Buddhist temples. Sets of large ceramic luohan from China's Liao dynasty (907–1125) survive in some numbers, and these may have influenced Korean artists during the Goryeo period, when there was much cultural influence from Liao and the Buddhist church was all-important and powerful.

The standing figure clasps his hands inside his sleeves. He is modeled in a solid, block-like manner with square ears and a flat nose, but his facial features have been applied with great care in underglaze iron-brown. He has hair, which is unusual, as most monks had shaved heads. He also has black stubble on his chin and black eyebrows, black pupils, and white eyes. There is a lot of kiln sand on the base as well as inlaid Chinese characters, two of which read *wang'ga*, meaning either Wang Family or King's Family. During the Goryeo period, Chinese characters were used for writing and for inscriptions such as this one.

Stoneware with celadon glaze and underglaze iron-brown painting
H. 18.3 cm (7 3/16 in.), base: 8.6 x 7 cm (3 3/8 x 2 3/4 in.)
Bequest of Charles Bain Hoyt—Charles Bain Hoyt Collection 50.1004

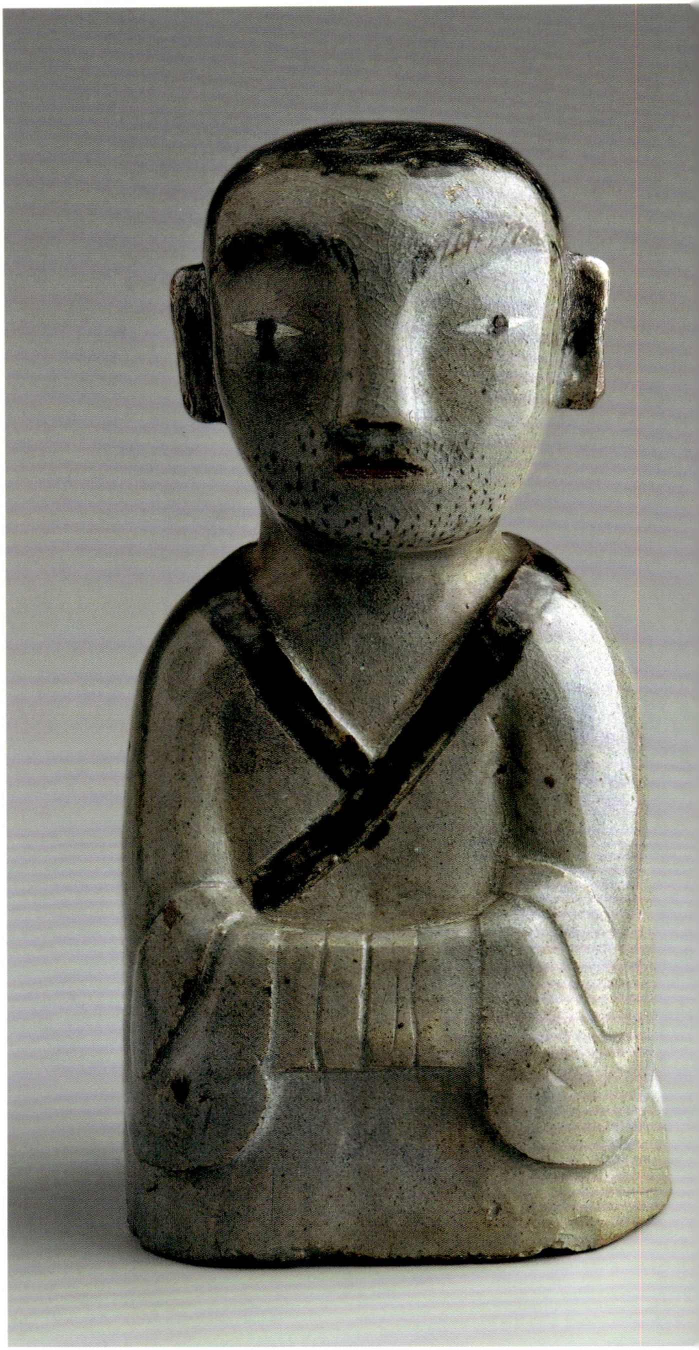

Conical cup

Goryeo period, 13th century

The pointed bottom of this cup made it impossible to put down when it was full of wine. Some scholars suggest that handle-less cups in this shape were used for making toasts, which would necessitate downing the wine in one go and then placing it upside down to show it had been emptied. Others surmise that they show influence from horse-riding Mongols, who could have used such cups while riding.

Three spur marks near the bottom and a glazed lip indicate that this cup was fired propped up on its pointed bottom instead of upside-down, which might have been easier. The decoration is a very good example of the reverse inlay technique. There are four bands, the uppermost one being a thin band of fret design inlaid in white slip. The chrysanthemum surrounded by a double circle in the second band, and the fourth band's large lotus petals, which use the pointed bottom of the cup as their center, are also reverse-inlaid in white slip. However, the rest of the second band and the third band below it are full of vigorous scrolls created when the background was scraped away and painted with white slip. The scrolls stood out on the original clay body as a result, and when the body was covered with celadon glaze, it turned the scrolls green.

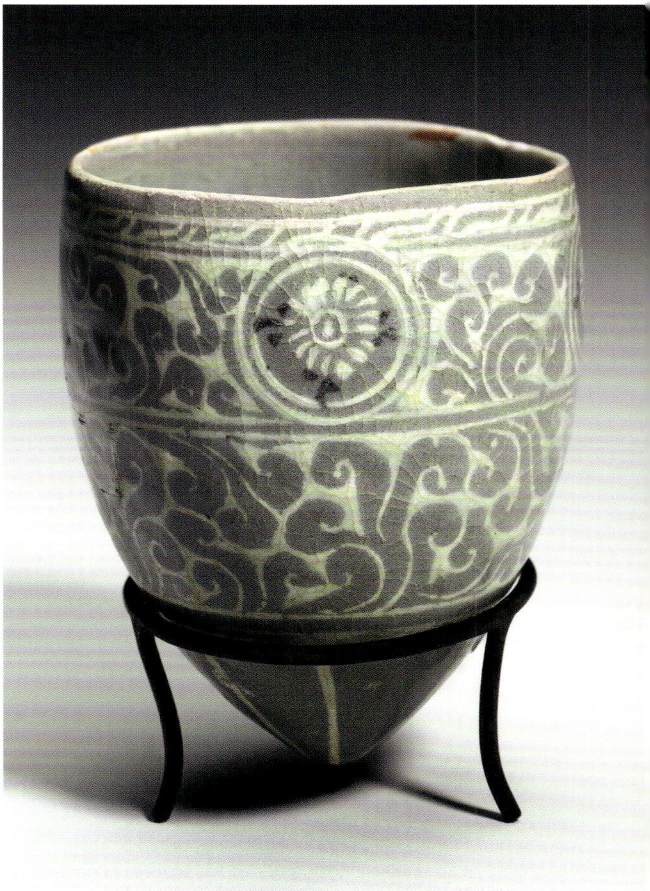

Stoneware with celadon glaze and inlaid decoration
H. 9 cm (3 9/16 in.), diam. of rim: 6.8 cm (2 11/16 in.)
Bequest of Charles Bain Hoyt—Charles Bain Hoyt Collection
50.999

Gourd-shaped ewer with inlaid grapevine

Goryeo period, 13th century

This tall wine ewer in the shape of an elongated gourd originally had a lid and might also have been accompanied by a warming basin. The ewer has a particularly elegant shape, a long spout, and a beautifully detailed handle that resembles part of a grapevine. The decoration of grapevines, leaves, and grapes, executed in a combination of inlay and reverse-inlay techniques, covers the entire surface of the vessel. The background surface was scraped away and inlaid with white slip so the leaves and vines stand out in green. Then the veins of the leaves were inlaid in black. The grapes are outlined in white slip and filled in with black slip. In some rare examples of this design, the grapes are filled in with underglaze red.

Grapes were introduced to Asia from the West along the Silk Road, first to China during the Tang dynasty and sometime thereafter to Korea. Grapevines became a popular subject for Korean artists and craftsmen, who used them through the nineteenth century on ceramics, lacquer, and paintings. The frequent combination of grapevine motifs with frolicking children has suggested to some scholars that the subject has an origin in Classical Bacchanalian imagery, and that its significance was transformed in Korea to symbolize abundance and many offspring.

Stoneware with celadon glaze

H. 32 cm (12⅝ in.); diam. of rim: 2.7 cm (1 1/16 in.); diam. of foot: 9.2 cm (3⅝ in.)

Bequest of Charles Bain Hoyt—Charles Bain Hoyt Collection 50.991a–b

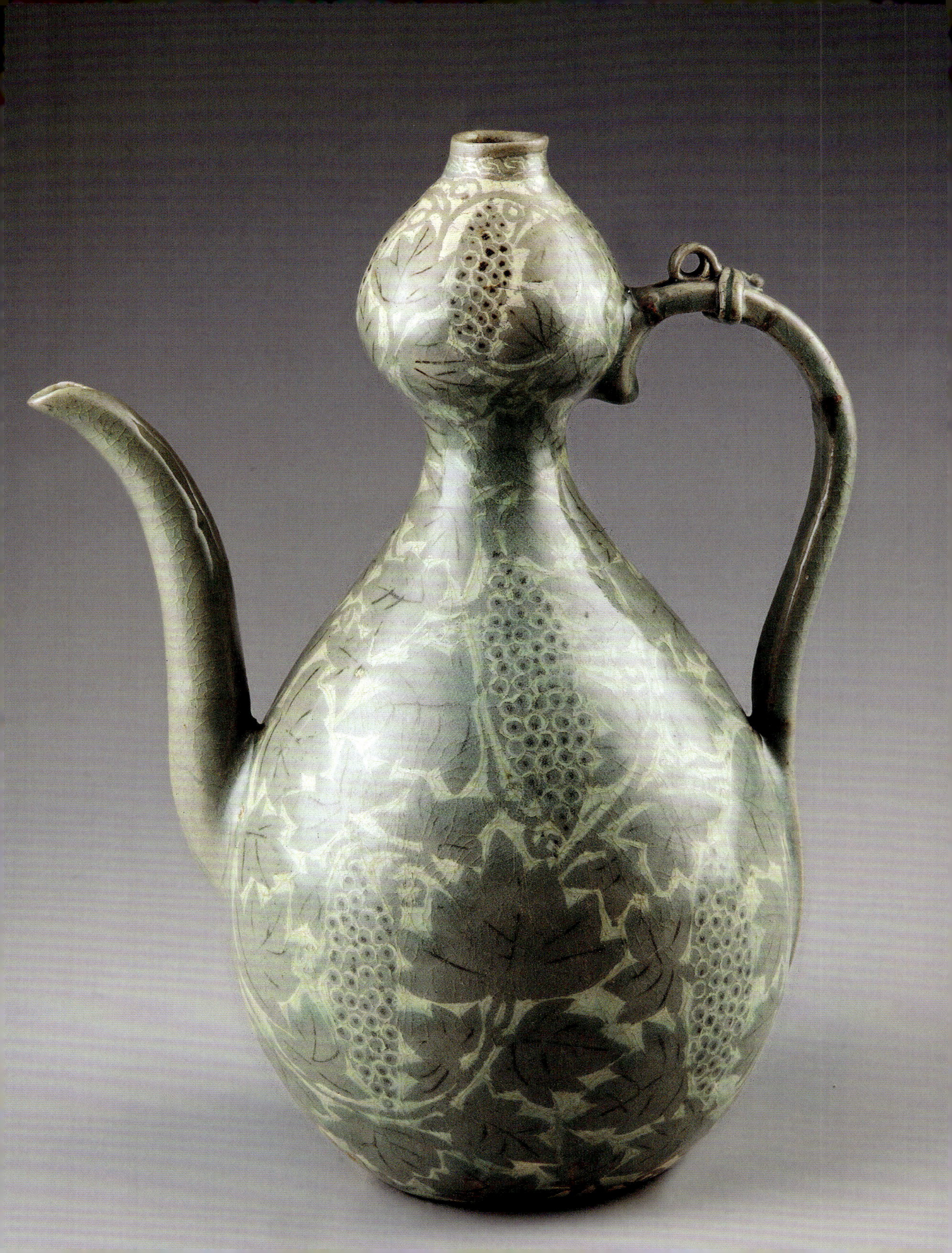

Melon-shaped ewer with inlaid peony and chrysanthemum

Goryeo period, 13th century

This wine ewer is formed in vertical sections to resemble a melon. Traders along the Silk Road introduced melons to Korea from the West via China. The melon's many seeds are auspicious symbols for many children. A warming basin may have originally accompanied the ewer.

Compared to earlier examples, this ewer has a relatively tall and elegant shape, deep vertical lobes, and a long spout and handle. The lid and the loop on the handle are replacements, but their shape and color reflect the originals. The loop on the handle was intended for attaching the lid by threading a cord through it and the loop on the lid.

The decoration consists of alternating peony and chrysanthemum sprays in the vertical lobes of the body, arabesques around the neck, and stylized lotus petals around the base, all inlaid in black or white slip. The grayish color of the glaze suggests a thirteenth-century date.

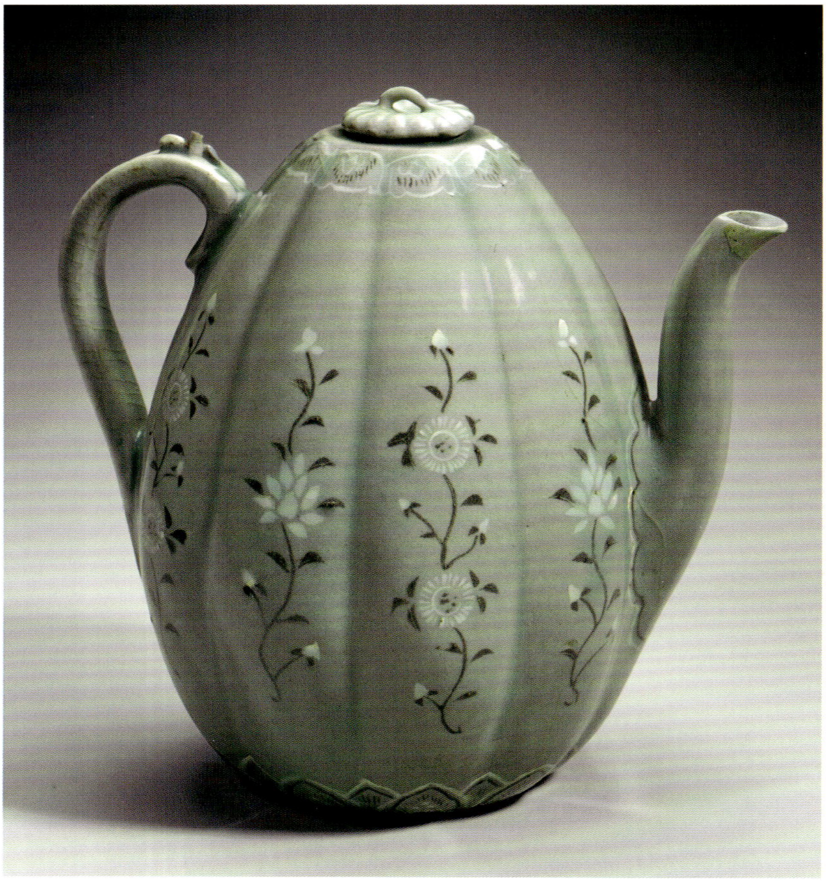

Stoneware with celadon glaze
H. 20.3 cm (8 in.); diam. of lid: 3.7 cm (1 7/16 in.); diam. of foot: 8 cm (3 1/8 in.)
Bequest of Charles Bain Hoyt—Charles Bain Hoyt Collection 50.985a–b

Flower-shaped cup with stand

Goryeo period, 13th century

Korean potters made cups and stands in sets for royal and aristocratic families living in the Goryeo capital of Gaeseong. Shards of similar vessels have been excavated from the Yucheon-ri kilns in North Jeolla Province in southwest Korea, where this type of set was probably made. Boats transported such tableware to the capital up the west coast of the Korean peninsula.

This small cup and stand may have been used for wine or tea. Xu Jing, the Chinese envoy who visited Korea in 1123, wrote, "The people of Gaoli have become much addicted to tea drinking and many kinds of tea implements are made." Based on silver prototypes, both the cup and its stand resemble flowers. The beautifully crafted ten-lobed cup has a high flared foot and a scalloped rim. Each lobe is decorated with a vertical row of four stylized chrysanthemum blossoms inlaid in white with black leaves. The saucer part of the stand has pairs of chrysanthemums inlaid on each lobe and its foot has single chrysanthemums. The raised central seat on which the cup rests is decorated with carved inverted lotus petals.

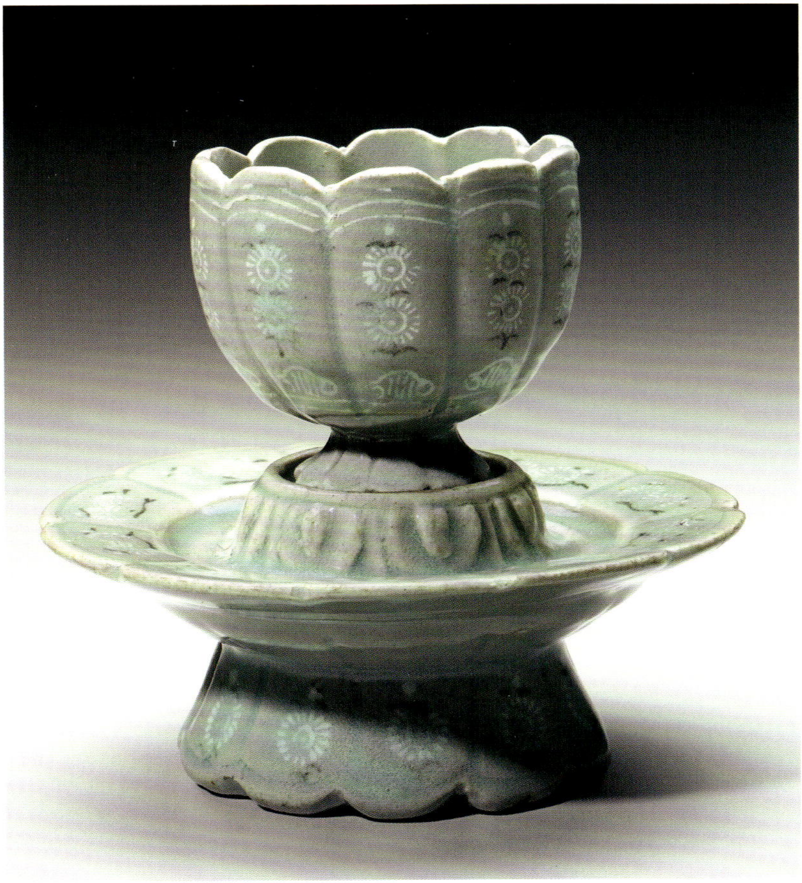

Stoneware with celadon glaze and inlaid decoration
Overall: H. 11.6 cm (4 9/16 in.)
Cup: H. 6.6 cm (2 5/8 in.); diam. of rim: 7.2 cm (2 13/16); diam. of foot: 3.6 cm (1 7/16 in.)
Stand: H. 4.8 cm (1 7/8 in.); diam. of rim: 12.8 cm (5 1/16 in.); diam. of foot: 7.8 cm (3 1/16 in.)
Gift of Frederick L. Jack
35.1353a–b

Oil bottle with stopper

Goryeo period, 12th–13th century

Stoneware with celadon glaze and incised floral design

H. 11.1 cm (4 3/8 in.); diam. of lid: 3.4 cm (1 5/16 in.); diam. of foot: 4.8 cm (1 7/8 in.)

Bequest of Charles Bain Hoyt—Charles Bain Hoyt Collection 50.977a–b

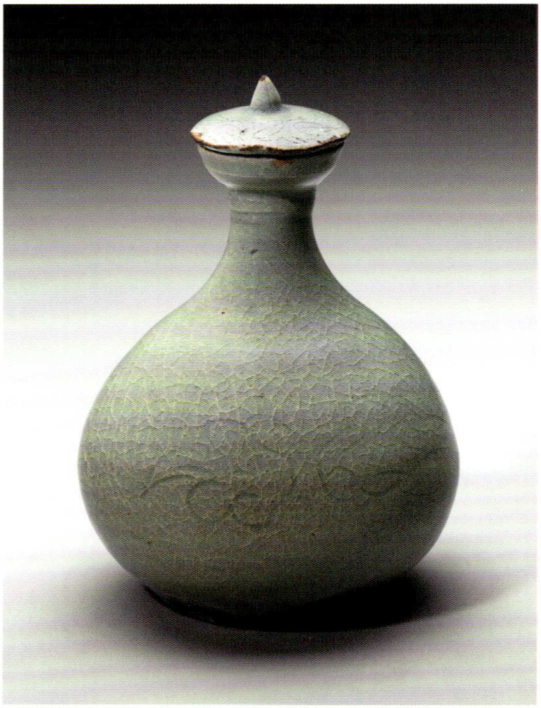

Oil bottle with inlaid chrysanthemums and cranes

Goryeo period, 12th–13th century

Stoneware with celadon glaze

H. 4.1 cm (1 5/8 in.); diam. of mouth: 2.2 cm (7/8 in.); diam. of foot 4.4 cm (1 3/4 in.)

Anonymous gift—Charles Bain Hoyt Collection 67.283

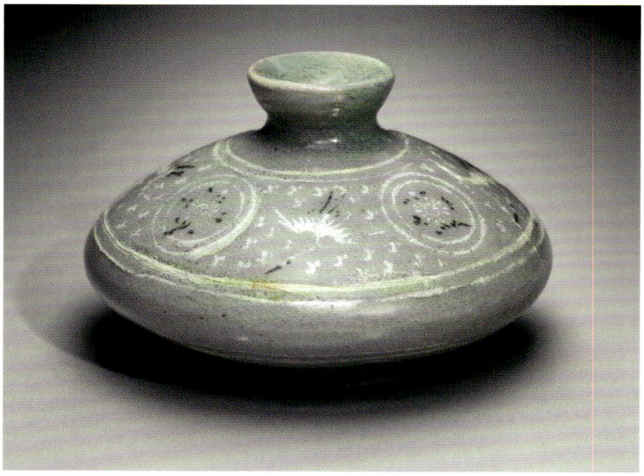

Elite women in the Goryeo period used oil from small ceramic bottles when combing their long black hair. Sometimes such bottles were part of cosmetic sets that also included lidded boxes for rouge and face powder. The taller oil bottle here is particularly rare because of its shape and size, and because it retains its lid with a knob in the shape of a lotus bud. Incised floral designs decorate the rest of the lid, and the entire vessel is covered with a finely crackled gray-green glaze.

The smaller, flatter bottle is a more common shape. The decoration of these bottles employs a variety of techniques, such as incising, inlay, and reverse inlay. This bottle has a band of inlaid decoration around the shoulder, within double lines of white slip. Small, stylized chrysanthemum florets, enclosed in double roundels, alternate with cranes flying among clouds.

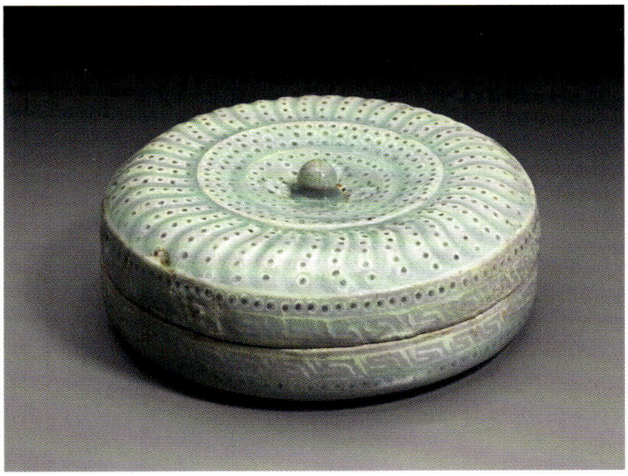

Lidded cosmetic box with bud-shaped knob

Goryeo period, 13th century

Some scholars have suggested that small lidded boxes like this one were used to hold incense, but they were more likely used as cosmetic boxes for face powder or rouge. This box is large compared to most other examples, and has a lid with a knob in the shape of a flower bud. The knob is unusual as most boxes of this type have flat lids. The inlaid decoration in black and white slip and the dip in the center of the lid are also rare. Four inlaid chrysanthemums are surrounded by rings of small beads or dots, perhaps extremely stylized chrysanthemums. The outer band of decoration consists of the same beads in rows radiating from the center.

Stoneware with celadon glaze
H. 4.3 cm (1 11/16 in.), diam. of base: 11.8 cm (4 5/8 in.)
Bequest of Charles Bain Hoyt—Charles Bain Hoyt Collection
50.1006a–b

Covered box with inlaid phoenix and floral patterns

Goryeo period, 13th century

This large box with vertical sides and an angular profile may be imitating a bronze or silver box and may be part of a set of boxes within boxes. It was used either for medicine or for Buddhist relics. The lively decoration of a pair of phoenixes and a flaming pearl in the center of the lid suggests that this box may have been a royal piece used by the Goryeo queen. The inlay is almost all in white, with no black details apart from the phoenixes' eyes. A band of inlaid white chrysanthemums encircles the phoenixes and a key fret band fills the side of the lid. The side of the box itself is decorated with undulating scrolls of peonies, also inlaid in white. There are thirteen small spur marks on the flat base of the box, proof that it was fired with great care. It has a subtle pale gray-green glaze.

Stoneware with celadon glaze
H. 10.8 cm (4 1/4 in.), diam. of foot: 20.2 cm (7 15/16 in.)
Bequest of Charles Bain Hoyt—Charles Bain Hoyt Collection
50.988a–b

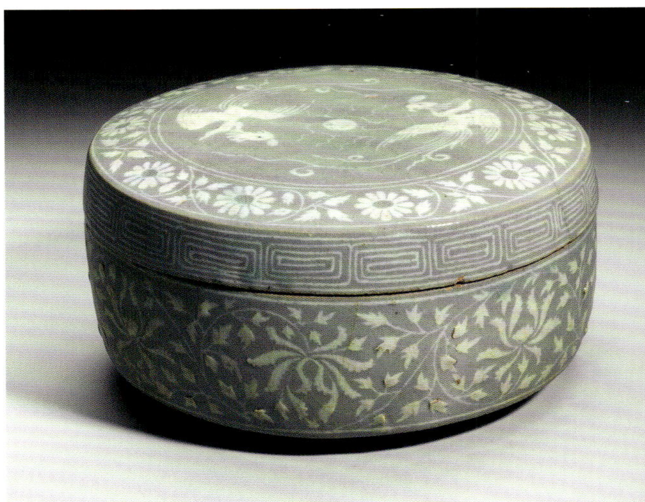

Plaque

Goryeo period, early 13th century

This celadon plaque or tile is a very rare piece and a testimony to the sophisticated craftsmanship of Korean potters who accomplished the difficult task of firing ceramics flat without warping. Its inlaid decoration has three rectangular bands, beginning at the outer edges, of white scrolls, black and white peony scrolls, and beads. The center has a lozenge-shaped panel filled with a scrolling spray of four peony flowers and seven buds. In the background are eight white cranes flying among clouds, with details of their beaks, eyes, and legs picked out in black. Probably used to decorate the wall of a royal building or a piece of wooden furniture, such plaques or tiles are evidence of the luxurious lifestyle of the Goryeo court at the capital, Gaeseong.

Stoneware with celadon glaze and inlaid decoration
L. 31.8 cm (12½ in.), w. 22.8 cm (9 in.), d. 0.4 cm (3/16 in.)
Edward Sylvester Morse Memorial Fund 33.25

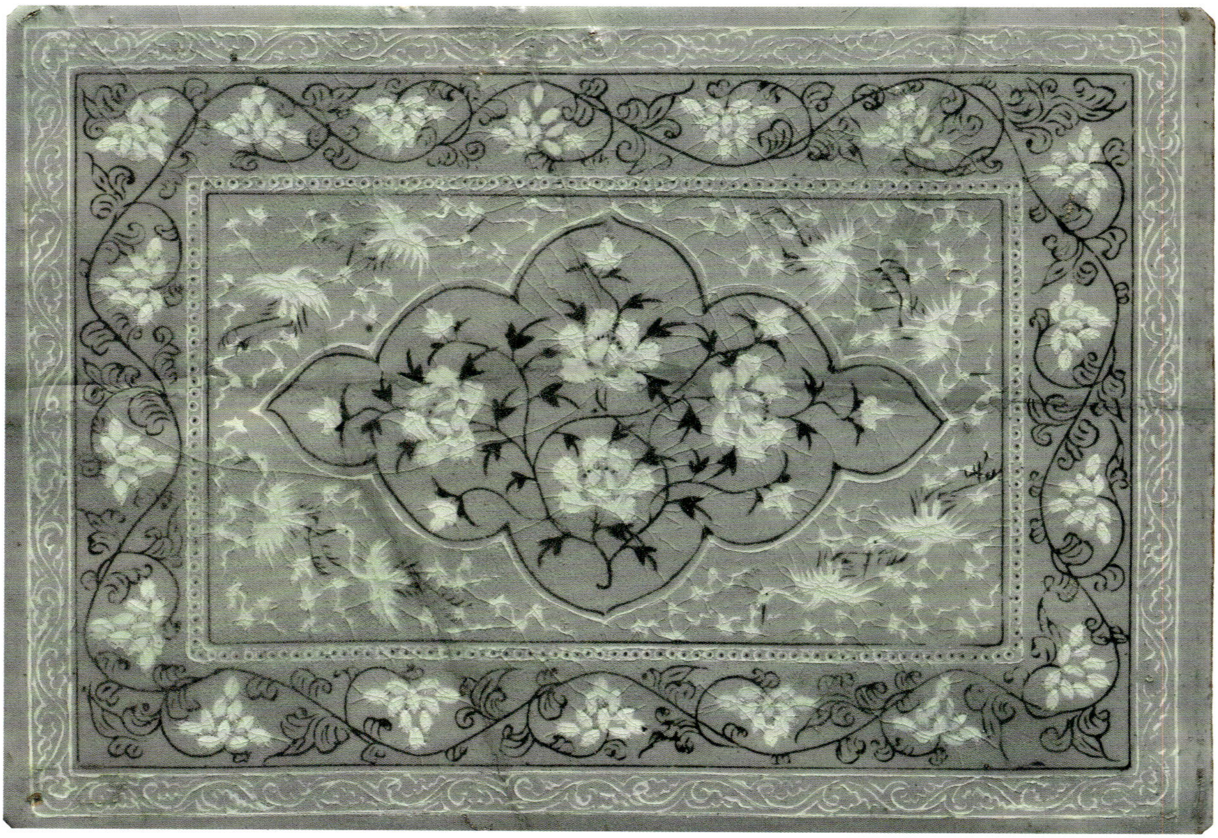

Wide-necked ewer with lid

Goryeo period, 12th century

Surviving examples make it quite clear that the shape of this wide-necked ceramic ewer copies that of ones made in bronze, as is the case with many ceramic vessels produced during the Goryeo period. The ewer's lid is flat with a dip in the center, and there are loops on the lid and the handle for a cord to keep the two pieces together. The decoration was painted on the surface in iron-brown under a thick gray-green celadon glaze. The design of two large peonies is splendidly free, covering the whole body and continuing up the spout. There are no border patterns but the shoulder is decorated with painted single strokes, perhaps in imitation of chrysanthemum petals.

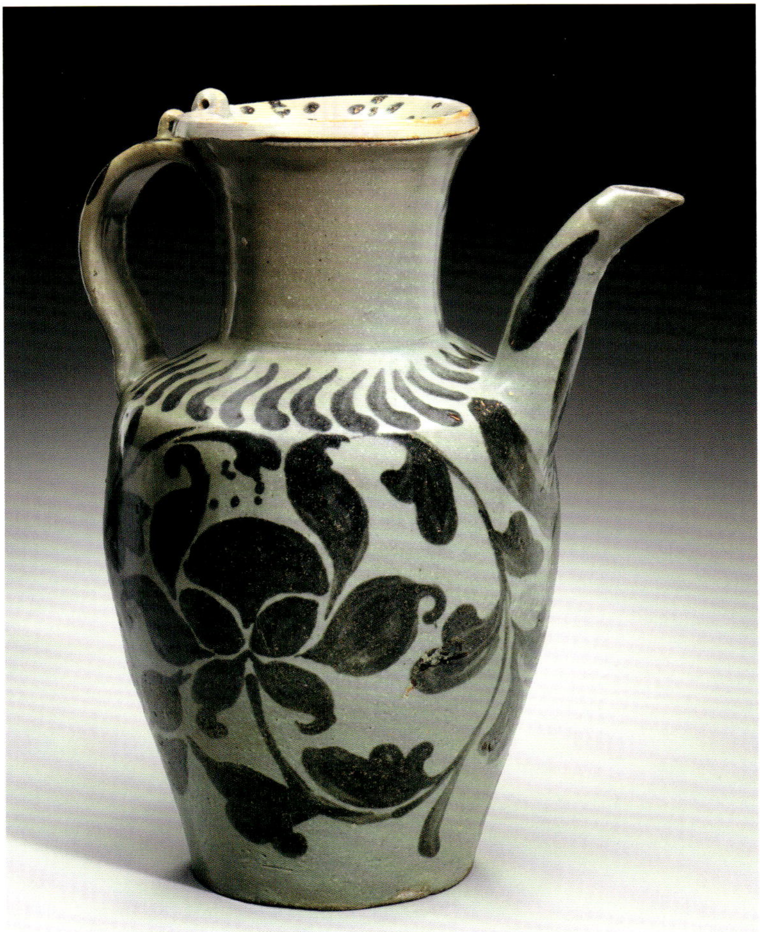

Stoneware with underglaze iron-brown
H. 25.8 cm (10 3/16 in.); diam. of mouth: 10 cm (3 15/16 in.); diam. of base: 9.2 cm (3 5/8 in.)
Bequest of Charles Bain Hoyt—Charles Bain Hoyt Collection
50.1022a–b

Prunus vase with coated iron-brown body

Goryeo period, early 13th century

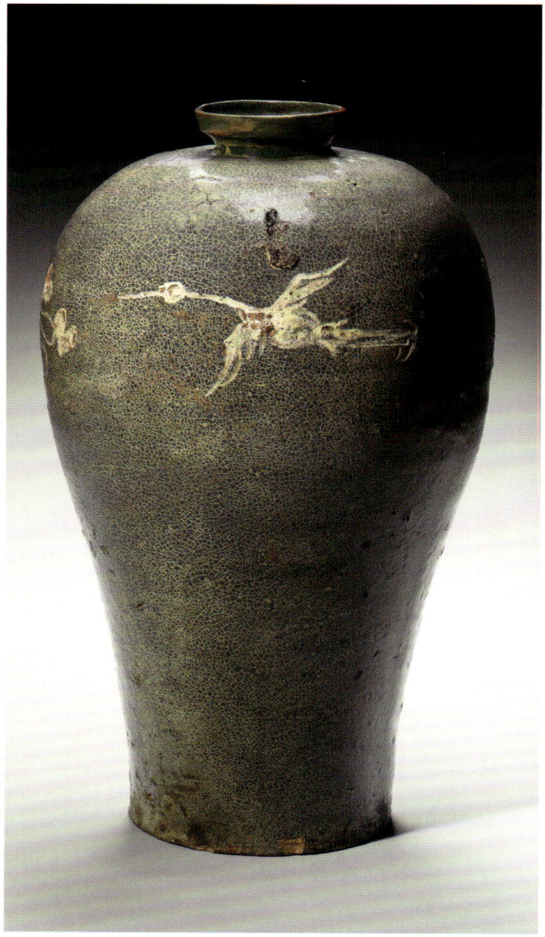

Although the shape of this maebyeong is similar to many celadons of the Goryeo period, the decoration is quite different. The design was incised in the leather-hard body of the vase through a blue-brown background coating of slip colored with iron oxide. The incised design was painted over with thick white slip and then the celadon glaze was applied. The resulting crackle is caused by the interaction of the undercoat and the glaze.

The design of clouds and cranes, associated with Daoist ideas of immortality and long life, was popular during the Goryeo period. Other such maebyeong are decorated with grass and foliage, and they are all characterized by having large areas of the body left undecorated. Many of them were produced at the Jinsan-ri kilns in Haenam, South Jeolla Province. They were probably originally used to hold wine.

Stoneware with celadon glaze and incised crane and floral design
H. 27.2 cm (10 11/16 in.); diam. of mouth: 5.5 cm (2 3/16 in.); diam. of foot 9.6 cm (3 3/4 in.)
Bequest of Charles Bain Hoyt—Charles Bain Hoyt Collection 50.2180

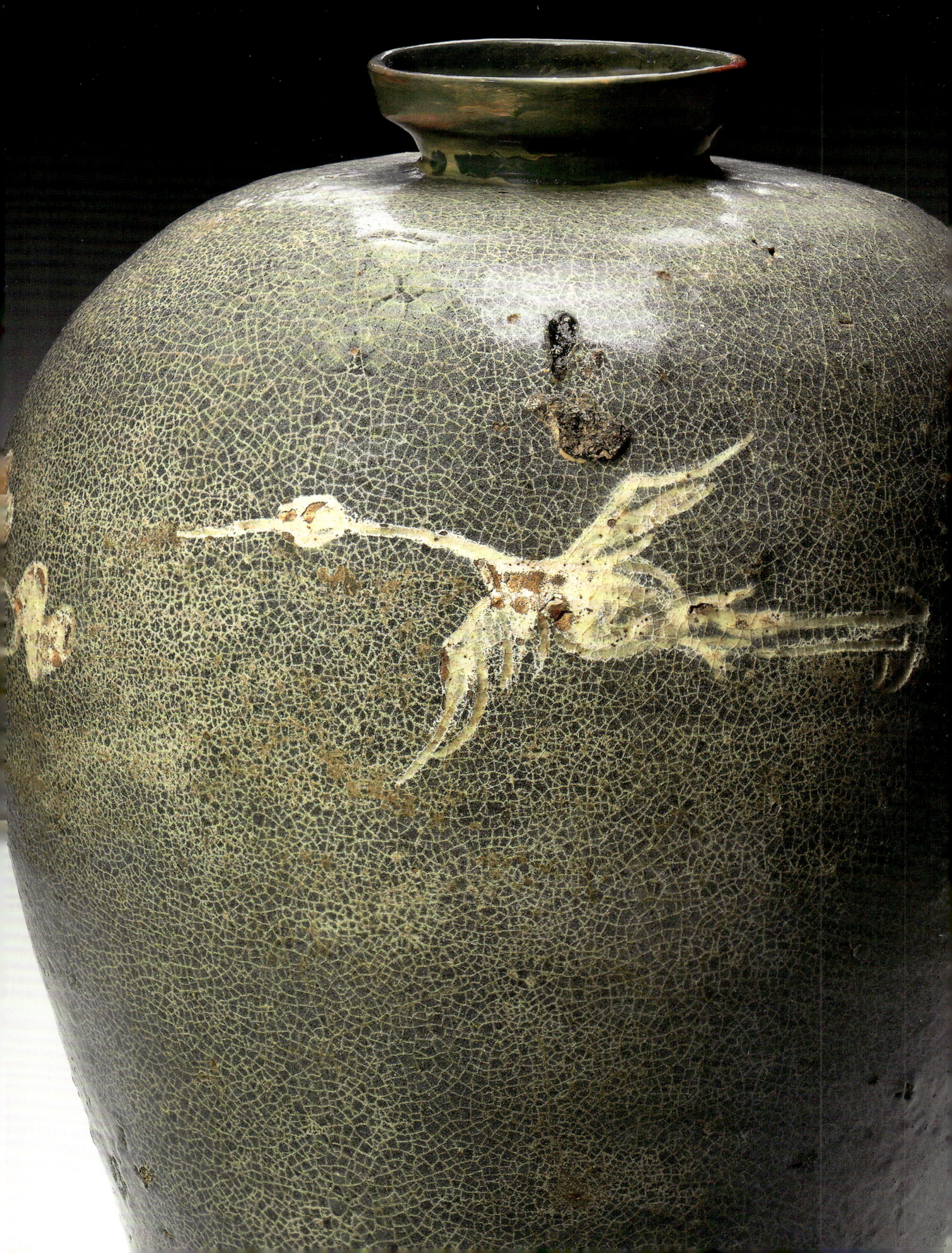

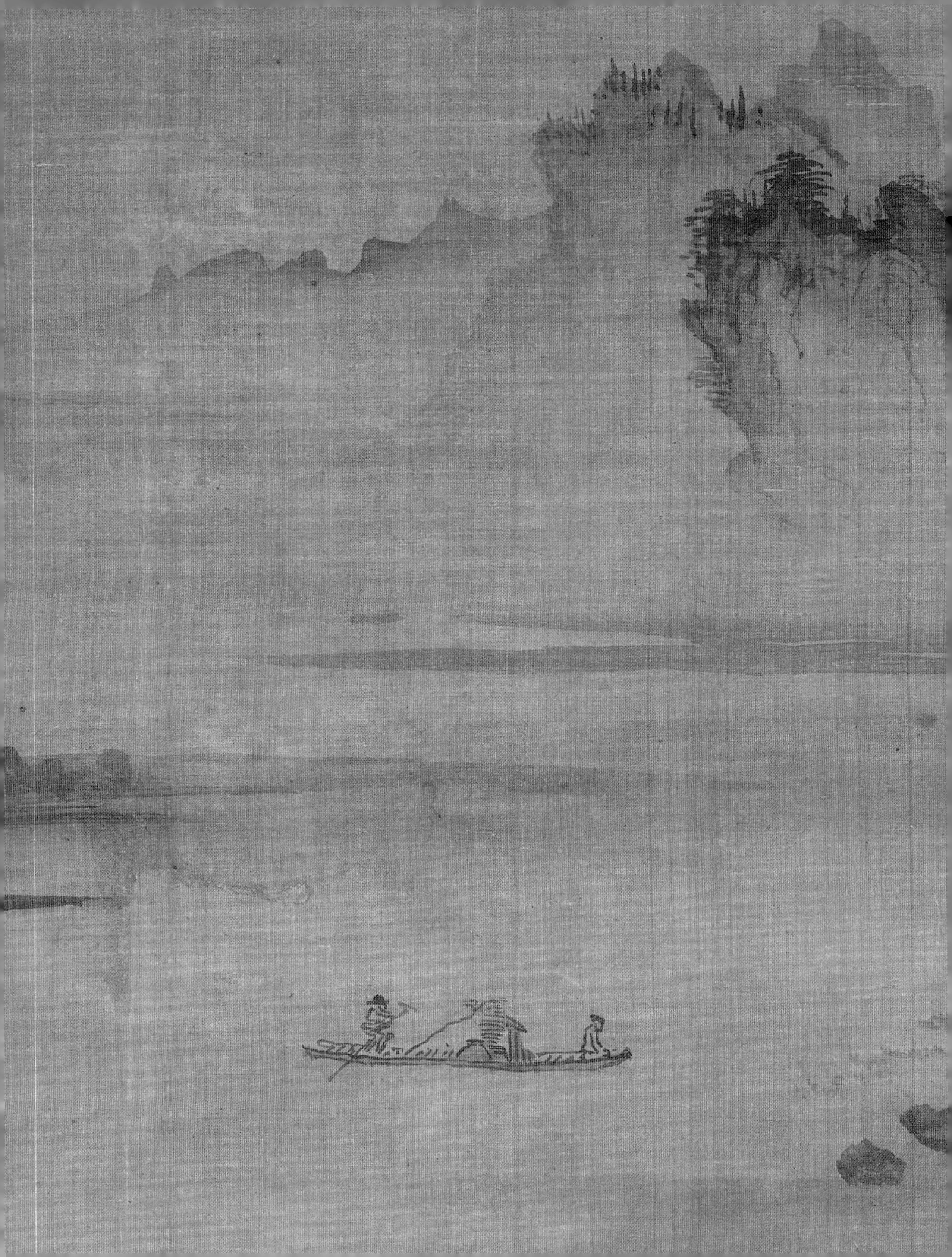

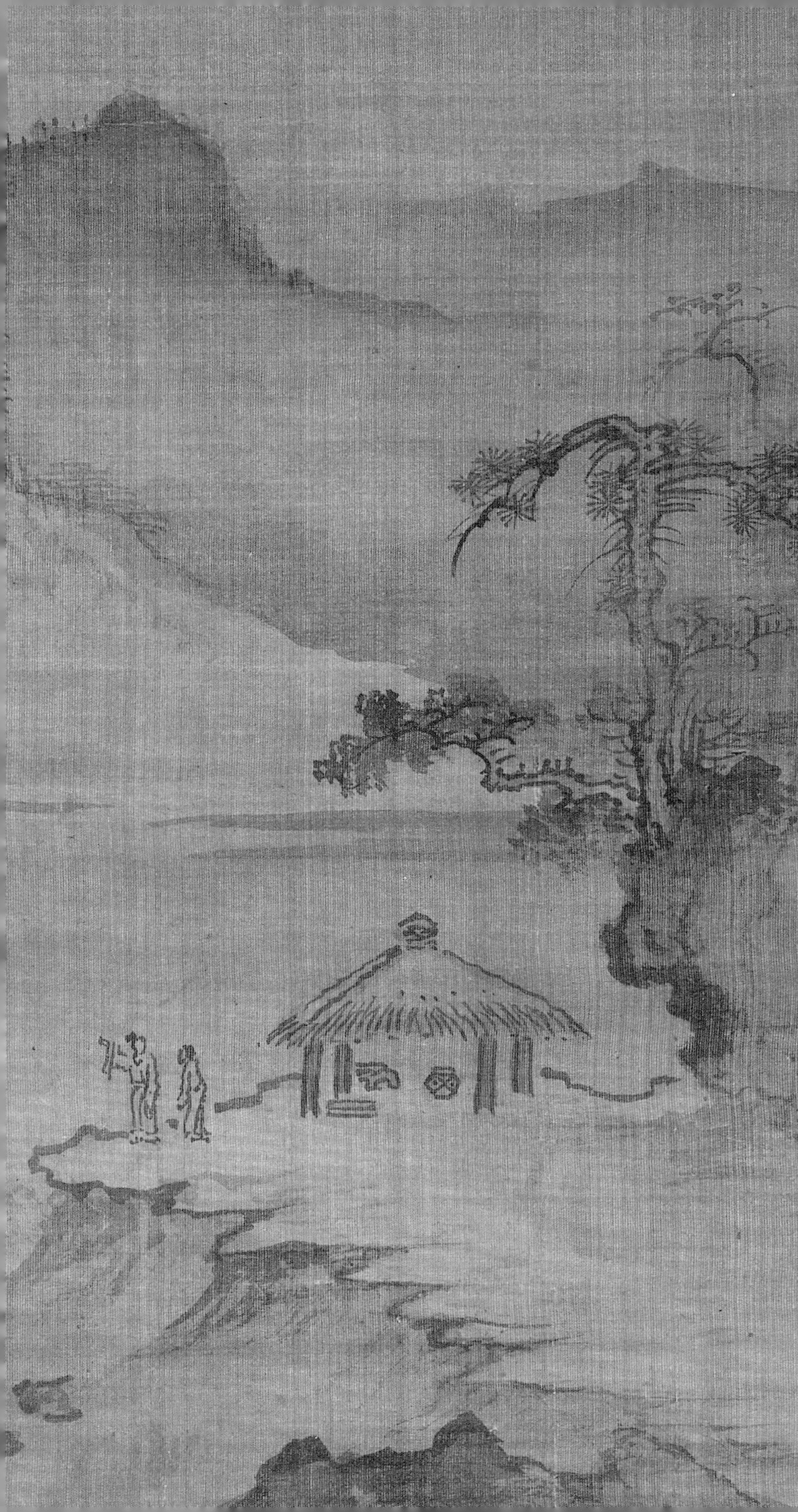

3 JOSEON PERIOD

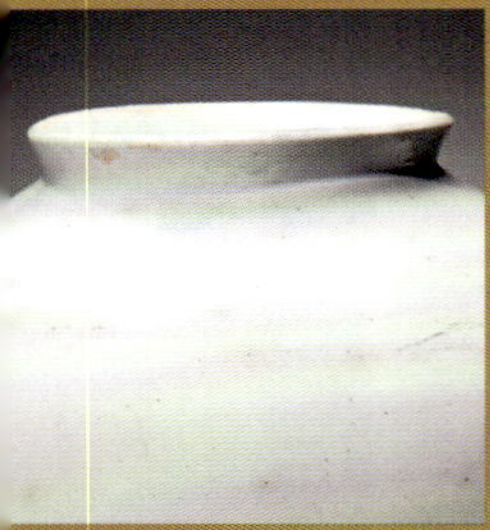
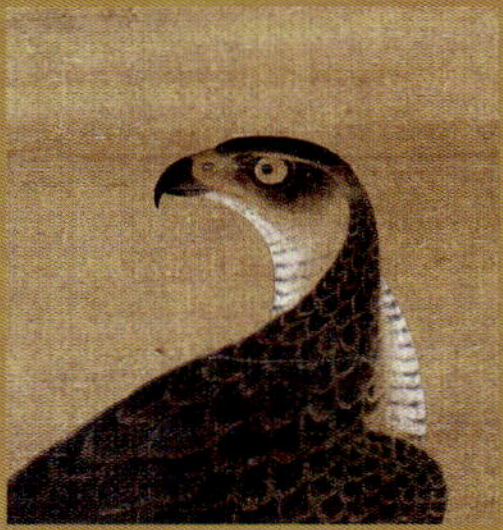
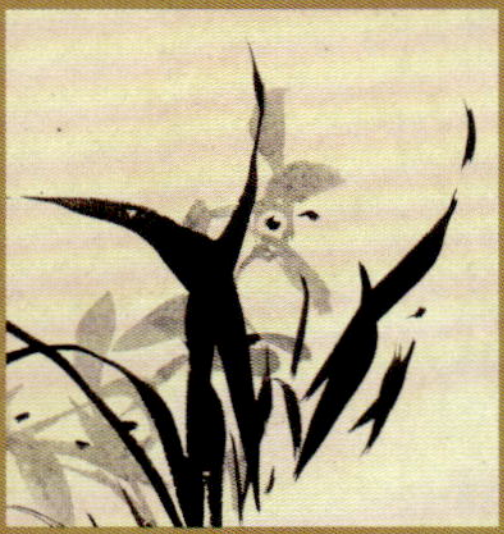
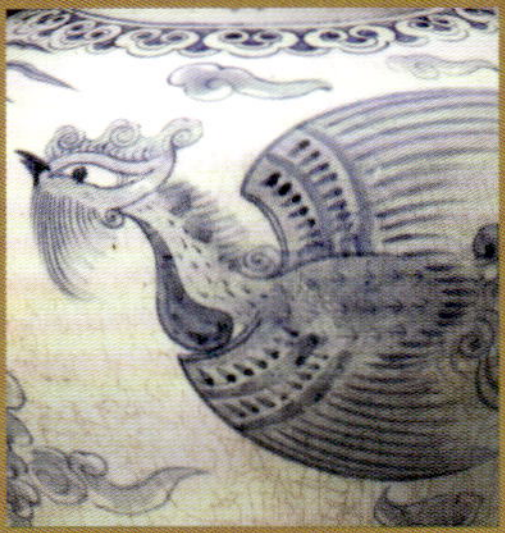
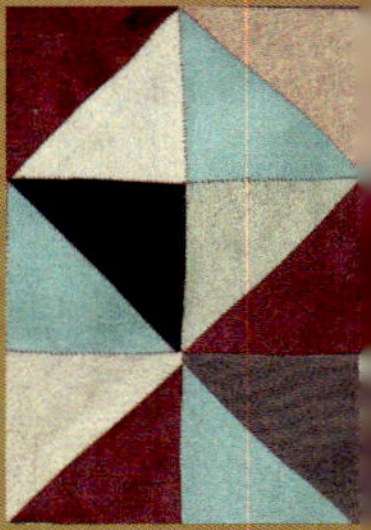

Joseon Period (1392–1910)

> The greatest merit of white porcelain lies in its absolute purity. Any effort to embellish it would only undermine its beauty.
>
> Yi Gyugyeong, Neo-Confucian scholar, early 19th century

The Joseon period is often called the Yi period, after the surname of its founder, Yi Seonggye, who defeated the Goryeo dynasty and established a new capital at Seoul in 1392. An austere form of Neo-Confucianism prevailed under the five hundred years of Yi rule. This philosophy as it was practiced in Korea was much stricter than in China, where it had originated. Much like the Chinese version, Korean Neo-Confucianism theoretically centered on ancestor worship based on the male line, and on the distribution of official positions based on merit gained through a system of examinations. In practice, however, the basically egalitarian principles of Confucianism were irreconcilable with the traditional Korean social hierarchy. Social discrimination was a major factor in Joseon society, which was divided into three distinct status groups or classes: the elite *yangban*, the commoners called *yang-in*, and the slaves or base people called *cheon'in*. Only the yangban could take the official examinations and hold positions of authority in the government and at court.

Taste among the yangban tended toward the austere and undecorated, epitomized by plain white porcelain and plain white clothes, plain white paper-lined walls, simple wooden furniture, and monochrome ink calligraphy and landscape painting. This aesthetic is often referred to as scholarly or literati taste because yangban culture was aimed at men of letters, scholars who practiced painting and calligraphy as amateurs without a care for gainful employment. At least in theory they were not professional artists or, even worse, businessmen or merchants.

Private academies supported by the Confucian literati grew in importance and influence during the Joseon period. Many such institutions received royal patronage and ended up being as central to Joseon culture as Buddhist temples had been to Goryeo culture. Buddhism was officially suppressed, but was in fact still practiced both at court and by many levels of Joseon society.

Due to the important role played by pure white porcelain in Confucian rites, the government strictly controlled its production beginning in 1479, when it established the official kilns called Bunwon to the southeast of Seoul. These kilns had to be moved from time to time in order to be near sources of firewood. Private regional kilns also developed in a kind of contract relationship with the Joseon government and eventually spread all over the country.

The two cultural and economic highpoints in the Joseon period are the fifteenth and the eighteenth centuries. During the early part of the fifteenth century, King Sejong the Great (reigned 1418–50) presided over many scientific and technological inventions, such as the vernacular Korean phonetic script, Hangeul. This logical system of twenty-four graphic signs representing consonants and vowels was originally intended as a way of helping less-educated people read Chinese characters and did not really flourish in its own right until the eighteenth century.

Dividing the two highpoints were the Japanese invasions of 1592 and 1596 under Toyotomi Hideyoshi and the Manchu invasions of 1627 and 1636. Great loss of life and of cultural treasures characterized these periods. Many wooden palace and temple buildings were burned, and many prisoners were taken to Japan in the sixteenth century. These included potters, who subsequently had a great influence on the development of Japan's porcelain industry.

The two reigns of King Yeongjo and his grandson King Jeongjo, from 1724 to 1800, formed a second period of great cultural development and confident Koreanization. For example, there was a proliferation of realistic paintings of actual places in Korea, as opposed to the previous trend for idealized landscapes that followed a tradition originating in China. Scenes of everyday life were also a new development in painting, and there was a surge of writing in Hangeul. A school of thought aimed at addressing social problems also emerged at this time. Called *Silhak*, or Practical Learning, it led its followers to try to reform agriculture and develop commerce and industry. Catholicism, known as Western Learning, was also introduced to Korea during the eighteenth century, when Korean envoys to China came into contact there with Jesuit missionaries from Europe.

The late Joseon period was one of economic decline, factional politics, and de facto rule by royal in-laws. The Prince Regent Daewongun, who came to power in 1864 as father of the twelve-year-old King Gojong, carried out an isolationist policy because he was afraid of contamination by Western ideas. Ironically, it was the Japanese who, after the Meiji imperial restoration and their own rapid modernization, finally succeeded in opening Korea up to trade and diplomacy in the 1880s. After Korea established diplomatic relations with Western countries in 1882, there followed a period when Western travelers were able to view late-Joseon Korea at firsthand. The forcible annexation and colonization of Korea by Japan in 1910 brought the long Joseon period to an end.

Some of the Western travelers to Korea in the late nineteenth and early twentieth centuries were able to build up collections of everyday items and works usually characterized as folk art. These include paintings and objects produced for use by ordinary people and associated with folk customs and folk beliefs. Compared to the monochrome ink paintings and white porcelains favored by the yangban elite, the painted screens, embroideries, and utilitarian ceramics of the common people are more decorative, with bright colors and auspicious symbols. However, some themes, formats, and motifs are common to all Korean art, whether produced by professional artists, scholar painters, or itinerant village artisans.

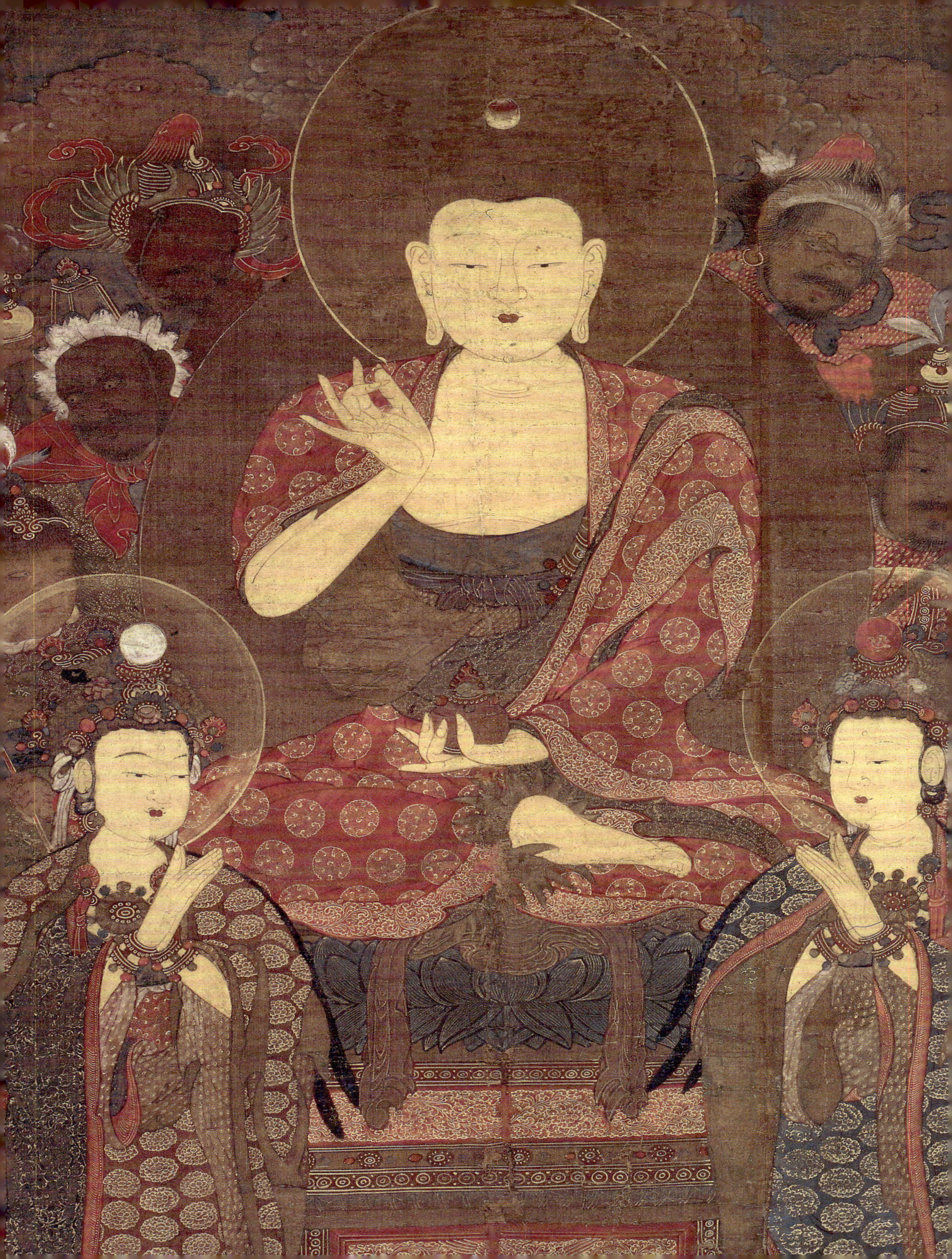

Medicine Buddha Triad with Twelve Guardians

Joseon period, late 16th century

This Medicine Buddha triad was commissioned in the second half of the sixteenth century by the Dowager Queen Munjeong to pray for the longevity of her son, King Myeongjong. The Dowager Queen was an avid Buddhist who employed artisans from the temples and the court to produce hundreds of Buddhist works. One of the most venerated deities in Korea even when Buddhism was officially suppressed, the Medicine Buddha was said to be able to cure all human illness, both physical and mental. His healing nature is so powerful that just seeing his image or hearing his name is sufficient to alleviate any suffering.

This superb painting is perhaps one of the best-preserved early Joseon depictions of the Medicine Buddha. The healing Buddha is sitting in an upright posture on a lotus-shaped throne. His left hand is placed on his lap to signify that he is in meditation. The palm is turned up to hold a medicine jar full of the nectar of long life. Buddha's right hand is raised; the circle formed with the thumb and middle finger signifies the Wheel of Law, the Dharma, or the Path of Righteousness. Suryaprabha, who represents sunlight, attends him on his right, and Candraprabha, who represents moonlight, stands on his left. The Twelve Guardians symbolizing the Buddha's twelve vows to cure all suffering are lined up behind the triad. The richly decorated garments with many florets and scrolls in delicate lines of gold are a legacy of the aristocratic taste of the previous Goryeo period, when Buddhism flourished as the state religion.

Panel; ink and colors on silk
123 x 127.5 cm (48 7/16 x 50 3/16 in.)
Gift of the heirs of Henry Adams 19.265

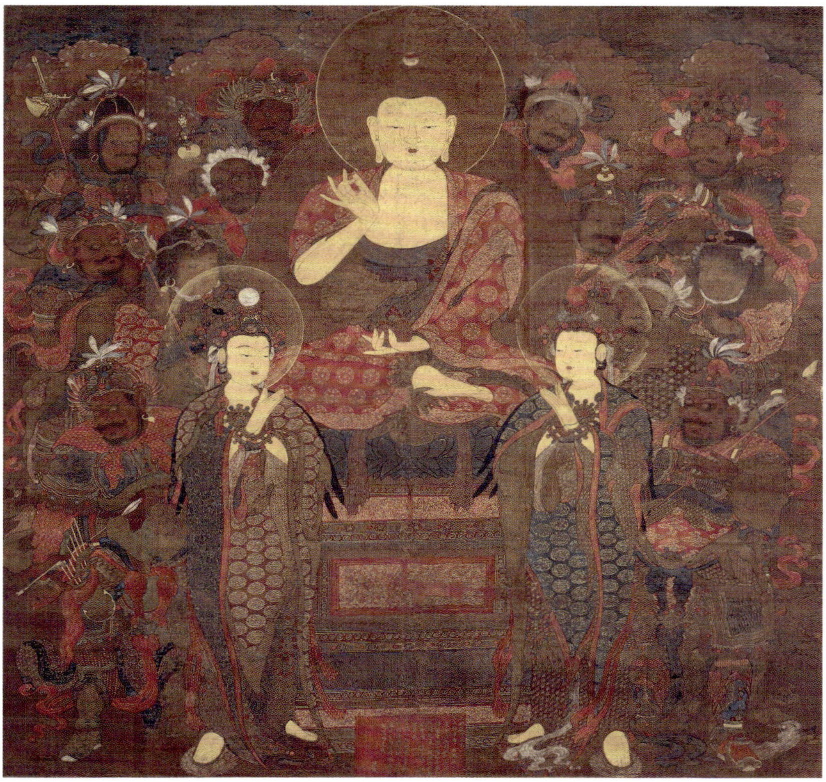

Avalokitesvara with Water and Moon

Joseon period, late 17th–18th century

Avalokitesvara is the Bodhisattva of Compassion, who vowed to lead all sentient beings to the Western Pure Land of Amitabha Buddha. This benevolent bodhisattva was widely worshipped in Korea beginning in the sixth century. He gained a prominent following in Korea during the Goryeo period, when belief in the Western Pure Land became popular. Avalokitesvara may be identified by his jeweled headdress, fluid gossamer gown, feminine body, and the celestial atmosphere symbolizing his abode, Mount Potalaka. He is often shown with a kundika vessel, willow branch, bamboo, blue bird, moon, rock, or water.

This depiction, *Avalokitesvara with Water and Moon*, is one of a few paintings of this triad created during the late-seventeenth to eighteenth centuries, when Buddhism experienced a brief revival and temples that had been demolished by successive foreign invasions were reconstructed. Avalokitesvara is sitting on the rocky waterside with his back upright and his eyes looking slightly down. The bodhisattva looks relaxed, with his right arm softly placed on his lap and his left lightly touching the ground, a pose called "the posture of royal ease." Sudhana, the boy described in the *Flower Garland Sutra*, appears on the left.

Panel; ink and colors on silk
136 x 121 cm (53 9/16 x 47 5/8 in.)
Francis Gardner Curtis Fund 17.1636

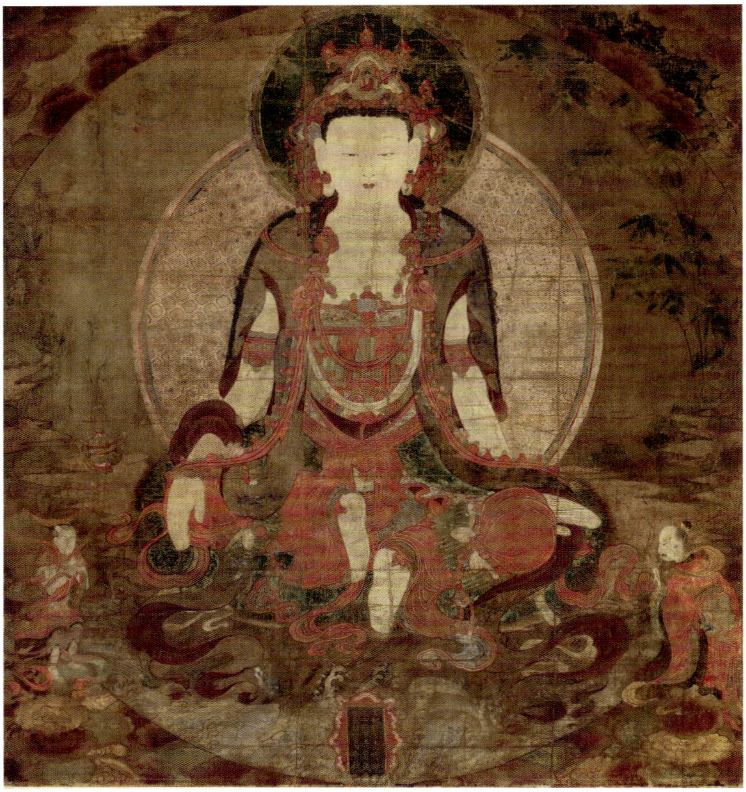

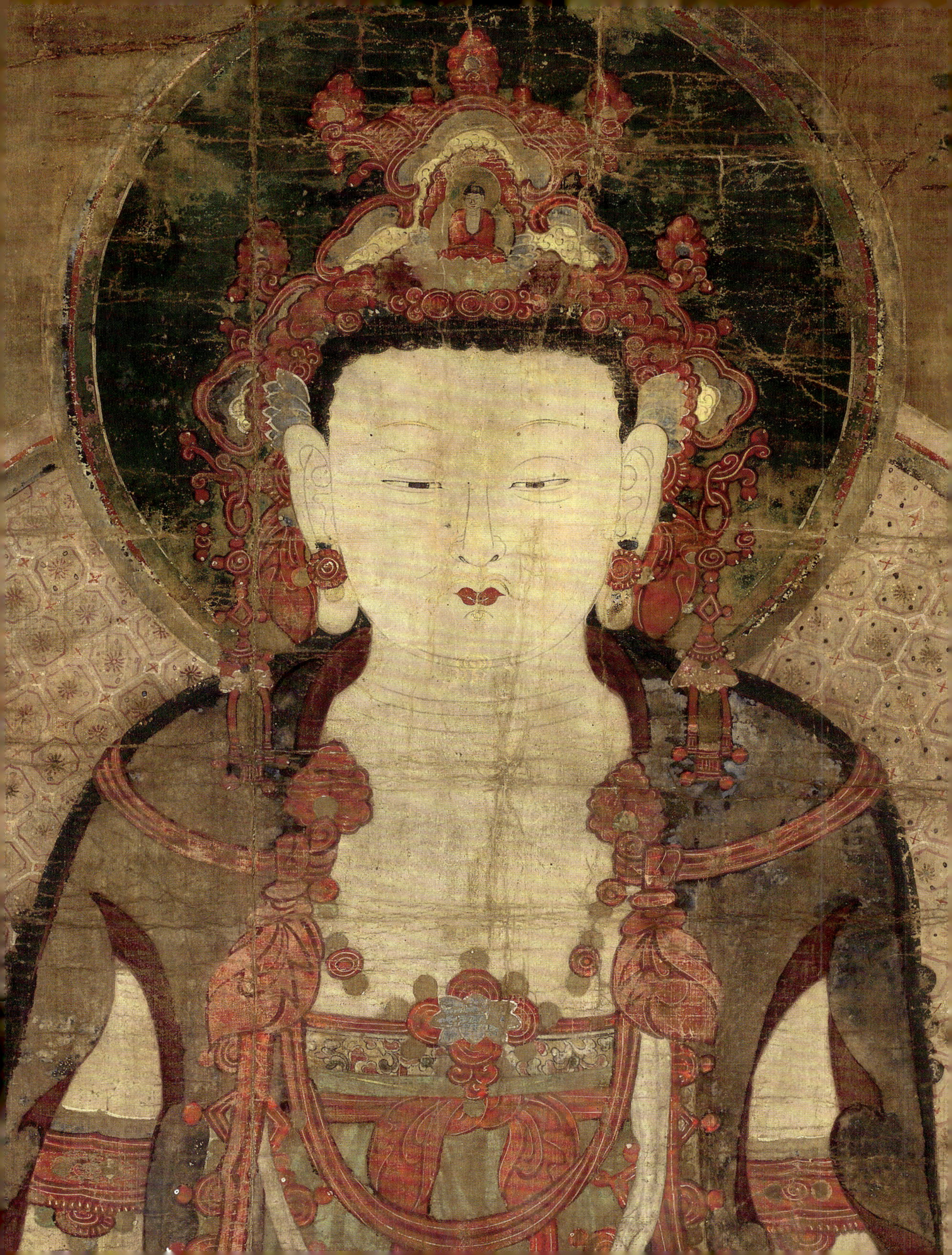

Taesan, the Seventh King of Hell

Joseon period, 19th century

This painting depicts Taesan, the seventh of the Ten Kings of Hell who collectively preside over the Buddhist purgatory. Worship of these ten kings took root in Korea during the eleventh century and developed under the strong influence of Tang-dynasty China. Examples of Tang Kings of Hell paintings can be seen in the caves of Dunhuang on the Silk Road. It was not until the late Joseon period that demand for Ten Kings of Hell paintings grew in Korea, along with the development of various temple rituals centered on the kings. Depicted individually or in groups of ten, five, or two, the kings were enshrined in the Hall of Judgment, where people made votive offerings and prayers for rebirth in a better place on behalf of their ancestors as well as for themselves.

This King of Hell painting has a typical two-tier composition. In the upper part, the king is sitting on a high-backed chair behind a wooden desk. He holds a scroll or a scepter in his left hand and touches his beard with his right hand. These features signify his dignified status as a judge who knows the sins of all. The king's numerous attendants, including both boys and girls, surround him. The lower part of the composition illustrates a gruesome hell scene. The bodhisattva Ksitigarbha stands with hands in prayer for the half-naked sinners being cut in half. Animal-headed wardens apply torture according to records and instructions held by assistant judges in official attire. The delivery messenger on horseback hurriedly drags an unwilling sinner by the hair.

Panel; ink and colors on silk
153.5 x 108.7 cm (60 7/16 x 42 13/16 in.)
Denman Waldo Ross Collection 17.86

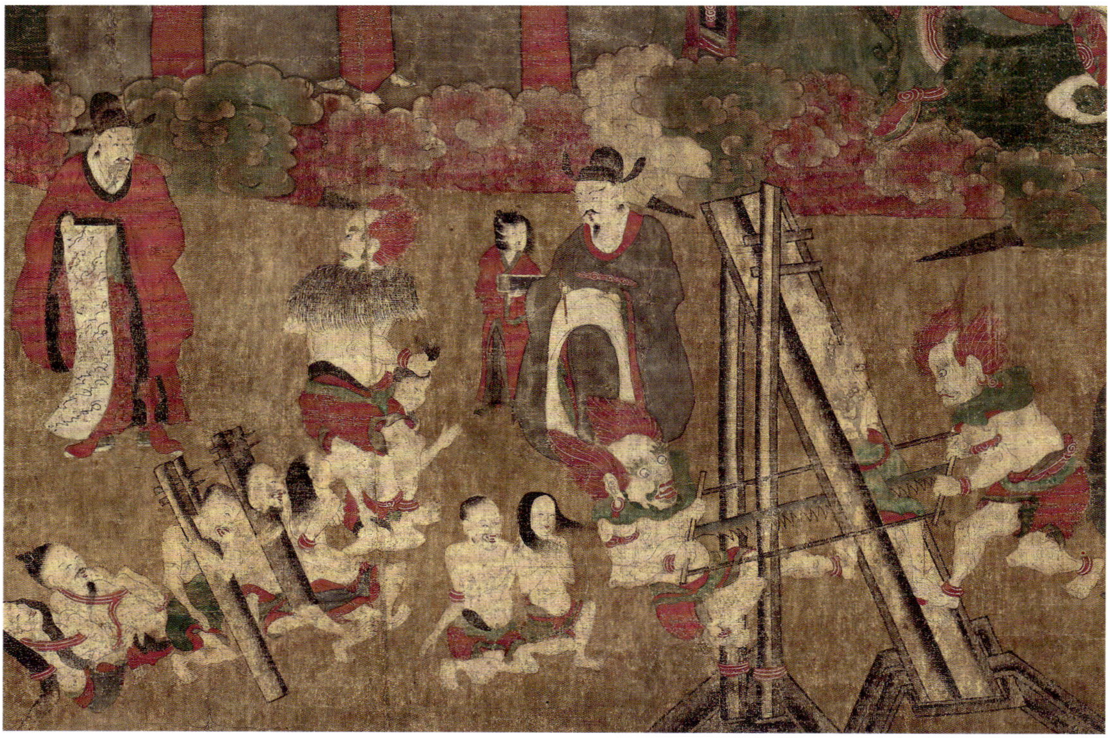

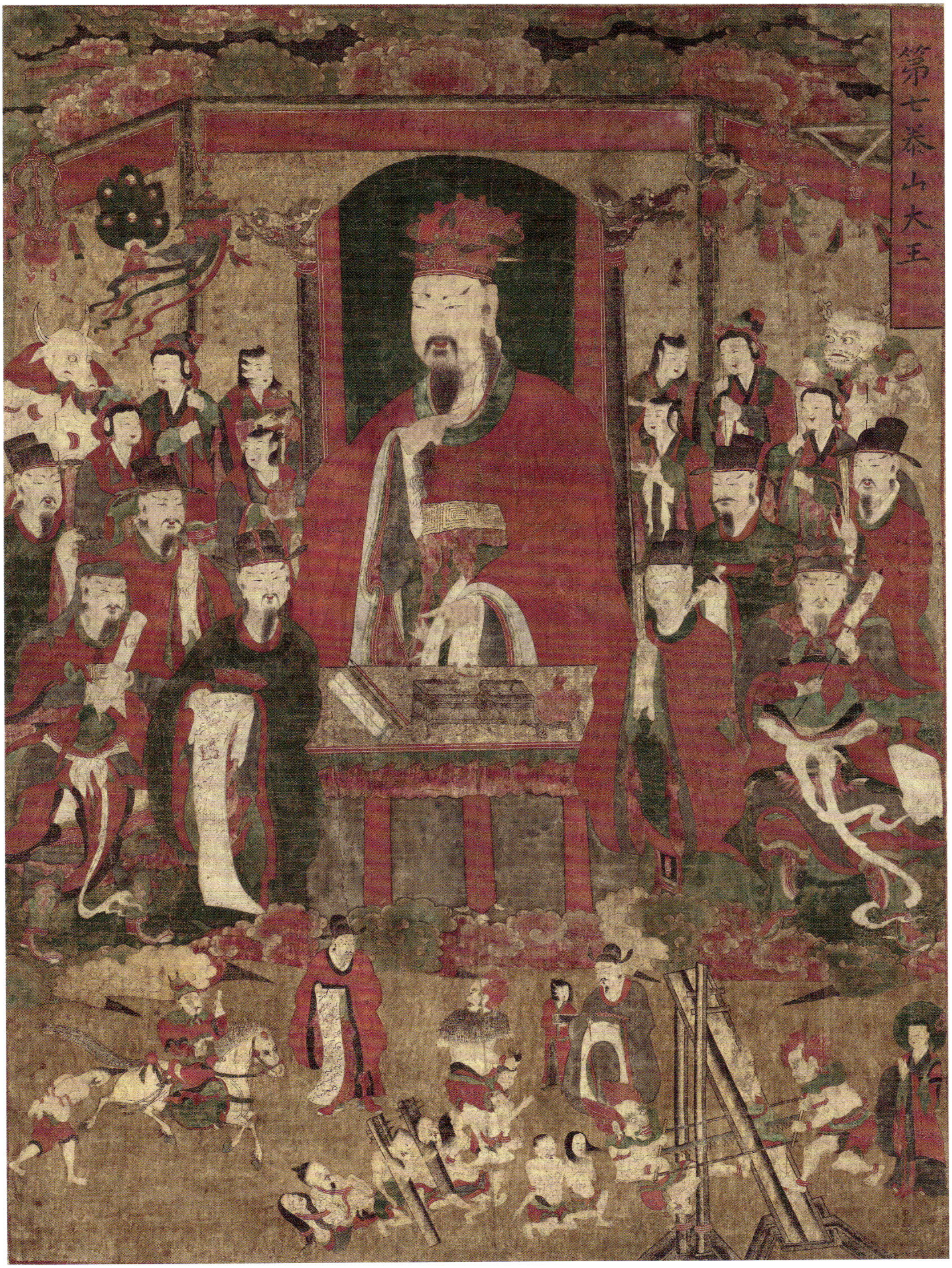
第七泰山大王

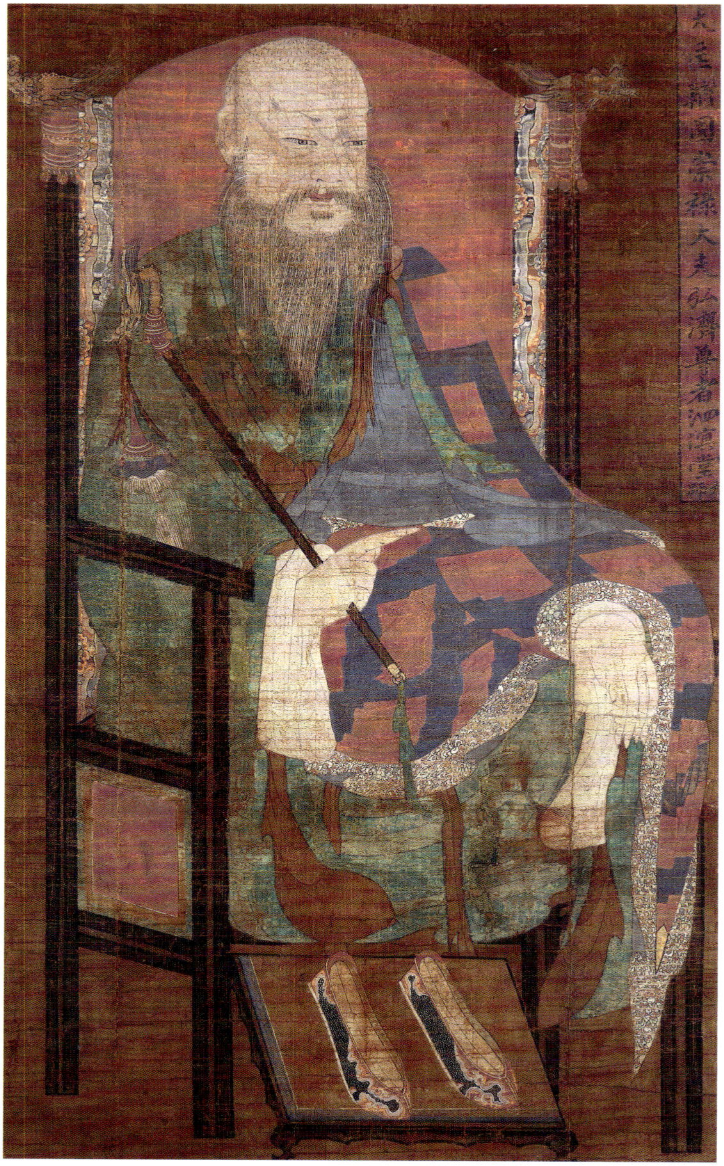

Portrait of Priest Samyeongdang

Joseon period, 17th century

The monk known as the Venerable Samyeong was an unusual man of the cloth, because he was also a military leader and diplomat during the turbulent time of the Japanese invasions in the late sixteenth century. He voluntarily led his fellow monks in battle and won several critical victories. Later, he joined the Korean king's envoys sent to sign a peace treaty with Tokugawa Ieyasu. After the war, in recognition of his role as a protector of the nation, Samyeong's portrait was housed in temples throughout the country.

In this portrait, the Venerable Samyeong is seated on a chair with his feet crossed under his regalia. The three-quarter view is a characteristic posture of seventeenth- and eighteenth-century Korean portrait painting, both religious and secular. Most portrait paintings in the Joseon period were intended for worship in rituals dedicated to notable figures in the household, clan, school, or temple; they tend to depict the sitter as a generalized type for ceremonial purposes rather than realistically capturing a moment's emotion. Samyeong's portrait shows his austere character and authority as a military leader through his commanding gaze, masculine physique, and the elaborate decoration on his clothes.

Panel; ink and colors on silk
105.5 x 63.5 cm (41 9/16 x 25 in.)
Denman Waldo Ross Collection 25.188

Lidded bowl with peony and raindrop patterns

Joseon period, early 15th century

Buncheong stoneware marks a transition that slowly but surely replaced the earlier celadon tradition of the Goryeo period and led to the subsequent taste for white porcelain. Potters formed the bodies of buncheong wares with gray clay and then applied a generous amount of white slip. The name *buncheong* means "powder green" or "grayish green," indicating the process whereby gray stonewares were made to look a bit like white wares.

This lidded bowl is a typical early example of buncheong ware. It combines the inlay technique carried on from the Goryeo period with stamping, which developed in the early Joseon era. After shaping the body on a wheel, an artisan pressed stamps with various motifs into the body before the whole piece was covered with white slip. The slip was then wiped off the surface, leaving it in the stamped decoration. Stamping alleviated the need for the laborious manual carving process necessary in the inlay method. This simplification allowed for the mass production of ceramics. Stamping also served to conceal imperfections in the clay and glaze, whose quality declined after the late Goryeo period.

The main motif on this bowl is a peony, a much-loved symbol of fame and wealth. The background is filled with repetitive stamped dots in "raindrop" patterns. The rims of the bowl and lid are decorated with inlaid scroll designs. Round bowls with covers were often used to serve sticky rice, a staple of the Korean diet. In Japan, buncheong wares with this type of stamped decoration are called mishima ware.

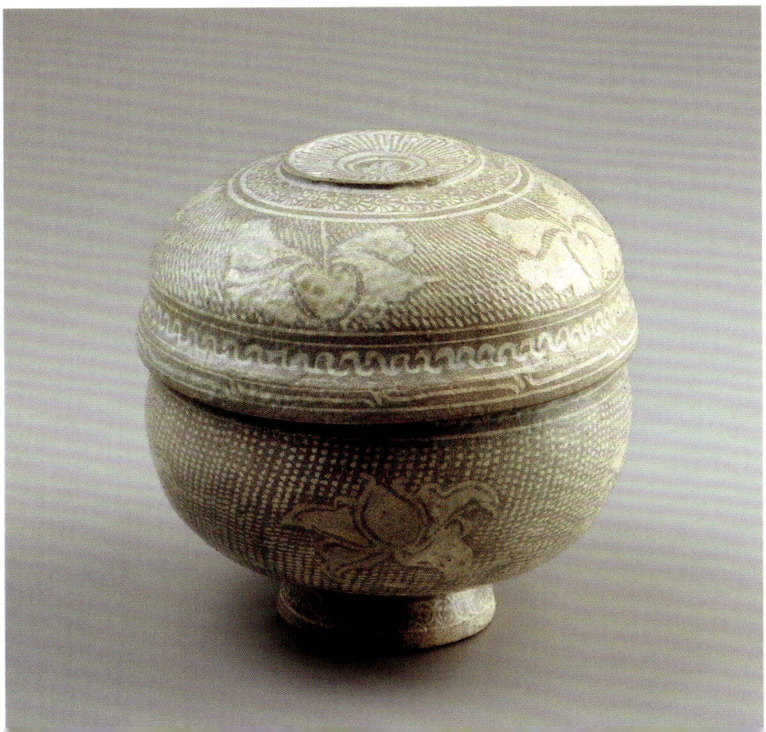

Buncheong stoneware with inlaid and stamped decoration
H. 15.2 cm (6 in.); diam. of lid: 17.2 cm (6¾ in.); diam. of foot: 7.7 cm (3⅛ in.)
Bequest of Charles Bain Hoyt—Charles Bain Hoyt Collection
50.1025a–b

Bowl with chrysanthemum and rope-curtain patterns

Joseon period, 15th century

This bowl is decorated with impressed chrysanthemum and "rope-curtain" patterns on the inner and outer surfaces. The combination of these two designs was popular for stamped buncheong wares, which reached their height during the reign of King Sejong in the early fifteenth century. Buncheong wares of that time tend to have densely applied, highly stylized stamped designs, as on this bowl. In some cases, these wares had office names stamped on them, evidence that these vessels were put to daily use in the court as well as in central and local offices.

Buncheong wares were used in both ordinary and royal households, and high-quality examples were offered as tributary goods. The government closely watched over ceramic production as an important source of state revenue. *The Annals of King Sejong* document a control measure imposed on potters so local administrative offices could monitor and maintain the quality of the region's ceramics.

Buncheong stoneware with stamped decoration
H. 8.3 cm (3¼ in.); diam. of rim: 18.3 cm (7³⁄₁₆ in.); diam. of foot: 5.8 cm (2⁵⁄₁₆ in.)
Bequest of Charles Bain Hoyt—Charles Bain Hoyt Collection 50.1129

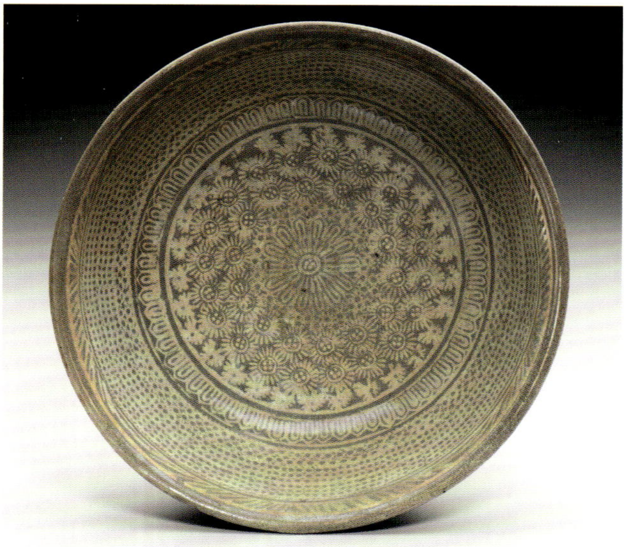

Prunus vase with dragon and chrysanthemum florets

Joseon period, early 15th century

This stoneware bottle was decorated using the slip-inlay technique called sanggam, which reached its height during the twelfth century in the preceding Goryeo period. Fifteenth-century inlay designs, as demonstrated by this piece, tend to be more elaborate than those of the Goryeo. Buncheong wares with inlaid designs were widely produced up until the 1420s.

This vessel features a dragon motif, a favored and prestigious subject for the Korean aristocracy. The decoration on the bottle is divided into three parts: the main dragon motif is inlaid in the central section, and the upper and lower sections are adorned with chrysanthemum florets. This three-part composition was typical of fifteenth-century bottles of this maebyeong shape and can be compared with underglaze blue decoration on Chinese Yuan- and Ming-dynasty porcelains. The added element of humor in the facial expression of the dragon differs from dragons depicted during the preceding Goryeo period. Buncheong ceramics appealed to the Joseon taste for modest and unpretentious art. A change in the vessel's shape is also evident. In the eleventh and early twelfth centuries, maebyeong had straighter sides; by the fifteenth century, the trend was toward a more curvaceous shape.

Buncheong stoneware with inlaid decoration
H. 33.7 cm (13¼ in.); diam. of mouth: 7.3 cm (2⅞ in.); diam. of foot: 9.7 cm (3¹³⁄₁₆ in.)
Bequest of Charles Bain Hoyt—Charles Bain Hoyt Collection 50.2176

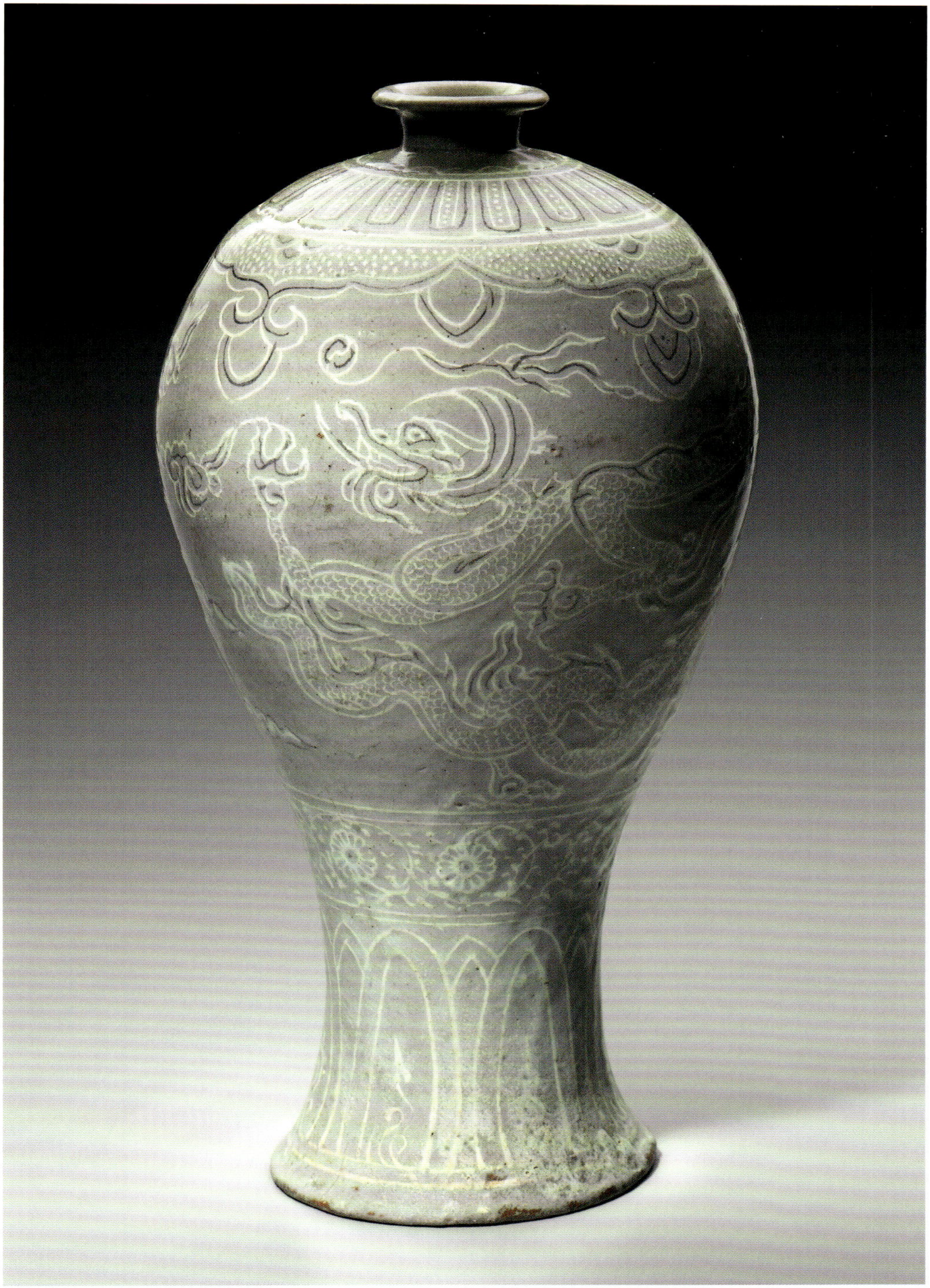

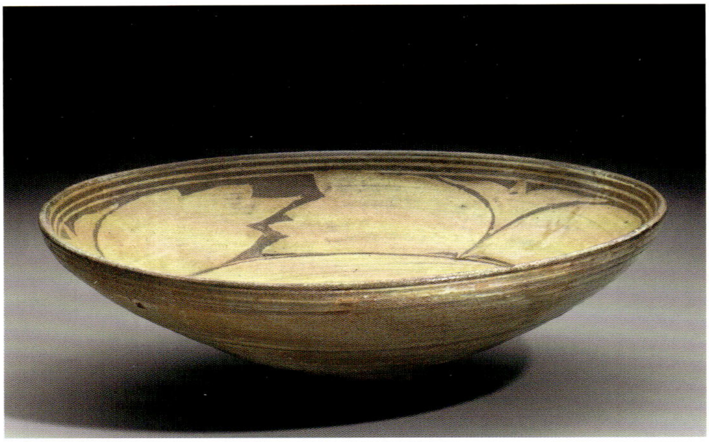

Dish with leaf design

Joseon period, late 15th century

Early Joseon-period buncheong wares tend to show a certain originality and freedom in their design. Working in local, often private kilns in contrast to the centralized, government-controlled ceramic-making centers of the Goryeo period, the early Joseon potters were able to take advantage of a less rigid production system. The freedom of design they exhibited was something that appealed to Japanese taste, particularly to twentieth-century potters such as Hamada Shoji.

The entire body of this deep dish is decorated with bold leaf patterns made by the application of white slip. To achieve this effect, the potter first applied white slip over the entire body and then scraped away the background of the pattern to expose the gray body underneath before firing. The result is a shallow relief pattern. This technique, known as *sgraffito*, is also called reverse inlay, as the ground rather than the motif is cut away.

Buncheong stoneware with sgraffito decoration
H. 6.2 cm (2 7/16 in.); diam. of rim: 19.1 cm (7 1/2 in.); diam. of foot: 5 cm (1 15/16 in.)
Bequest of Charles Bain Hoyt—Charles Bain Hoyt Collection
50.1112

Bottle with floral design

Joseon period, late 15th century

This slender pear-shaped bottle is decorated with incised floral designs. The incising technique is similar to sgraffito in that decorative patterns are cut away from a body that has been covered with white slip. However, only the outlines of the motifs are engraved, leaving all other surfaces white. Joseon potters were able to incise a wide range of both realistic and abstract outline patterns with relative ease.

The long neck and full-volume base of this bottle are typical of early Joseon ceramics. Both the shape and the decorative scheme are reminiscent of Chinese blue-and-white porcelain of the Yuan dynasty. The decoration is divided into three parts: the mouth and neck have little decoration; the shoulder has a stylized supplementary design of lotuses; and the lower portion features the main motif, a boldly engraved floral design that reveals the gray body underneath the white slip.

Buncheong stoneware
H. 33.5 cm (13 3/16 in.); diam. of mouth: 6 cm (2 3/8 in.); diam. of foot: 8.3 cm (3 1/4 in.)
Bequest of Charles Bain Hoyt—Charles Bain Hoyt Collection
50.1027

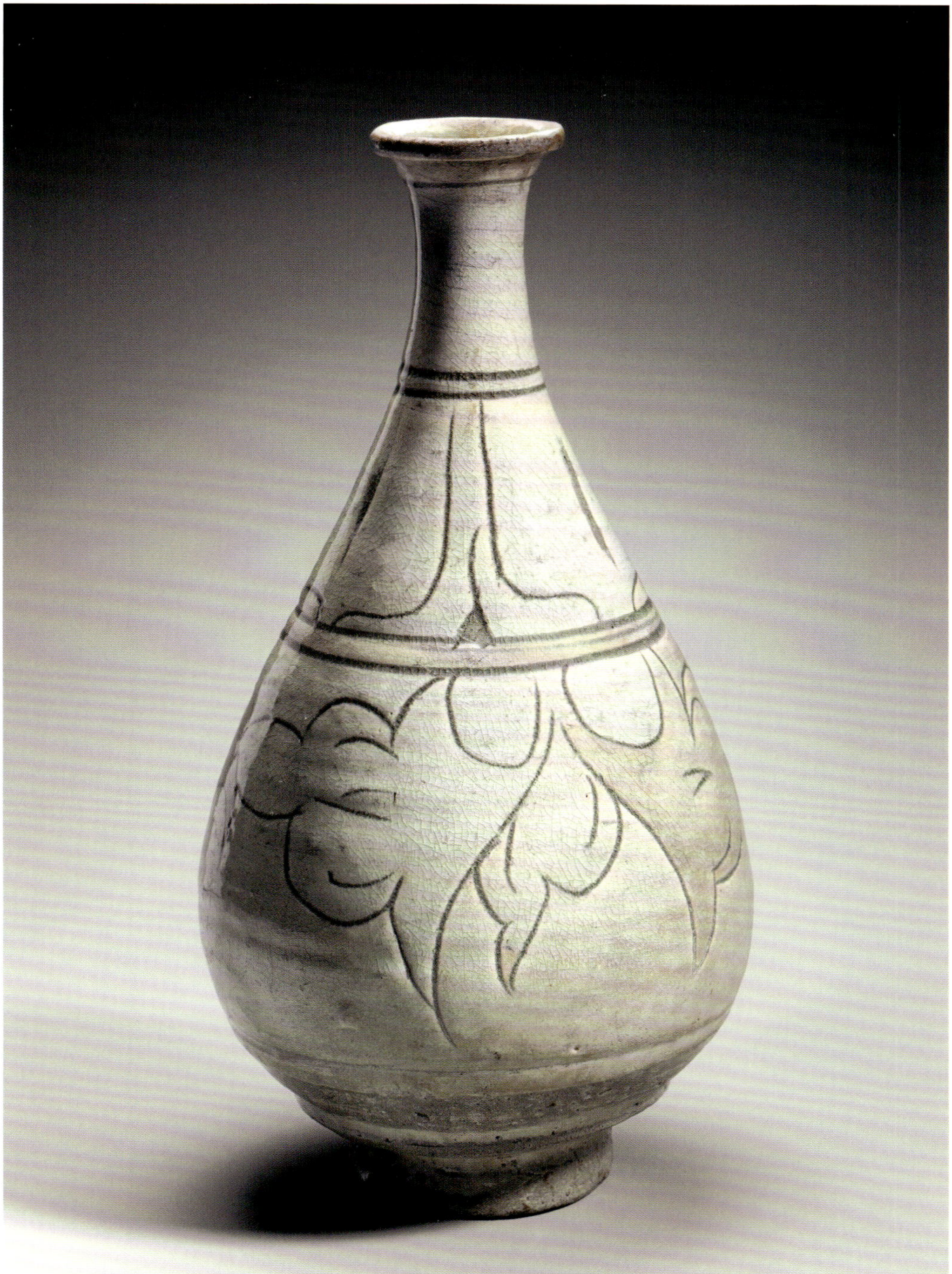

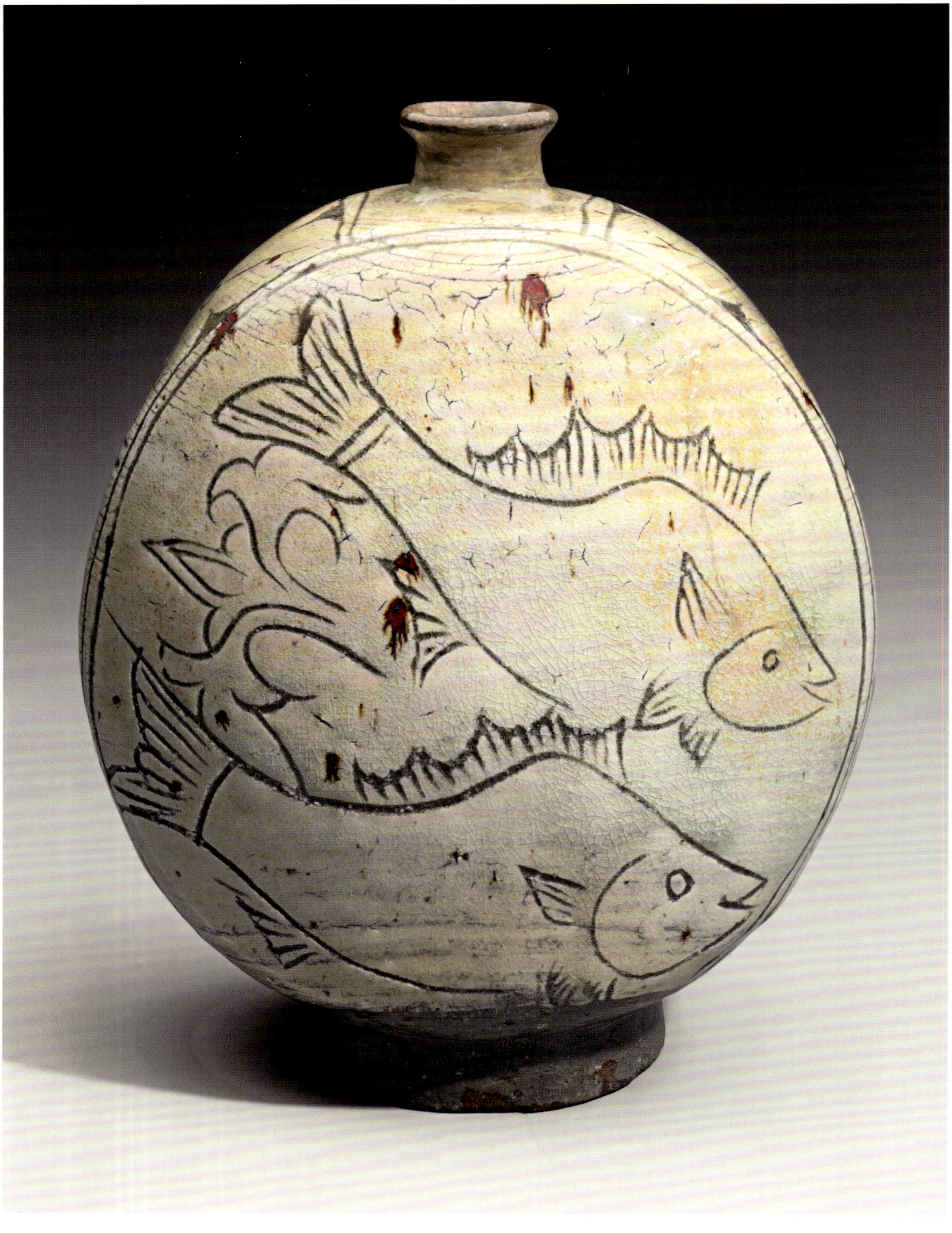

Flask with fish and scroll design

Joseon period, late 15th century

This boldly decorated flask, probably made for wine or sauce, is characterized by its flattened sides. The potter created it by first forming a round body and then hitting it on two sides. Flattened sides made such flasks easier to carry than globular jars, especially for outings and picnics. One side of this bottle has an incised double fish design, and the other side, along with the shoulders, is decorated with floral scroll designs in sgraffito. The combination of fish and scroll designs is common in fifteenth-century Joseon buncheong ceramics.

Fish patterns were popular in Korean art in many media. Fish were eaten and enjoyed widely and were also associated with wealth, prosperity, and fertility. Two fish were symbols of a happy marriage. The fish designs on this flask are executed with a lively and humorous simplicity. They are large and fat and seem to be diving around the surface of the flask. Part of this flask's neck is a modern repair.

Buncheong stoneware with incised and sgraffito decoration
H. 22.8 cm (9 in.); diam. of rim: 8.6 cm (3 3/8 in.);
diam. of body: 18.3 x 13.9 cm (7 3/16 x 5 1/2 in.)
Gift of William Sturgis Bigelow and Denman Waldo Ross—
William Sturgis Bigelow Collection 99.298

Jar with painted scrolls

Joseon period, late 15th century

Wide-mouthed and full-bodied jars were generally used for food storage. On this jar, white slip was applied to the entire gray stoneware body with a rough broom-like brush before the main motif was painted on top. The potter applied the white slip unevenly, leaving some areas only partly covered and the brush marks visible. High levels of iron oxide account for the brownish-black color of the pigment. The design is rendered with a free and bold hand, emphasizing the infinite possibilities of the brush.

Buncheong wares with iron-brown decoration were mainly produced in private kilns located in the middle of the Korean peninsula, most notably in Gongju or around Gyeryongsan. These kilns are dated to the period from the late fifteenth century to the early sixteenth century, when buncheong ware was being replaced by plain white porcelain or underglaze cobalt-blue decorated porcelain.

Buncheong stoneware with underglaze iron-brown painting
H. 15.1 cm (15 15/16 in.); diam. of rim: 9.8 cm (3 7/8 in.);
diam. of foot: 6.6 cm (2 5/8 in.)
Charles Bain Hoyt Fund 59.492

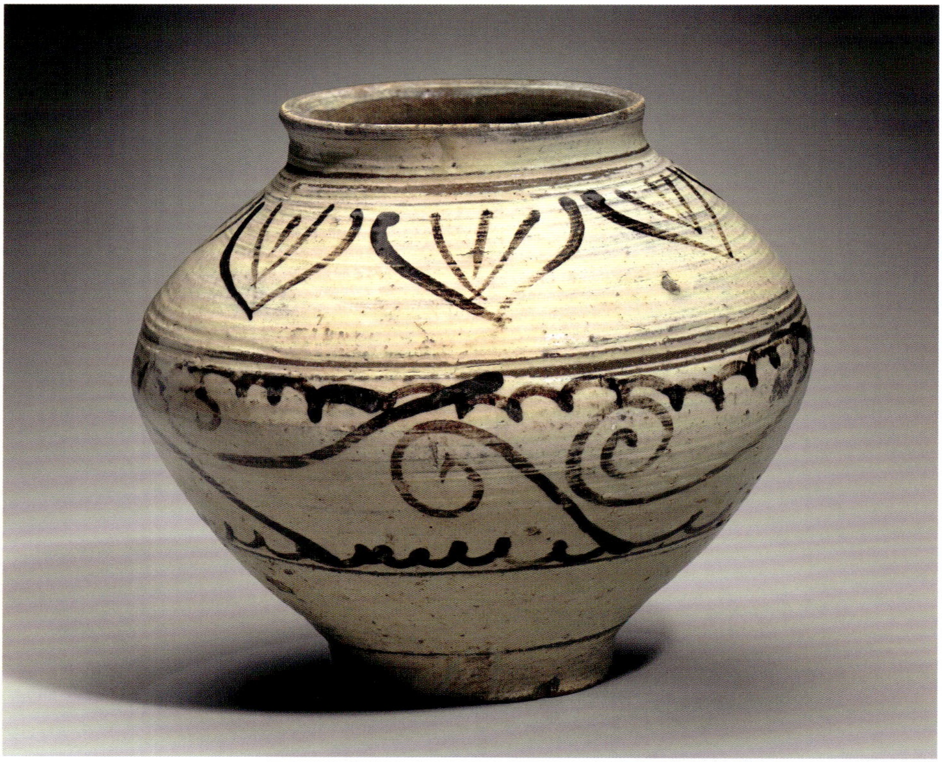

Jar with lotus and floral design

Joseon period, late 15th–16th century

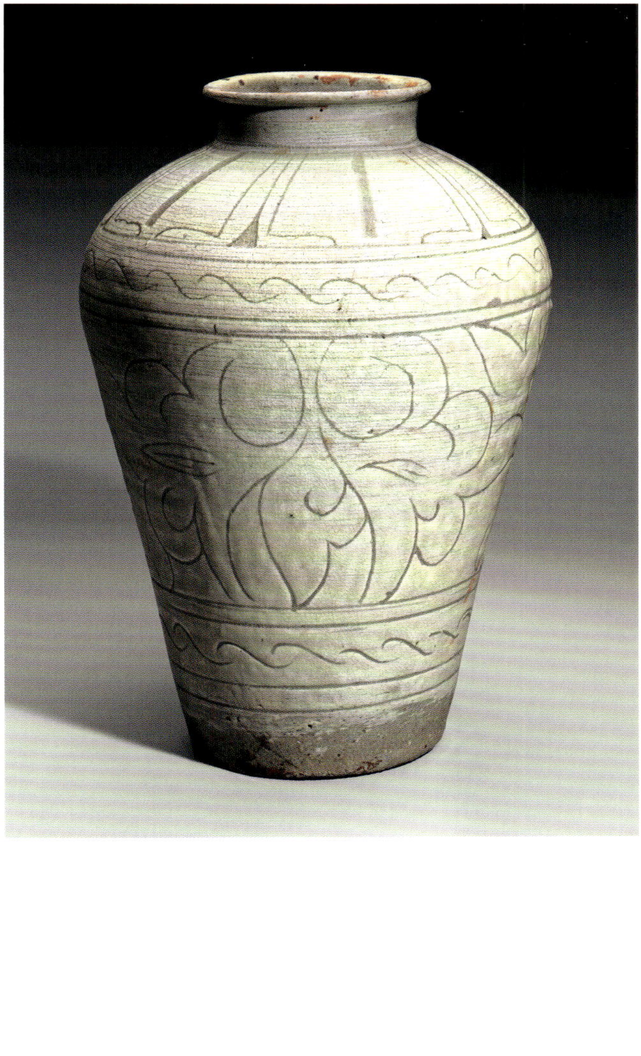

This large jar with wide shoulders and tall proportions was used for storing food or wine. The rather carelessly brushed-on white slip and the stylized motifs are typical characteristics of buncheong wares of the late fifteenth and early sixteenth centuries. As is common on large jars, the patterns are horizontally divided into four sections that feature incised designs of lotus flowers on the upper shoulder and more general floral designs in the middle of the body.

This jar, with its abstract freedom of design and rather slapdash execution, epitomizes the end of the relatively short tradition of buncheong ware, a uniquely Korean product.

Buncheong stoneware with incised decoration
H. 32.5 cm (12 13/16 in.); diam. of rim: 11.1 cm (4 3/8 in.); diam. of foot: 11.7 cm (4 5/8 in.)
Bequest of Charles Bain Hoyt—Charles Bain Hoyt Collection 50.1115

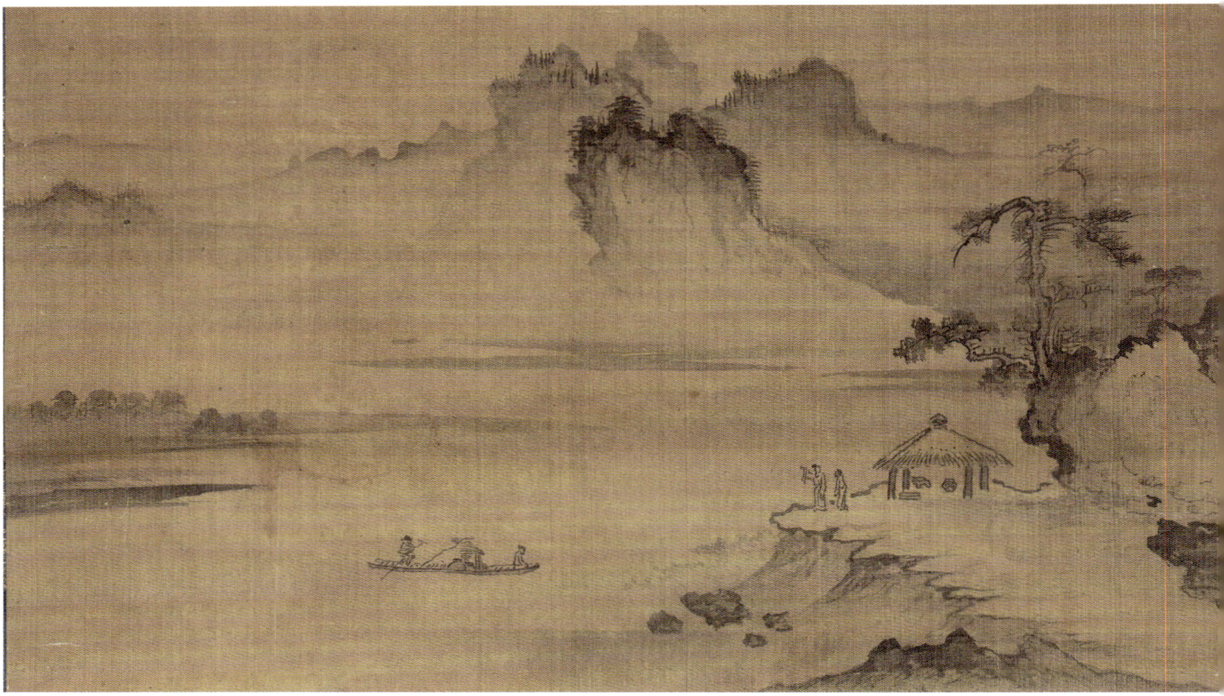

Landscape

Joseon period, 15th century

In Korea as in China, landscape painting was regarded as a high art second only to calligraphy and bamboo painting. By the fifteenth century, Korean painters were diligently studying newly emerging styles from China and blending them with existing Korean styles and techniques. The nostalgic scenery depicted in this landscape is reminiscent of the style of the fifteenth-century master An Gyeon, who is famous for his Korean-style interpretation of Chinese classical landscape painting. An's distinctively sloping landscape composition and subtle brush strokes—said to resemble crab claws—as well as his choice of themes all had an enduring influence on Korean painters of the time. The extended, foggy, space in the middle ground of this painting and the rough execution of the rocks and mountains in the background are other examples of An's legacy.

Hanging scroll; ink on silk
30.5 x 51.8 cm (12 x 20⅜ in.)
William Sturgis Bigelow Collection 11.6174

Falcon on a Perch

Attributed to Yi Am (1507–1566)

Joseon period, 16th century

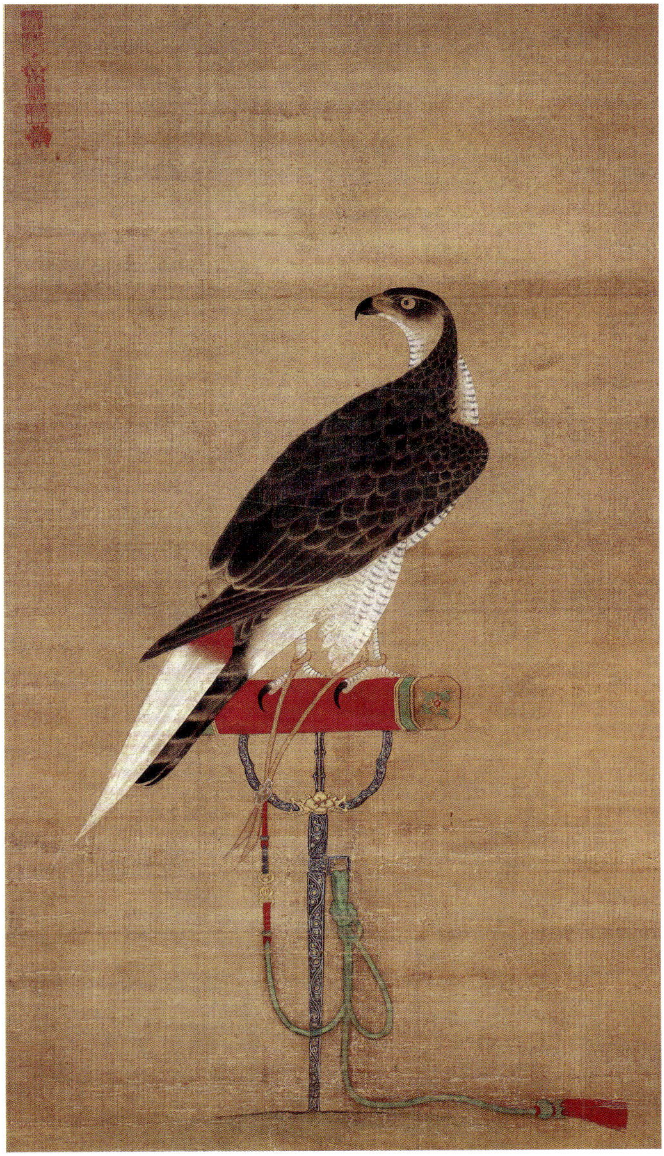

This painting of a falcon sitting on an elaborately decorated perch had long been attributed to Xu Ze, a Chinese painter working in the late fourteenth century, but it was recently reattributed to the renowned Korean painter Yi Am. Yi Am was known for his realistic yet poetic portrayal of animals and birds. The reattribution was made on the basis of two of the six seals present on the painting, which bear the artist's official title and his family origin, and a third seal, which is in the shape of a Chinese ceremonial bronze vessel.

Falcons were kept in captivity and trained for hunting. An ardent advocate of falconry, King Chungnyeol (reigned 1274–1308) instituted a governmental division that mainly dealt with matters relating to it. Due to such close association with the court, falcons symbolized authority and power. The use of gold and the intricate decoration of the perch in this painting suggest that the bird depicted might have been owned by the king, and that the painter, as a member of the royal Yi family, had access to it.

Hanging scroll; ink, color, and gold on silk
98.1 x 54.2 cm (38⅝ x 21$\frac{5}{16}$ in.)
Gift of William Sturgis Bigelow—William Sturgis Bigelow Collection 11.6164

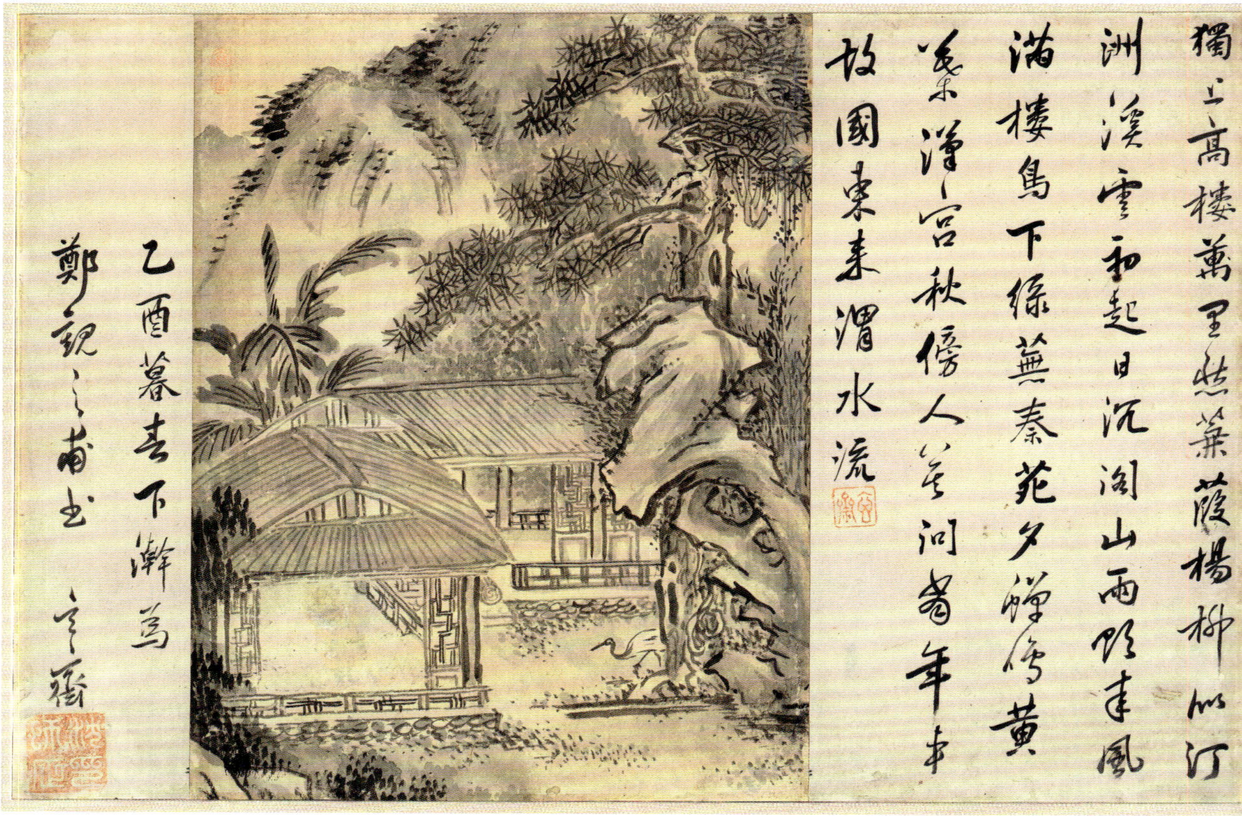
獨上高樓萬里愁蒹葭楊柳似汀
洲溪雲初起日沉閣山雨欲來風
滿樓鳥下綠蕪秦苑夕蟬鳴黃
葉漢宮秋傍人莫問當年事
故國東來渭水流
乙酉暮春下澣為
鄭觀之甫書

Landscape

Sim Sajeong (1707–1769)

Joseon period, 1765

Sim Sajeong was an ink painter whose artistic style was inspired by Chinese painting. In particular, this painting was influenced by the traditions of the Chinese Wu School, whose members liked to paint garden scenes. A giant rock can be seen next to an empty L-shaped house belonging to a Confucian scholar. The rock, pine tree, giant banana plant emerging from behind the roof of the house, and crane in the foreground are all symbols of Confucian literati.

According to the written commentary (added later), this painting was commissioned by a person named Jeong Gwanji and accompanied by an early- to mid-ninth-century poem by Xu Hun of the Tang dynasty. As a professional painter, Sim made his living by commission, although he came from a prominent scholar-official family. Its members held high-ranking official titles for many generations until Sim's grandfather was ousted amid factional disputes. Despite the financial and psychological hardship this unfortunate family history brought him, Sim was nonetheless able to maintain his connection with mainstream literati circles in his own time and earn respect from succeeding generations of artists.

Panel; ink on paper

34.4 x 53 cm (13 9/16 x 20 7/8 in.)

Gift of Mr. and Mrs. George H. Rockwell 63.629

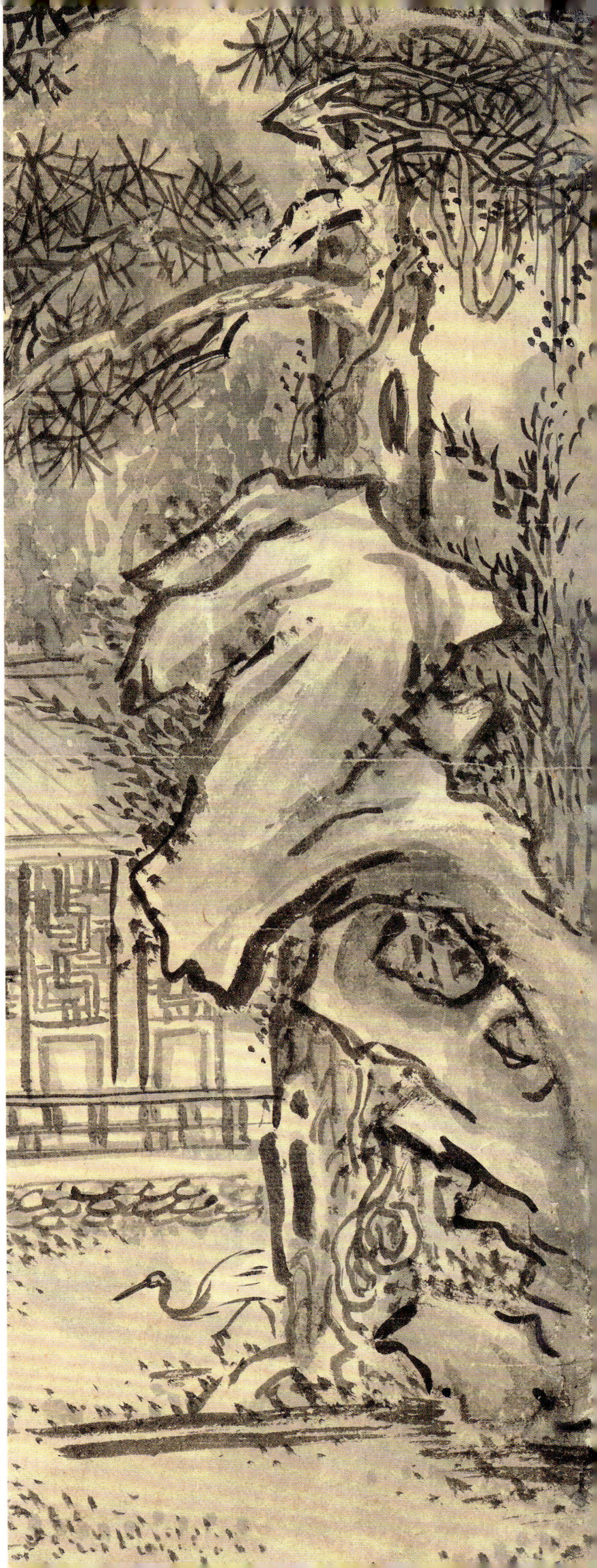

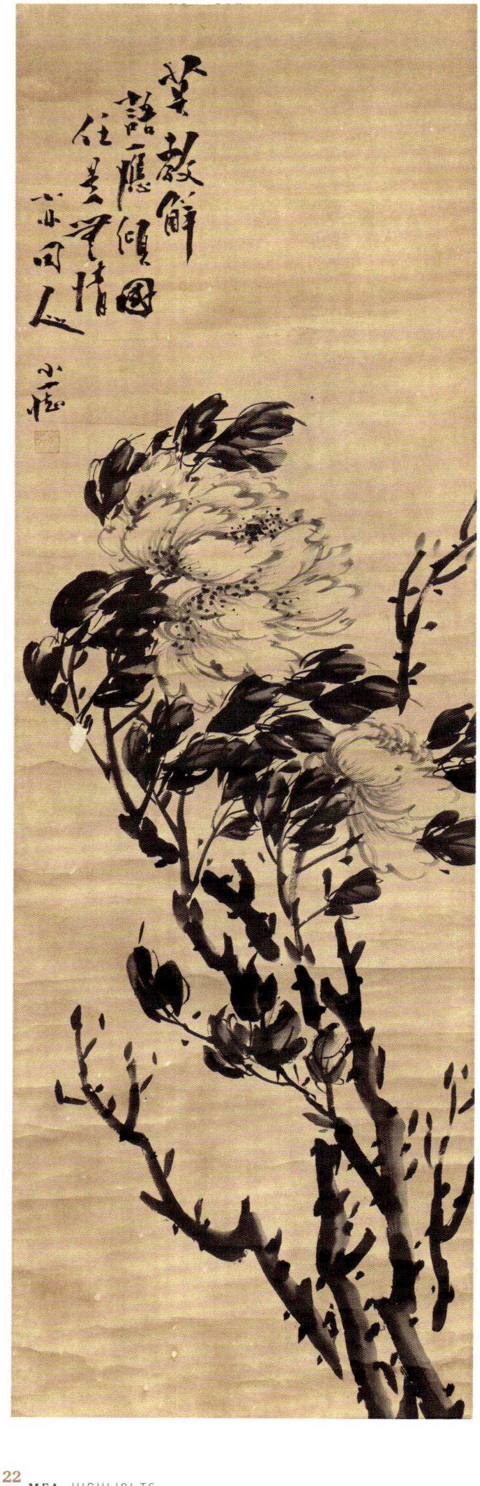

Peony

Heo Ryeon (1808–1893)

Joseon period, 19th century

A commoner by birth, Heo Ryeon received little professional training as an artist until he met his teacher, Kim Jeonghui, a leading figure in the Korean literati painting tradition. Heo's close connection to Kim enabled the unknown regional artist to become famous in literati circles. Kim gave Heo a pseudonym, Small Fool, as a reflection of Heo's keen interest in the famous Chinese Yuan-dynasty painter Huang Gongwang, whose own self-deprecating pseudonym was Big Fool. Kim said of Heo: "In the past, there was Huang Gongwang and now there is Heo. Heo's painting is outstanding."

Heo showed mastery over a variety of subject matter including landscapes, figures, and traditional plants. The great number of peony paintings he created throughout his life gave him another name, Heo Peony. As symbols of riches and honor, brightly colored peonies were popular subjects for paintings. Heo consistently painted his peonies using exclusively black ink to identify himself as a literati painter. He frequently accompanied his monochrome images with verses written in the manner of his teacher, also as evidence of his association with the literati tradition.

Hanging scroll; ink on paper
116.5 x 37.2 cm (45⅞ x 14⅝ in.)
Gift of Paula, Marta, and Erin Bennett in memory of Paul and Helen Bernat 1994.342

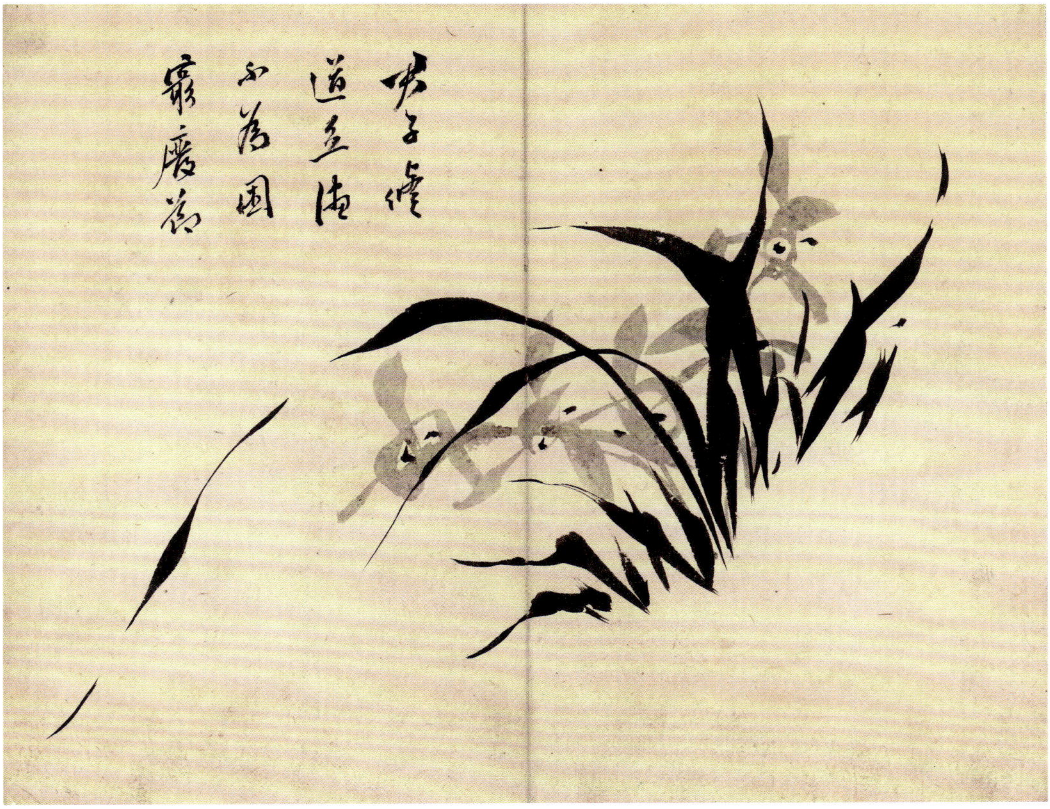

Flower, Birds, Rocks, and Fish

Yang Gihun (1843–1897), painter

Yi Huisu (1836–1909), calligrapher

Joseon period, late 19th century

This work is from an album composed of thirty individual ink paintings by Yang Gihun and three calligraphic works by Yi Huisu. As a court painter affiliated with the Royal Painting Bureau, Yang remained faithful to the Chinese-inspired literati style of painting that dominated artistic trends in Korea from the eighteenth century. He became best known for his reed-and-wild-geese paintings. The calligrapher Yi was also a professionally trained painter. He was versed in landscape painting as well as in the illustration of orchids and bamboo, and gained renown for his mastery of various styles of calligraphy. The topics of the paintings in this album range from strangely shaped rocks, the Four Gentlemen (pine, prunus, rock, and bamboo), and birds and flowers, to aquatic creatures, all of which were popular subjects among educated gentlemen in Joseon society at that time.

Accordion-folded painting album of thirty-four leaves; ink on paper

Each leaf: 23.5 x 29.2 cm ($9\frac{1}{4}$ x $11\frac{1}{2}$ in.)

Charles Bain Hoyt Fund and Museum purchase with funds donated anonymously 2000.829.3

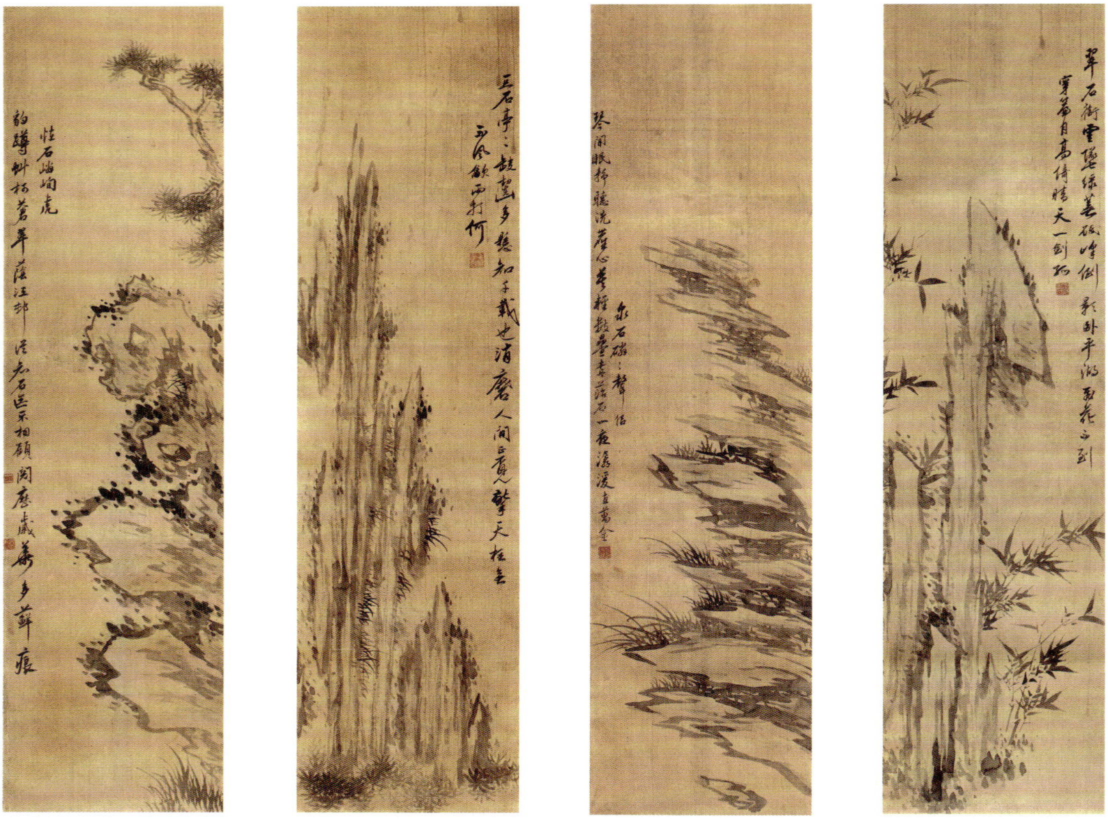

Rock, Pine, and Bamboo

Kim Yeong (born 1837)

Joseon period, late 19th–early 20th century

Confucian scholars revered rocks as one of the Ten Symbols of Longevity as well as for their natural dignity. The tradition of painting rocks, especially those with strange shapes, entered the Korean repertoire as an independent subject from China during the late Joseon period. To the Korean aristocrats whose main concern was to attain scholarly and moral eminence, painting the eccentric and unusual shapes of rocks was regarded as a way to express their inner feelings.

These four paintings are presumed to be a set because of their similarity in style and size. All four were executed primarily in ink. The artist Kim Yeong was a professional painter who belonged to the Royal Painting Bureau. He was particularly good at landscape painting and depictions of bamboo trees in ink. In each of these paintings he described the theme in an inscription on the left or right side. Two of the four paintings depict rocks alongside trees, a pine and a bamboo. These trees were also widely revered, symbolizing constancy, fidelity, and scholarly integrity.

Hanging scrolls; ink and light colors on silk

121.3 x 32.3 cm ($47\frac{3}{4}$ x $12\frac{11}{16}$ in.)

121.5 x 32.4 cm ($47\frac{13}{16}$ x $12\frac{3}{4}$ in.)

121 x 32.5 cm ($47\frac{5}{8}$ x $12\frac{13}{16}$ in.)

125.5 x 32.4 cm ($49\frac{7}{16}$ x $12\frac{3}{4}$ in.)

Gift of Mr. and Mrs. George H. Rockwell 63.2676–79

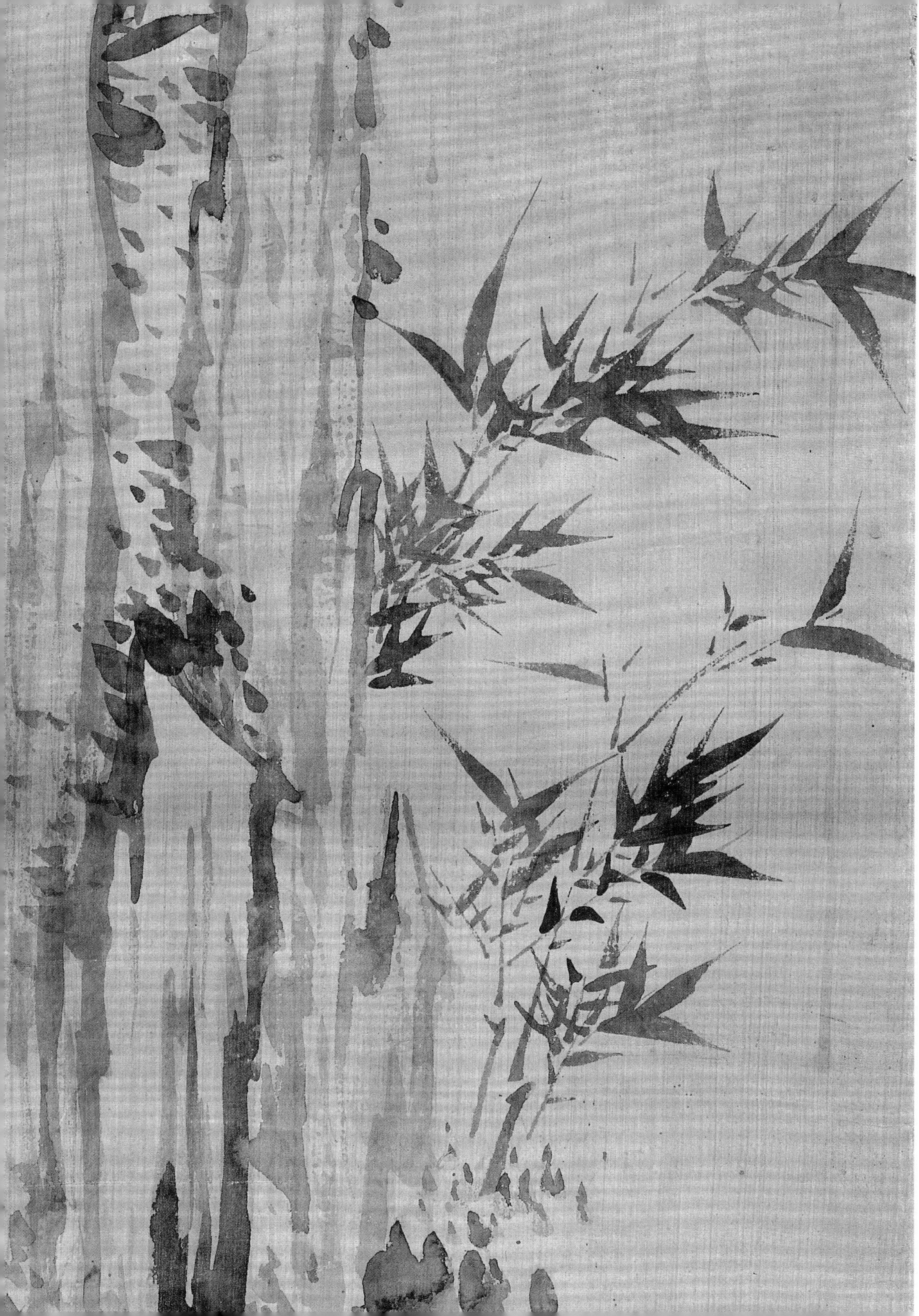

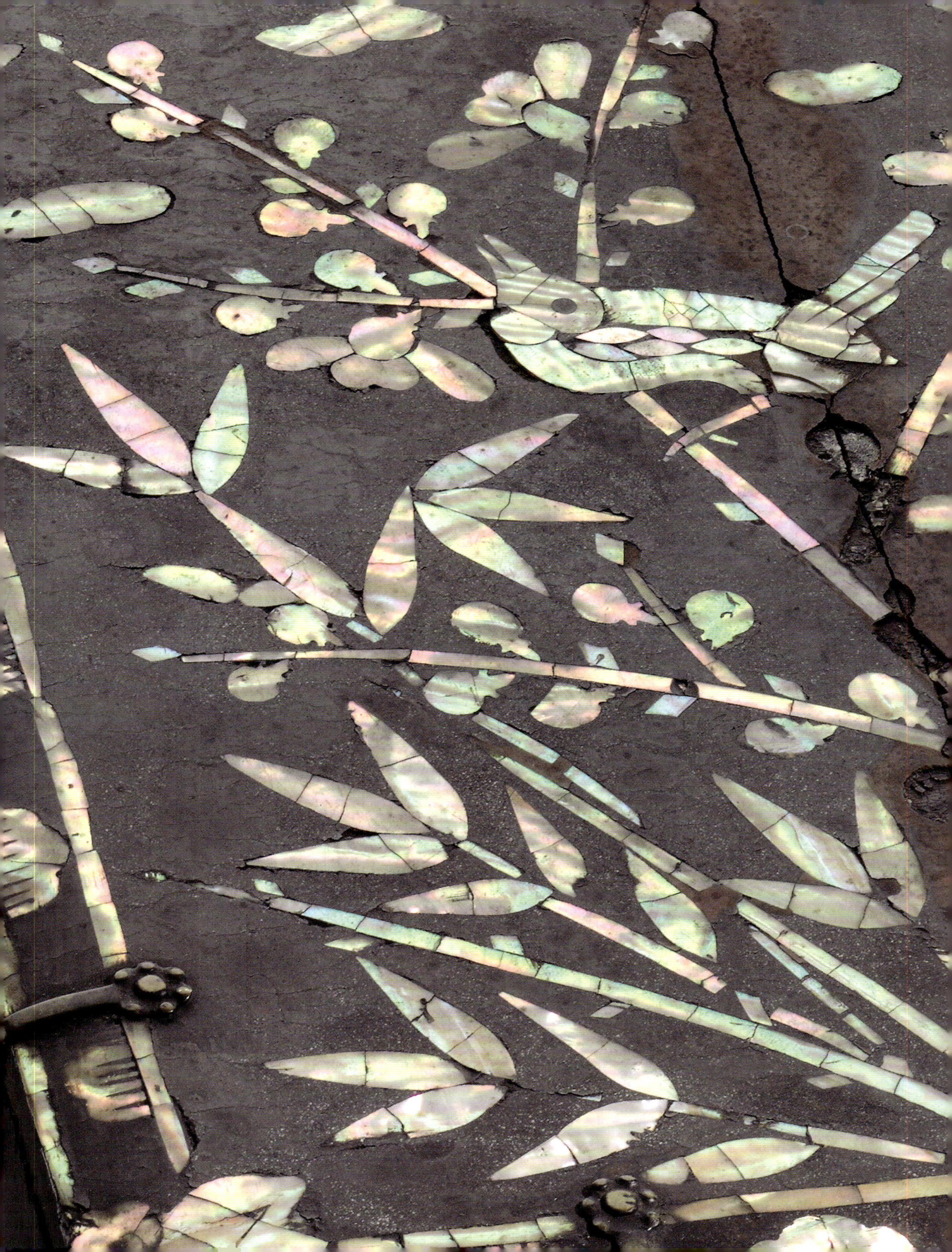

Box with mother-of-pearl inlay

Joseon period, 17th–18th century

This box is a fine example of Korean inlay work from the mid–Joseon period, when the yangban elite could afford such high-quality secular items in their homes. An aristocratic family probably used this ornate box for storing papers, stationery, or clothes. It is solidly constructed with metal fittings to secure the joints in the wood, and these fittings are decorated with chrysanthemum-shaped finials. The lid, which fits over the entire box, leaving only the base uncovered, is unusually decorated with a bird and flower scene reminiscent of literati ink painting. The bird perched on a prunus branch emerges from bamboo branches and clouds. The entire scene is inlaid using large and thick slices of mother-of-pearl, which have been scored to produce a crackled look. The sides of the lid are alternately decorated with sprays of bamboo and pinks originating from a central point at the base. Bordering the top of the lid is a double line, where six-petal flowers are either cut in half and applied along the lines or cut into four pieces to decorate the four corners. This method of inlaying with mother-of-pearl developed during the Joseon period out of the more complex, geometric, and regular chrysanthemum patterns (in very small and thin slices of shell) characteristic of the preceding Goryeo period, when precious lacquer boxes were used primarily in a Buddhist context.

Lacquer on wood with inlaid mother-of-pearl decoration and metal fittings
L. 26.5 cm (10 7/16 in.), w. 26.5 cm (10 7/16 in.), h. 9.5 cm (3 3/4 in.)
Bequest of Charles Bain Hoyt—Charles Bain Hoyt Collection
50.1685a–b

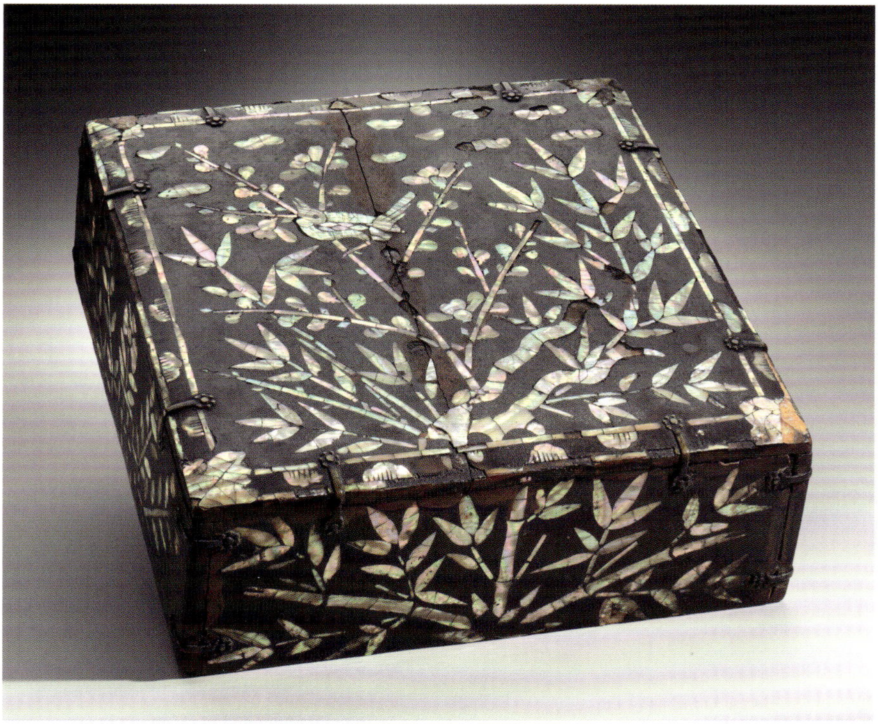

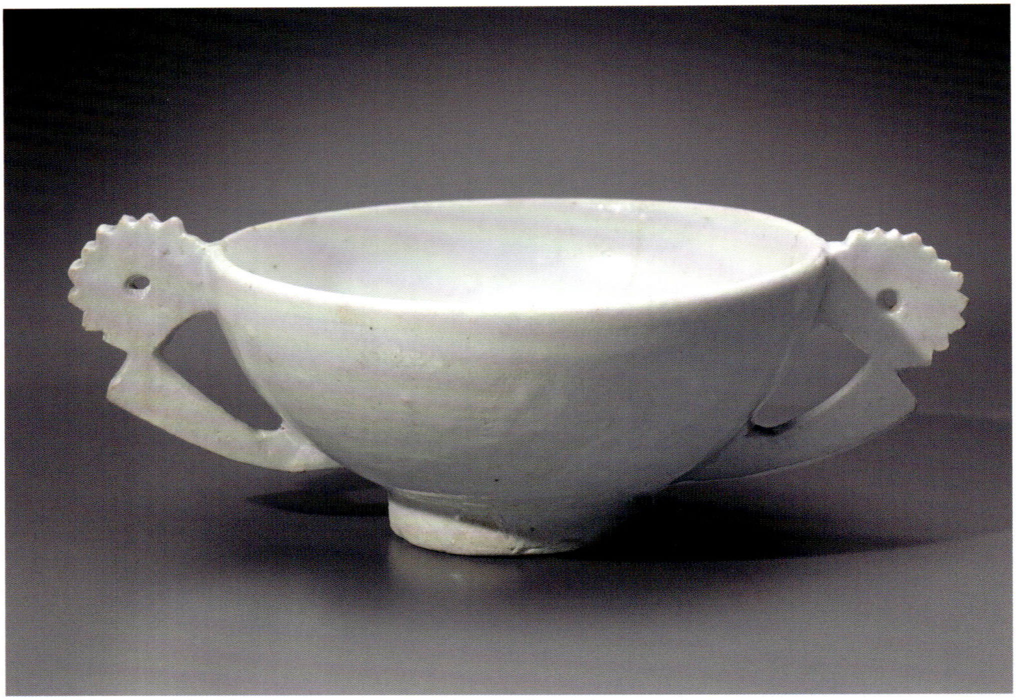

Cup with two handles

Joseon period, late 15th century

This vessel was meant to be held with both hands when offering wine in Confucian ancestor-worship ceremonies. A dish with a high foot for food offerings often accompanied such cups on the altar. An early example of Joseon white porcelain, this piece dates to the late fifteenth century.

The production of white porcelain on the Korean peninsula can be traced back as far as the tenth century, but the later Joseon-period white porcelain tradition is more closely related to that of the Ming dynasty. Ming porcelains were known to the Koreans through gifts and unofficial, private imports in limited circulation among members of the upper class. In the early fifteenth century, Korean potters produced white porcelain in small quantities alongside buncheong ware. They crafted the white wares with much care, then encased them in protective stands (called *saggars*) when firing them to ensure flawless results. The resulting fine white porcelain was reserved for the king. He sometimes used it to entertain Chinese envoys, who requested Korean white porcelain as tributary goods.

White porcelain

H. 5 cm (1 15/16 in.); diam. of rim: 9.6 cm (3 3/4 in.);
diam. of foot: 4 cm (1 9/16 in.)

Bequest of Charles Bain Hoyt—Charles Bain Hoyt Collection

50.1038

Ritual bowl

Joseon period, 17th century

The flanges at the sides of this seventeenth-century bowl imitate the flanges that appeared at first by accident on ancient Chinese bronze ritual vessels, where the joins on the ceramic piece molds leaked molten bronze. Such ceramic bowls were used instead of more expensive metal vessels to hold rice and other grain offerings in Confucian ceremonies. The clean and austere appearance of white wares made them particularly fitting as ritual vessels. Plain white undecorated porcelain was continually produced throughout the Joseon period and was popular even after porcelain decorated with underglaze blue was introduced. The white color accorded not only with the aesthetic that favored simplicity and natural charm but also with Confucian ideals of humility and integrity.

The overall shade of white wares depends on the quality of the clay. Court documents attest to the enormous efforts made to ensure high quality: officials employed at the royal kiln carefully selected clays from locations throughout the country, sampling and testing them for color and purity. Gyeonggi Province was an ideal place to establish the official court-supported kilns, thanks to the availability of good clay and abundant firewood—two key resources required to operate a kiln. Its proximity to the Han River was another advantage, as completed white wares could easily be shipped to palaces and central offices in the capital.

White porcelain
H. 15. 8 cm ($6\frac{1}{4}$ in.); diam. of mouth: 24.5 cm ($9\frac{5}{8}$ in.);
diam. of base: 9 cm ($3\frac{9}{16}$ in.)
Bequest of Charles Bain Hoyt—Charles Bain Hoyt Collection
50.1145

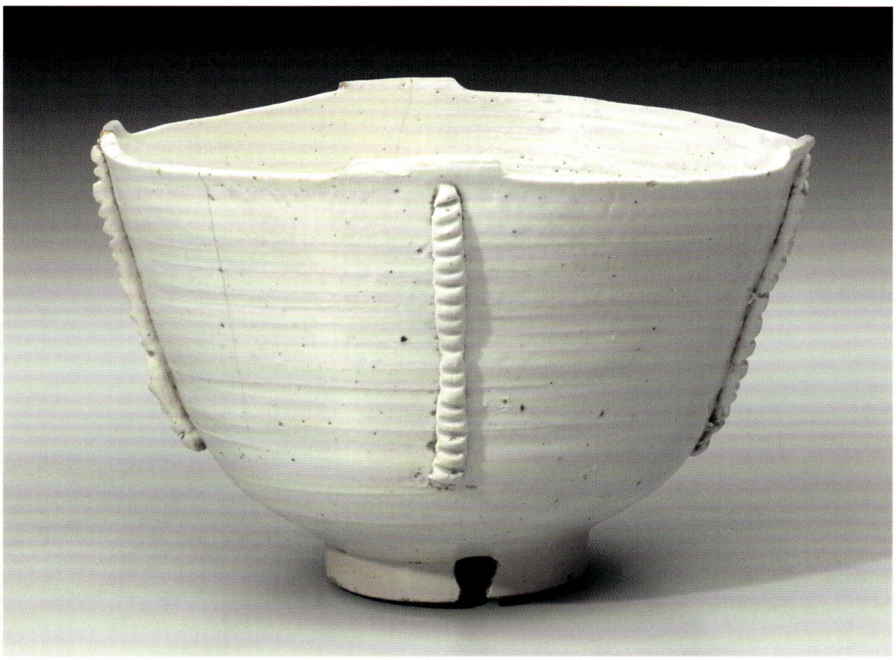

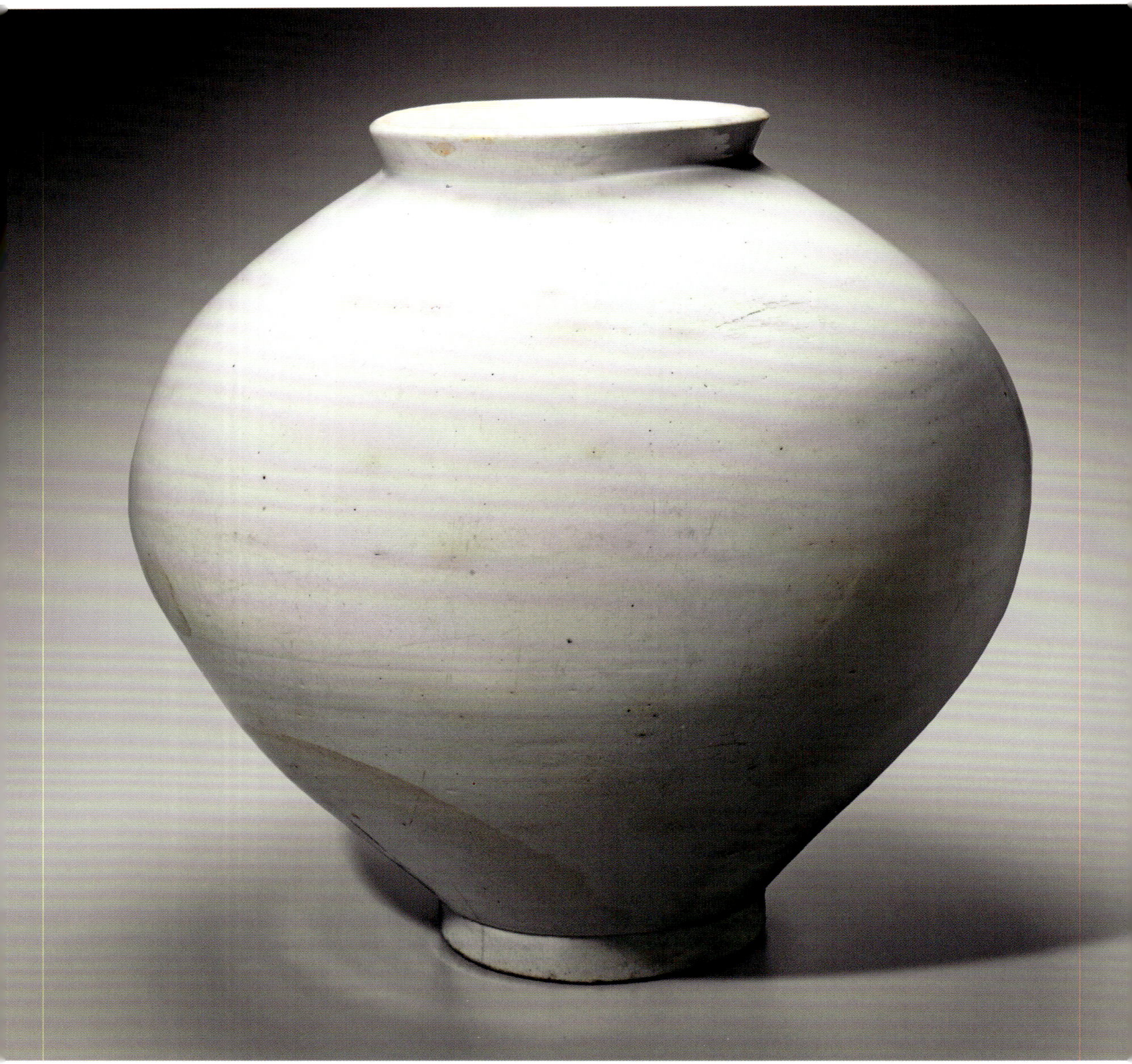

Moon jar

Joseon period, early 18th century

The imperfect symmetry and generous, full volume of this bulbous, moon-shaped jar epitomize the austere Confucian aesthetic of the Joseon Period. There are only a few examples throughout the world that have survived in such perfect shape. Moon jars were typically fired in two parts (upper and lower) before being luted or fused together to form a complete work. This jar has a visible horizontal ridge across the center of the jar where the two parts were joined.

Moon jars were popular in the late Joseon period, from the seventeenth century to the eighteenth century. They were used for food storage, with their contents ranging from grains to salted fish, both of which were essential winter side dishes, to condiments.

The hint of blue in the glaze of this piece dates it to the eighteenth century. White porcelain tended to be snowy, creamy white in color until roughly the sixteenth century, after which it tended to have a blue tint until the late eighteenth century. Nineteenth-century white wares are gray with a cloudy glaze. Later moon jars also tend to have an elongated oval shape.

Moon jars such as this one were popular in Japan among early twentieth-century folk craft scholars such as Yanagi Soetsu, who particularly appreciated their naturalistic asymmetry. They were also highly influential with Western studio potters such as Bernard Leach and Lucie Rie. Contemporary Korean potters such as Han Ikhwan (1921–2006) and Park Youngsook (born 1947) have also attempted to recreate their timeless beauty.

White porcelain
H. 44 cm (17 5/16 in.); diam. of mouth: 21.2 cm (8 3/8 in.);
diam. of foot: 16.3 cm (6 7/16 in.)
Bequest of Charles Bain Hoyt—Charles Bain Hoyt Collection
50.1040

Jar with phoenix design

Joseon period, 18th century

White porcelain with underglaze cobalt-blue decoration

H. 39 cm (15 3/8 in.); diam. of rim: 16.2 cm (6 3/8 in.);

diam. of foot: 17.3 cm (6 13/16 in.)

Bequest of Charles Bain Hoyt—Charles Bain Hoyt Collection

50.2211

Jar with orchid design

Joseon period, 18th century

White porcelain with underglaze cobalt-blue decoration

H. 40.2 cm (15 13/16 in.); diam. of rim: 15 cm (5 7/8 in.);

diam. of foot: 15.5 cm (6 1/8 in.)

The John Pickering Lyman Collection. Gift of Miss Theodora Lyman 19.871

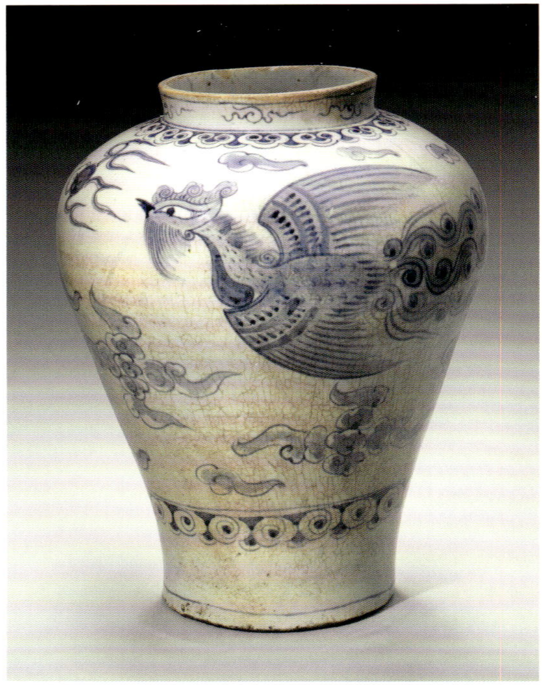

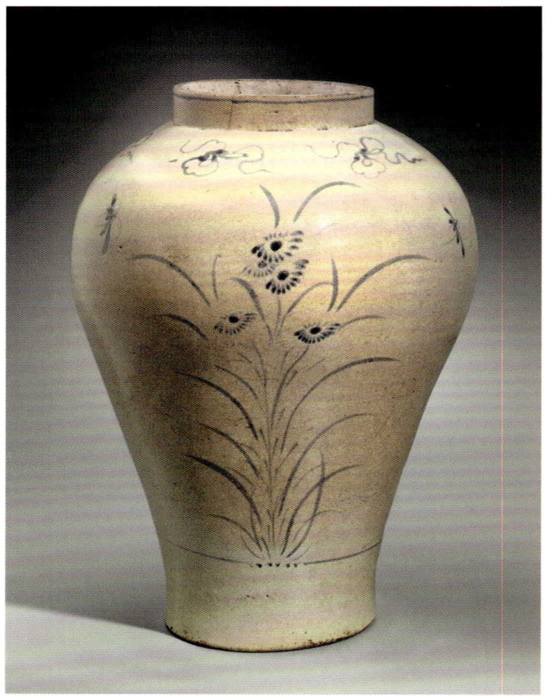

Excavations of the royal kilns from the eighteenth century reveal a considerable increase in blue-and-white ware production at that time. Korean potters took a uniquely Korean approach to blue-and-white motifs and shapes adapted from China. For example, many areas of the white surface of the jar pictured to the lower right were left undecorated, quite a different approach from the elaborate and dense decorative patterns of Chinese ceramics. The sparser Korean application of motifs may be attributed to the limited availability of the expensive cobalt pigment, which had to be imported from China, but also reflects the Korean tendency toward simplification and enhancement of natural beauty. Plant designs, especially orchids, pine trees, and cherry blossoms, were among the most frequently used patterns in early eighteenth-century Korean blue-and-white wares. The leaves of the orchid plant on this jar were sparingly drawn as fine lines. The horizontal line toward the foot denotes the earth from which the plants might have grown. Supplementary design elements include a somewhat stylized dianthus flower scroll along with butterflies and other insects.

The jar above right features a phoenix, a mystical bird associated with female royalty. Phoenixes were often accompanied by clouds to indicate the creature's heavenly status, but here the bird flies over a landscape. Compared to the orchid jar, this piece displays a more densely populated surface and a fuller shape toward the neck.

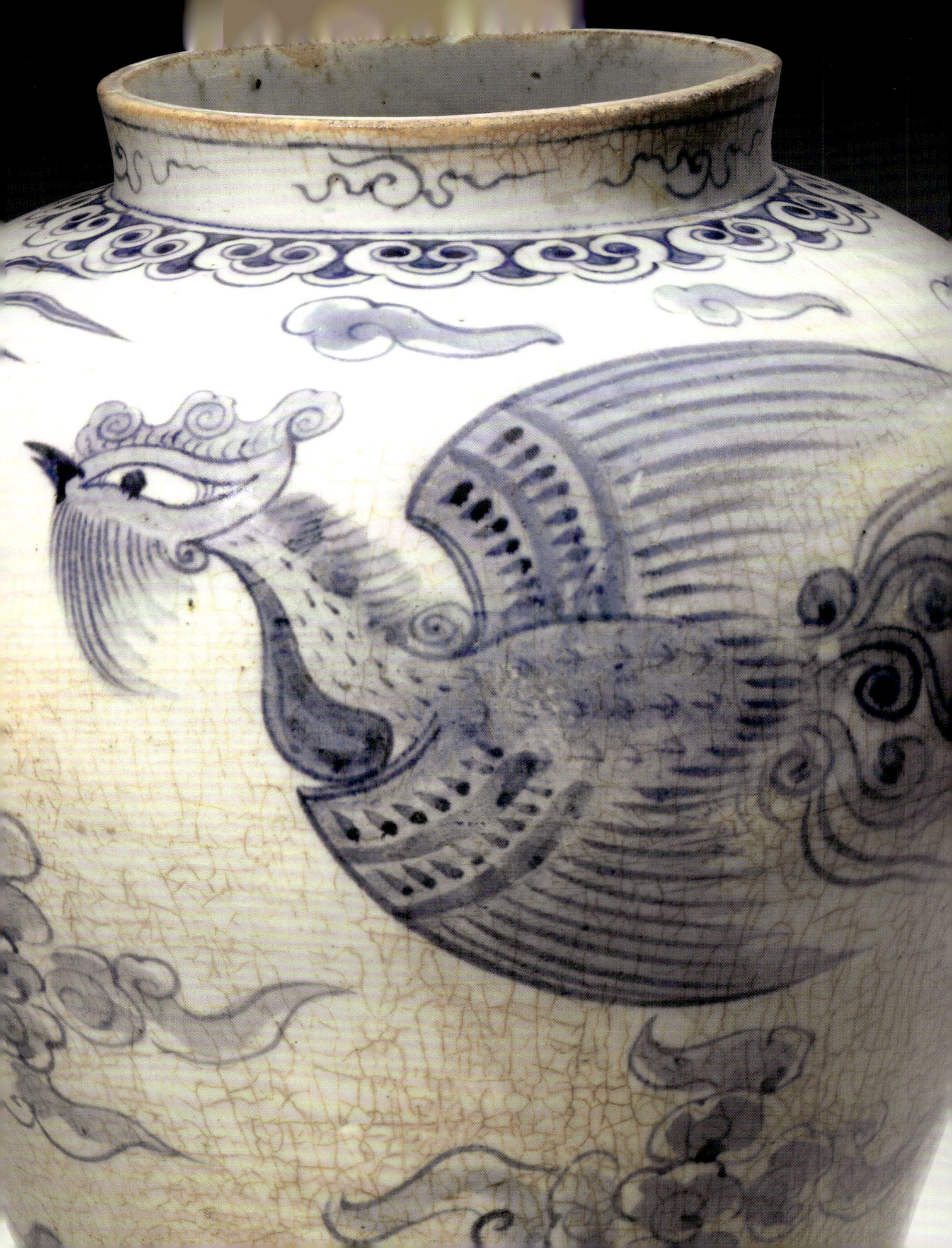

Jar with dragon and cloud

Joseon period, 18th century

A century of debilitating wars with Japan and China in the late seventeenth century resulted in the decline of overseas trade and a temporary weakening of the domestic ceramic industry. When obtaining cobalt blue from China became exceedingly difficult, readily available Korean iron-brown served as a practical substitute. Even the king's wares were produced with underglaze iron-brown during King Yeongjo's reign (1724–76) until affordable cobalt blue could be imported in the late eighteenth century. Local, private kilns also manufactured white porcelain with underglaze iron-brown. These local wares are characterized by simplified and humorous renderings of motifs derived from plants and animals. This jar's lively dragon among clouds is an example of one of the most frequently depicted designs. The scaly body of the auspicious creature wraps around the jar's surface, though the head and tail are missing. Such bold simplification, almost to the point of abstraction, occurred frequently in these locally produced iron-brown wares. The jar bears an inscription indicating that it was offered to a Buddhist temple.

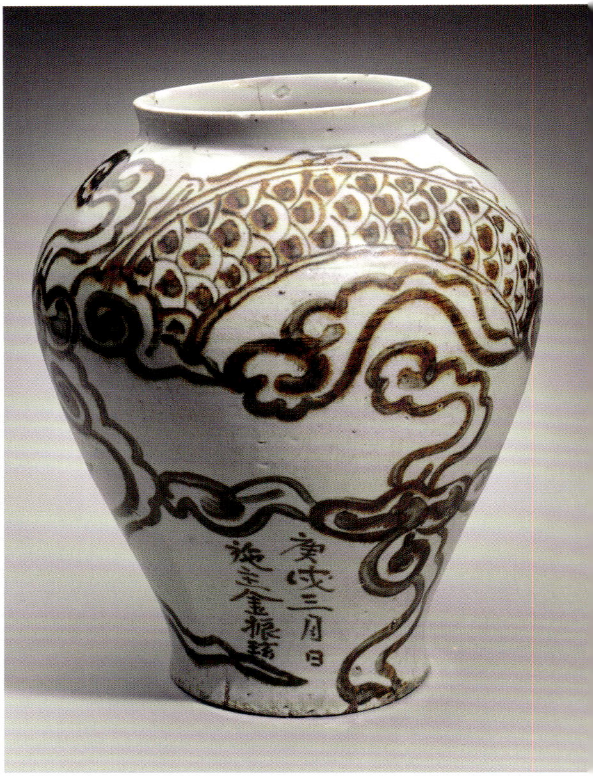

White porcelain with underglaze iron-brown painting
H. 32.5 cm (12 13/16 in.); diam. of mouth: 15.8 cm (6 1/4 in.); diam. of foot: 14 cm (5 1/2 in.)
Bequest of Charles Bain Hoyt—Charles Bain Hoyt Collection
50.2227

Flowerpot stand

Joseon period, late 18th century

Elaborate and ornate openwork ceramics appealed to members of the newly emerged middle classes in the late Joseon period. Increased private trade led to the accumulation of wealth and an increased demand for goods among members of those classes. Exposed to colorful and extravagant wares from Japan and China, they demanded more decorative wares than the austere ceramics favored by the elite in Korea. Changes in the operation of state kilns also affected the way ceramics were consumed during this period: potters who used to belong exclusively to court kilns were free to make ceramics privately for the general market.

Few Joseon examples of large white porcelain pieces with openwork designs survive. The openwork technique was usually employed for decorative objects, such as this flowerpot stand, since it was not practical for containers. Other items decorated with openwork include brush pots. The carved lotus patterns of this piece create an exceptional three-dimensional effect. The details of the petals and leaves have various depths, evoking a relief-like feel. Lotus designs representing purity regained popularity as a decorative pattern due to a resurgence of Buddhism in the later Joseon period. Buddhism had been strictly banned by the Neo-Confucian ruling class during the early Joseon period but was positively accepted by the ruling class of the later period, resulting in open worship of Buddhism by the broader public.

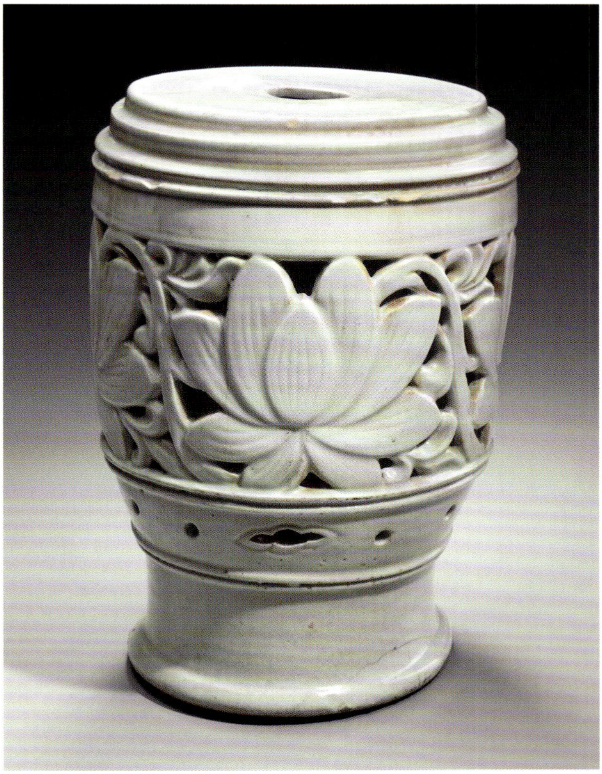

White porcelain with openwork lotus design
H. 34.2 cm (13 7/16 in.); diam. at widest point: 25.8 cm (10 3/16 in.); diam. of base: 19 cm (7 1/2 in.)
Bequest of Charles Bain Hoyt—Charles Bain Hoyt Collection
50.2141

Jar with painted grapevine

Joseon period, late 18th century

White porcelain with copper-red underglaze was popular in Korea during the eighteenth and nineteenth centuries. Many of the works produced have grape or lotus designs. The vine, leaves, and fruit of this jar were all painted in an impromptu and spontaneous style and only cover a small area of the body.

The imperfection in the clay and rather uneven finish of the surface, as well as gray color of the entire body, indicate that this jar was most likely produced in a provincial kiln. The court kilns located in Gwangju near Seoul at the time also used copper-red pigment, but rarely for the main element of the design. Instead, they limited the use of copper-red to supplementary areas and small details to enhance decoration painted predominantly with cobalt. The insufficient supply of cobalt blue outside of the government kilns may account for the primary use of copper-red in provincial ceramics. During the late eighteenth century, blue-and-white porcelain was considered to be a luxury and banned by order of the king. This led potters in the provinces to seek an alternative to prestigious blue-and-white wares and resulted in the production of pieces like this jar. The uneven shape and simple decoration of this type of pottery also appealed to Japanese taste.

White porcelain with underglaze copper-red painting
H. 21.6 cm (8½ in.); diam. of mouth: 11.6 cm (4$\frac{9}{16}$ in.); diam. of foot: 9.9 cm (3⅞ in.)
Bequest of Charles Bain Hoyt—Charles Bain Hoyt Collection
50.1113

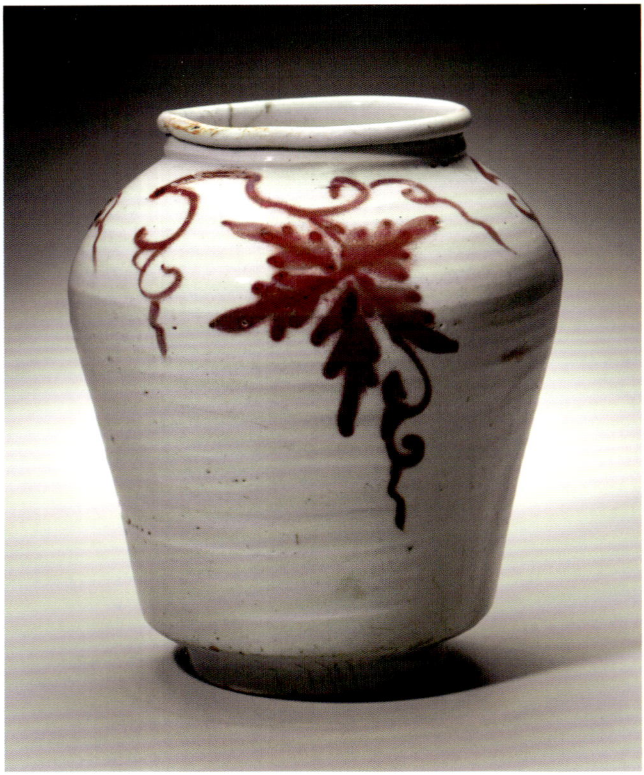

Octagonal bottle

Joseon period, late 18th century

The elite class of scholarly gentleman, known as yangban, became the new audience for and consumers of ceramics in the eighteenth century and they favored decoration based on landscape painting. The main design on this jar, a landscape and figure confined in a window in the shape of a Korean ivy leaf or neunghwa, is an example of the scholarly taste then in vogue. The practice of decorating ceramics with landscapes first emerged with the development of cobalt-painted ware in the late Joseon period. Professional, well-trained artists from the Royal Painting Bureau made regular visits to the court kilns. For this reason, the decoration on cobalt-painted wares tended to reflect contemporary trends in general painting. The practice of enclosing the design in a circle, a square, or a decorative scroll was also characteristic of the time.

This bottle is well proportioned with a full, globular body and a flaring lip. To create bottles with faceted sides, potters shaved off the rounded surfaces after throwing them. From the eighteenth century onward, these angular, usually octagonal, bottles became a popular shape for white porcelains produced in the official kilns, which were located at Geumsa-ri, Gyeonggi Province, at that time.

White porcelain with underglaze cobalt-blue decoration
H. 35.2 cm ($13\frac{7}{8}$ in.); diam. of rim: 5.8 cm ($2\frac{5}{16}$ in.); diam. of foot: 11.3 cm ($4\frac{7}{16}$ in.)
Bequest of Charles Bain Hoyt—Charles Bain Hoyt Collection 50.2213

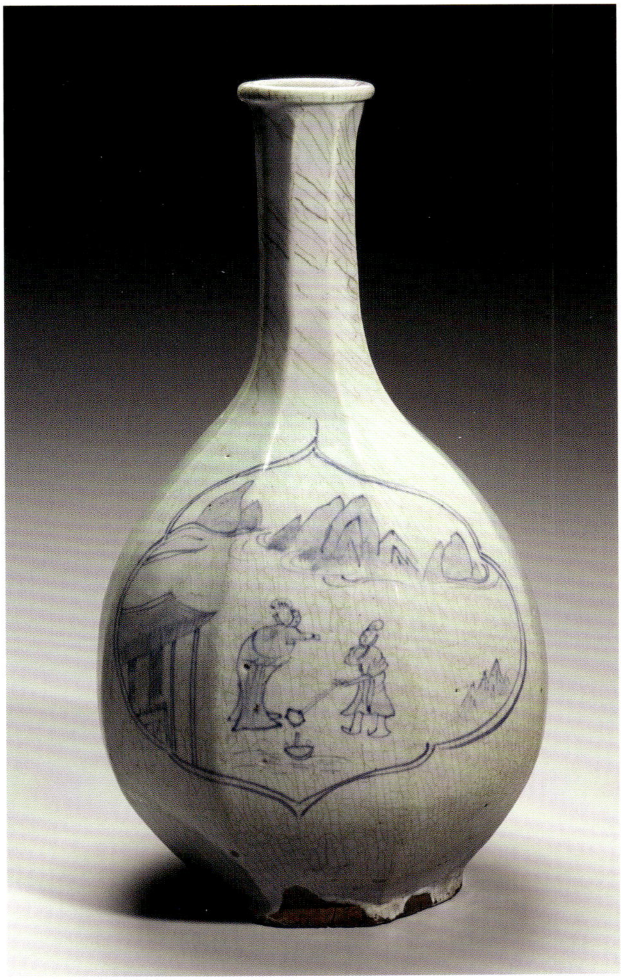

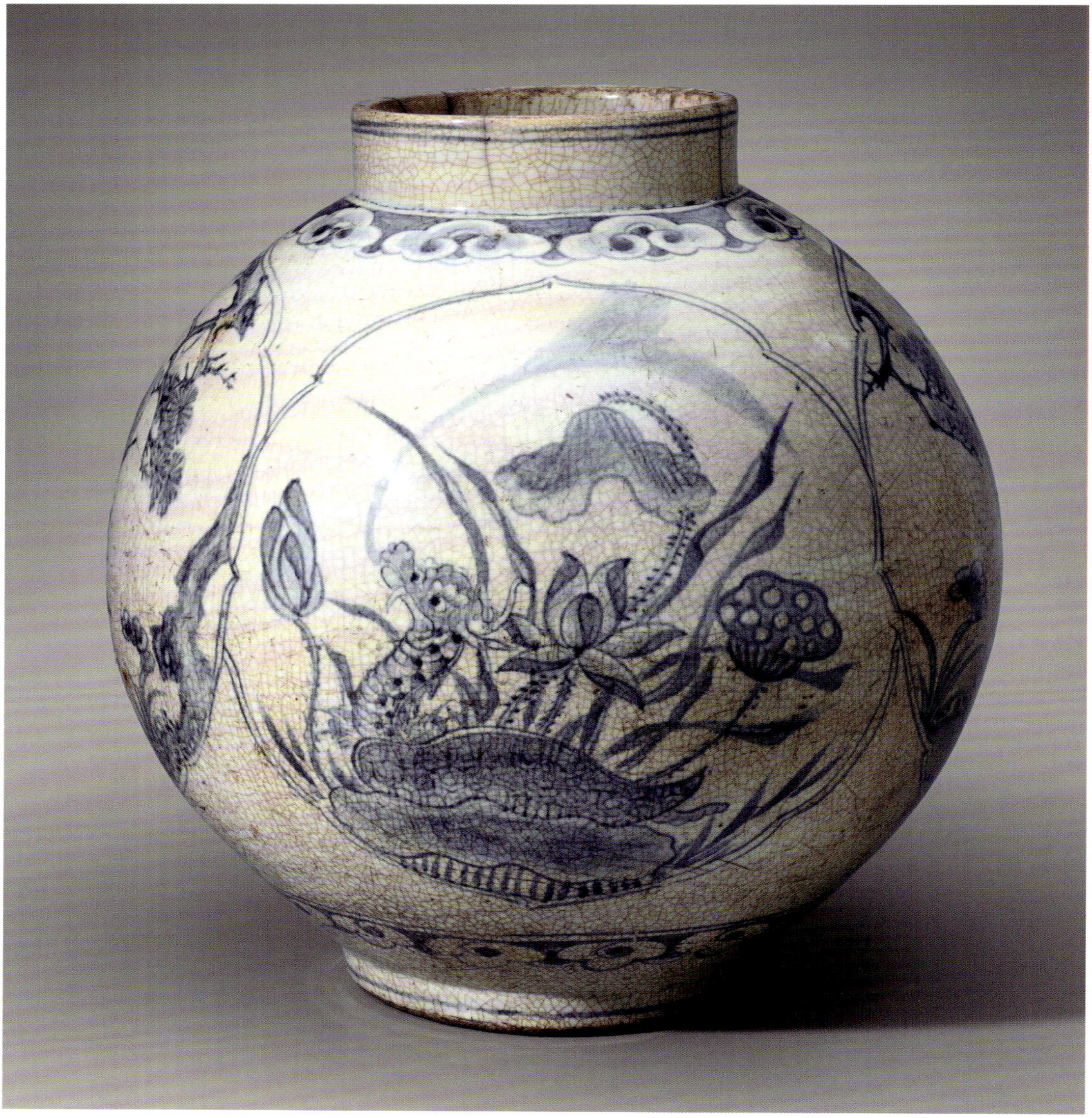

Jar with dragon and turtle

Joseon period, late 18th century

This globular jar was used as a wine vessel. Its remarkably fine and elaborate decoration in underglaze cobalt blue includes symbols of long life, such as the crane, tortoise, pine trees, and auspicious fungus, as well as lotus flowers. Most of these are counted among the Ten Symbols of Longevity. On this jar, the individual symbols are framed by four leaf-shaped cartouches. The shoulder and the foot of the jar are decorated with rows of auspicious *ruyi*, "as you wish" fungus scrolls. Sometimes such jars have four round cartouches instead. The painterly composition and brushstrokes suggest that trained artists painted the motifs. This jar has a crackled glaze and pale blue cobalt decoration and was probably made at the Bunwon-ri official kiln.

White porcelain with underglaze cobalt-blue decoration
H. 32.2 cm (12 11/16 in.); diam. of rim: 14 cm (5 1/2 in.); diam. of foot: 14.6 cm (5 3/4 in.)
The John Pickering Lyman Collection. Gift of Miss Theodora Lyman 19.949

Turtle-shaped vessel

Joseon period, 19th century

As commoners became significant consumers in the late Joseon period, potters increasingly adopted folk art motifs, as did the maker of this wine vessel shaped like a realistic turtle. The turtle is a popular symbol of long life. The spout is formed as the creature's head and open mouth, with fine details rendered in underglaze cobalt pigment. Incised lines indicate the divisions of the turtle's shell. The toes and legs of the animal serve as stands that support the body.

The constellation designs painted on the creature's back probably depict a specific horoscope of the owner. Astronomy was an important discipline not only in predicting weather patterns to benefit agriculture, but also to establish royal authority by providing insight into natural phenomena. Based on careful observation and recording of the movements of celestial bodies like the sun, moon, and stars, astronomy reached an advanced level during the Joseon period. In addition, worshipping stars, in particular the Seven Stars, was popular among the general masses, as the stars were believed to regulate human birth, life, and death. Ceramic wares with constellation designs therefore made auspicious gifts.

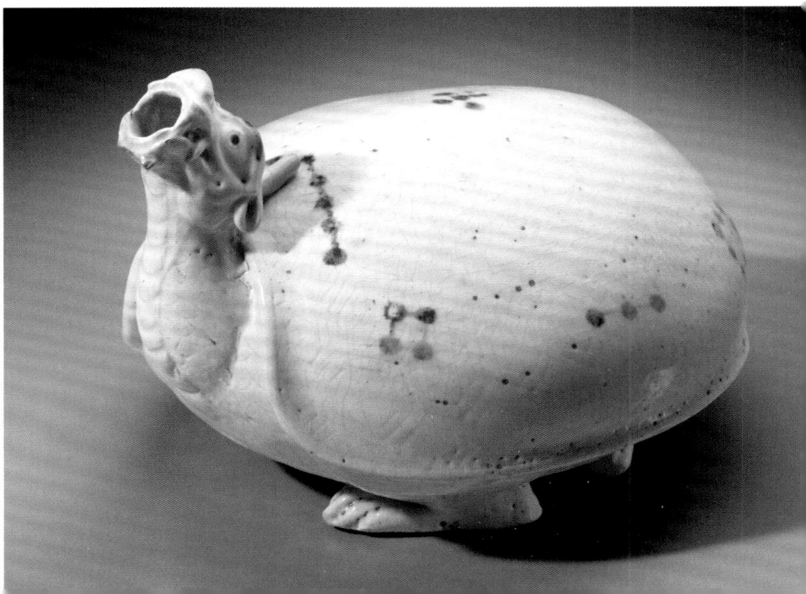

White porcelain with underglaze cobalt-blue decoration
H. 18.4 cm (7 1/4 in.), L. 26 cm (10 1/4 in.)
Bequest of Charles Bain Hoyt—Charles Bain Hoyt Collection 50.2212

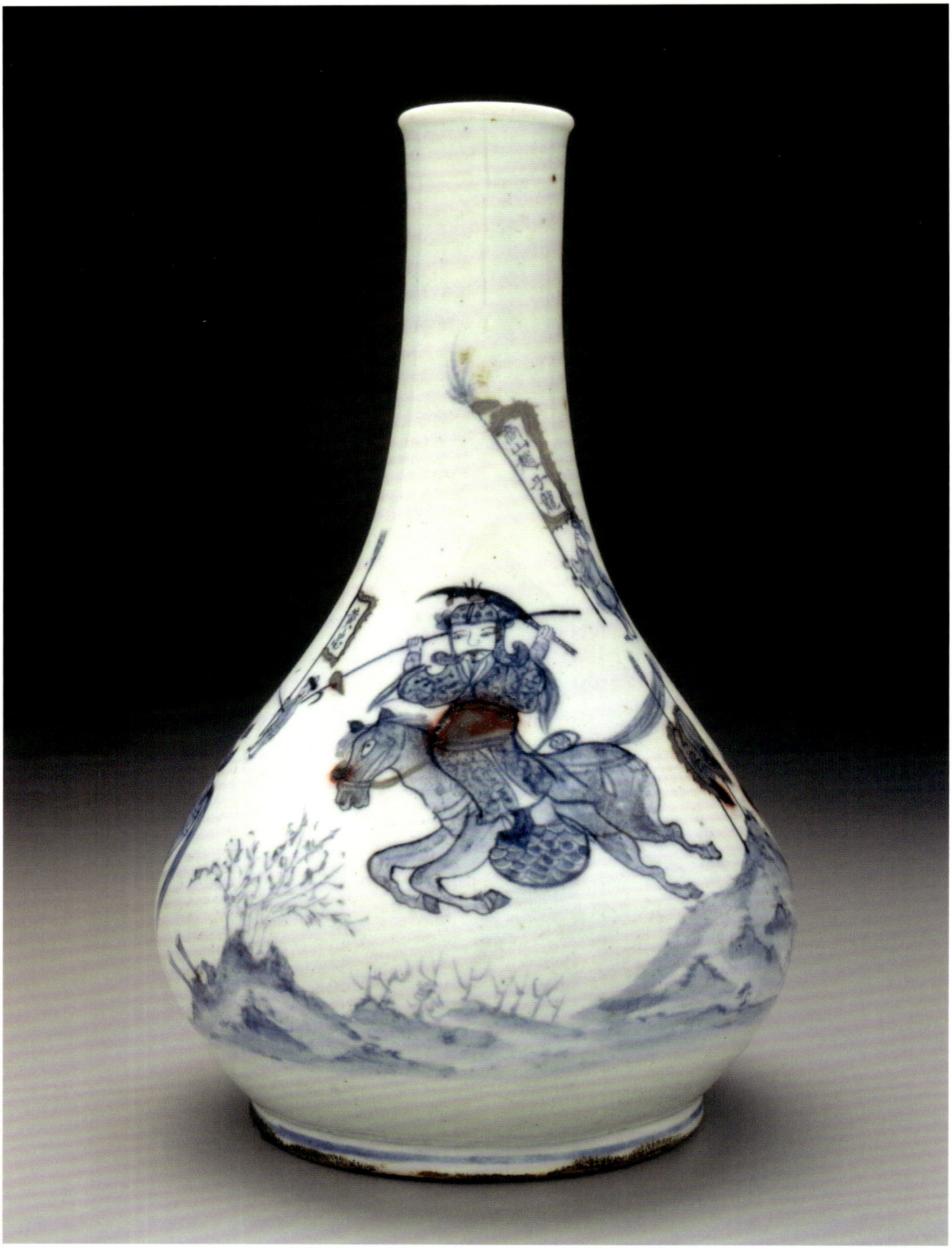

Bottle with painted figure and landscape

Joseon period, 19th century

The elongated neck and thick lower body of this vessel are typical for Joseon wine containers from the nineteenth century, but its decorative scheme is unusual. The narrative depicted in underglaze blue was adapted from the *Romance of the Three Kingdoms*, an Asian classic beloved in Korea as well as in China. Represented here are two of the Five Tiger Generals, Zhao Yun and Huang Zhong. Based on historical persons from the third century, these characters not only were favorite heroes of generations of readers, but also became objects of worship due to the valor and loyalty they demonstrate in the story. They confront one another here as though they are fighting a battle against the backdrop of a stylized landscape painting.

The poor application of copper-red on this vessel suggests that it may have been produced for the middle or lower classes in a private kiln. In addition, the figures, animals, and landscape painted on the flask are out of proportion to each other. The economic decline of the time caused a corresponding decline in ceramic craftsmanship, especially after 1884 when the government-controlled kilns shut down and were replaced by private kilns. Nonetheless, this piece stands out for its interesting and unusual decoration.

White porcelain with underglaze cobalt-blue and copper-red decorations
H. 27 cm (10⅝ in.); diam. of mouth: 4.4 cm (1¾ in.); diam. of foot: 11.6 cm (4 9/16 in.)
Bequest of Charles Bain Hoyt—Charles Bain Hoyt Collection
50.1041

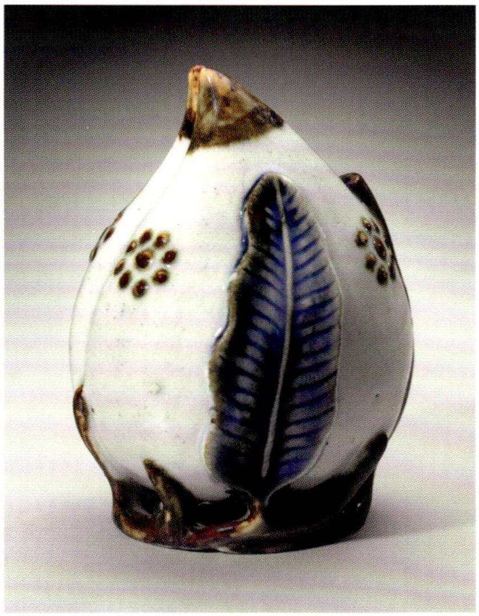

Peach-shaped water dropper

Joseon period, 19th century

This water dropper, used to drip water on the ink stone to mix with dry ink ground from a stick, takes the form of a ripe peach. With connotations of health, longevity, and even sexuality, the peach was a new shape for water droppers in the late Joseon period and may have been an invention of Korean potters. Other novel forms included carp, persimmons, toads, lions, houses, and mountains. Such sculpted water droppers were decorated with various underglaze pigments to achieve colorful and realistic effects. This trend was a departure from the previous era, when more reserved and simple wares were favored and a single pigment was used on each vessel. These changes can be attributed to growing exposure to foreign polychrome wares from China and Japan in the eighteenth century.

White porcelain with underglaze cobalt-blue and iron-brown decorations
H. 10 cm (3 15/16 in.), diam. of body: 7.4 cm (2 15/16 in.)
Bequest of Charles Bain Hoyt—Charles Bain Hoyt Collection
50.1142

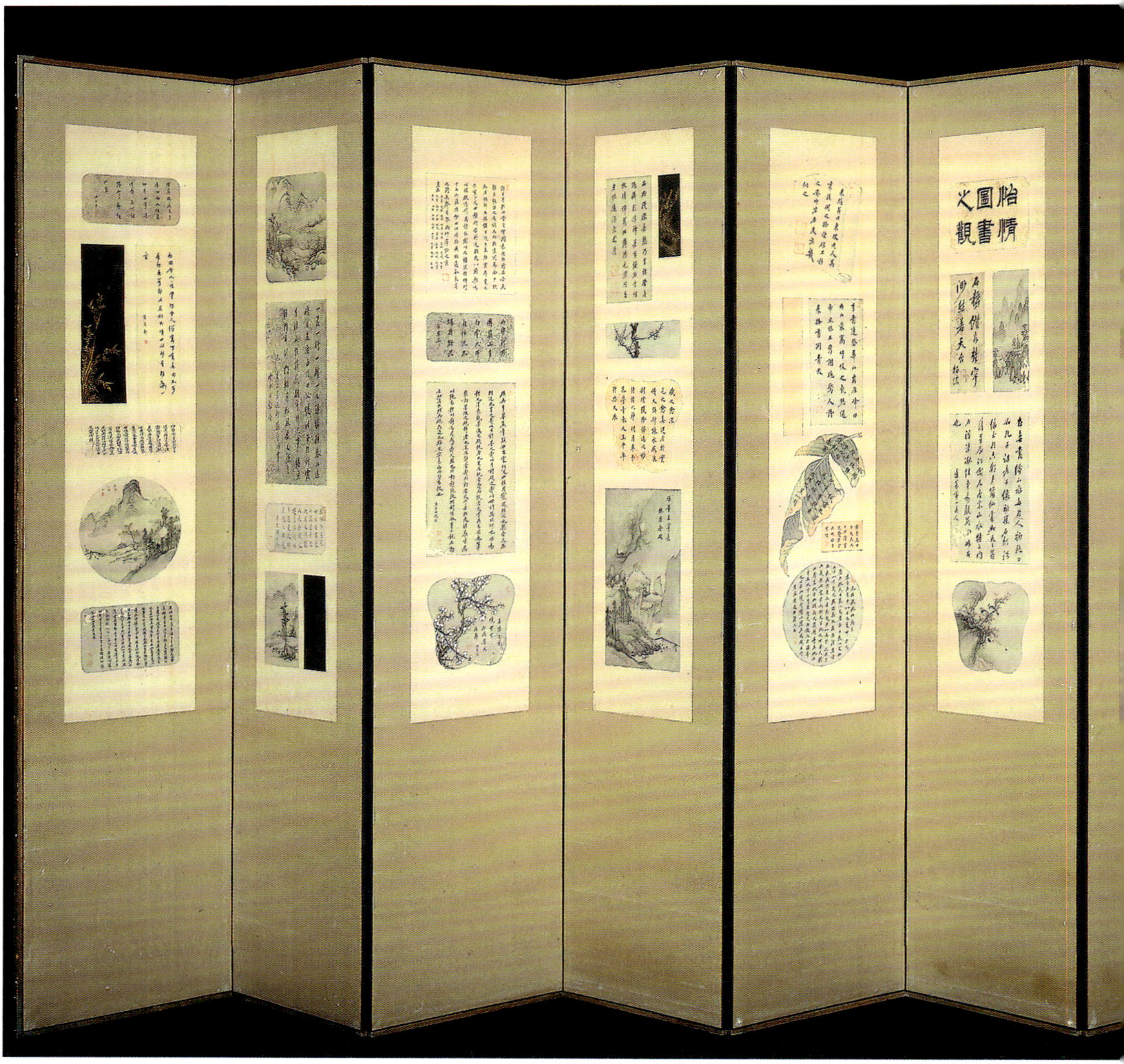

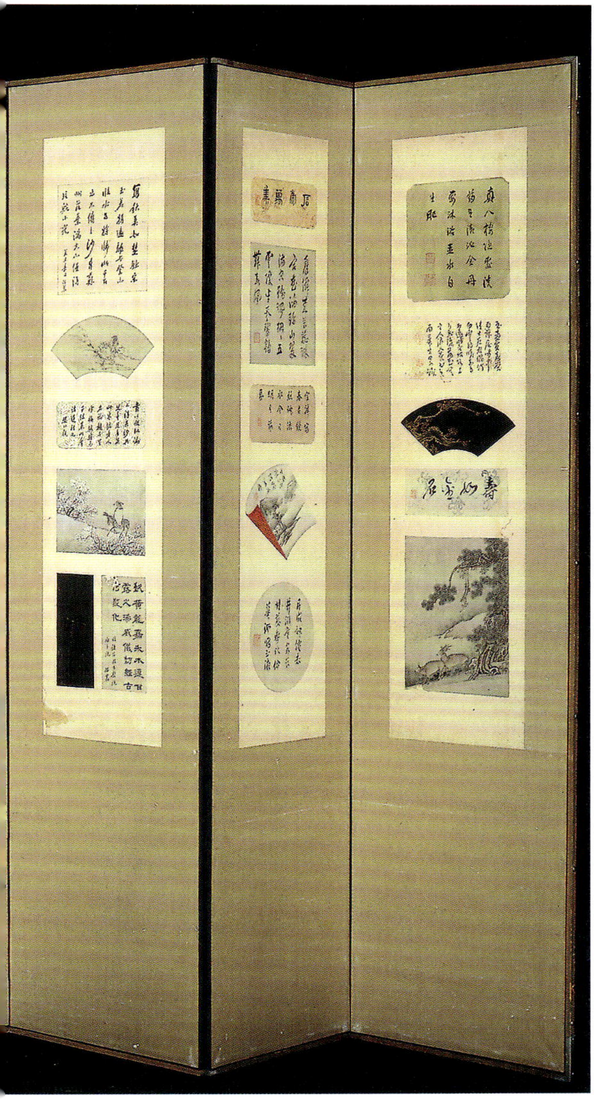

Screen with paintings and calligraphy

Joseon period, 19th century

Collage screens, a development of the late Joseon period, were in fashion among the upper classes in the nineteenth century. They reflect a similar development in China during this time, the production of collage scrolls. This screen, with five individual works of calligraphy and painting pieced together vertically in each of its panels, is typical of the genre. In this case the screen has ten panels altogether, but five such panels for a single screen was more common. The calligraphies and paintings differ in form and size and address a variety of subjects.

Collage screens served not only as decorative additions to a household, but also as symbols of a learned Neo-Confucian gentleman's ability to collect, appreciate, and exhibit highly valued works of art. Fan-shaped paintings were often included in the screen, as the fans were believed to expel bad luck and invite good luck into the household.

Ten-panel folding screen; ink and light colors on silk
188 x 450 cm (74 x 177 in.)
Charles Bain Hoyt Fund 1994.81

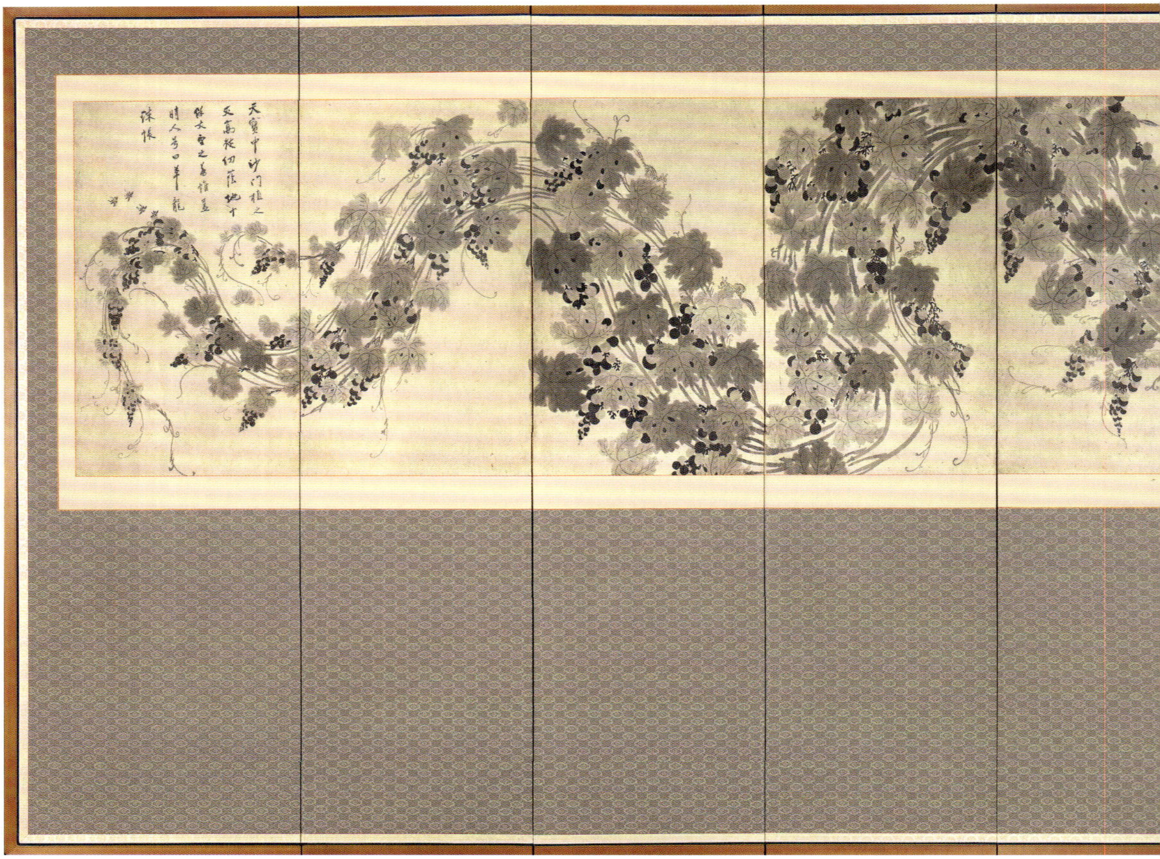

Screen with grapevine

Joseon period, late 19th century

The grapevine has a long history in Korean art. It was originally a favorite subject of literati painters, who thought its structure appropriate for sweeping brush strokes and ink wash. Later, in decorative Korean folk painting, the many seeds of the grapes became popular symbols for many male heirs. This grapevine screen reflects the nineteenth-century popular taste for spontaneity and artlessness. The vines sweep across all eight panels from right to left. There is vigor and liveliness emanating from the quick rendering and dramatic composition. This particular grapevine is thought to resemble a dragon, which also carries auspicious meaning, as dragons were believed to bring rain and therefore good harvests. The squirrels and bees enjoying themselves among the plump grapes demonstrate the humorous quality of late Joseon period decorative painting. The inscription at the top left is an excerpt from a collection of essays written by the ninth-century Chinese scholar Duan Chengshi extolling the good qualities of grapevines.

Eight-panel folding screen; ink on paper
153 x 342.9 cm (60¼ x 135 in.)
Charles Bain Hoyt Fund 2009.342

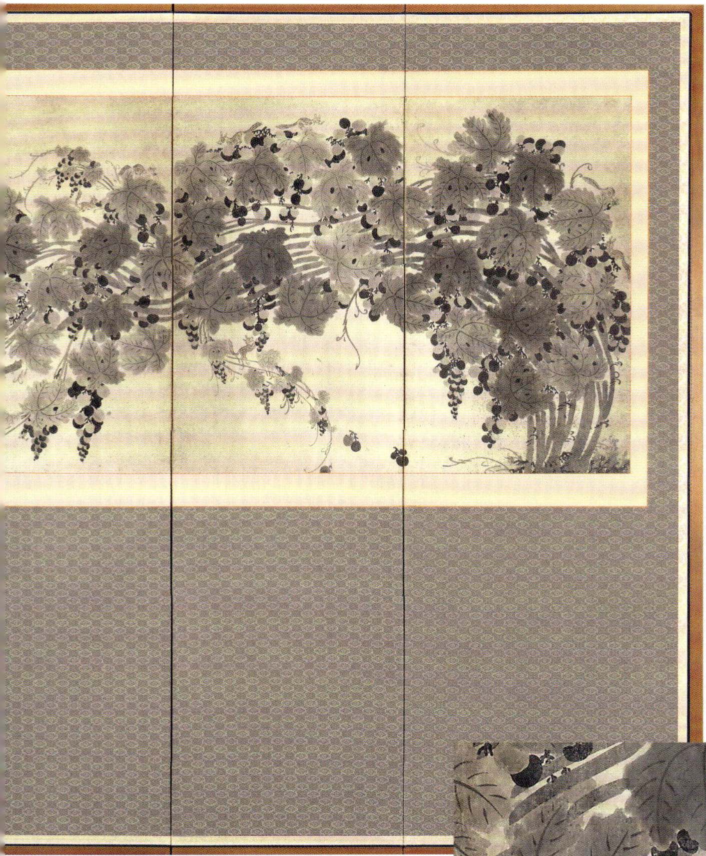

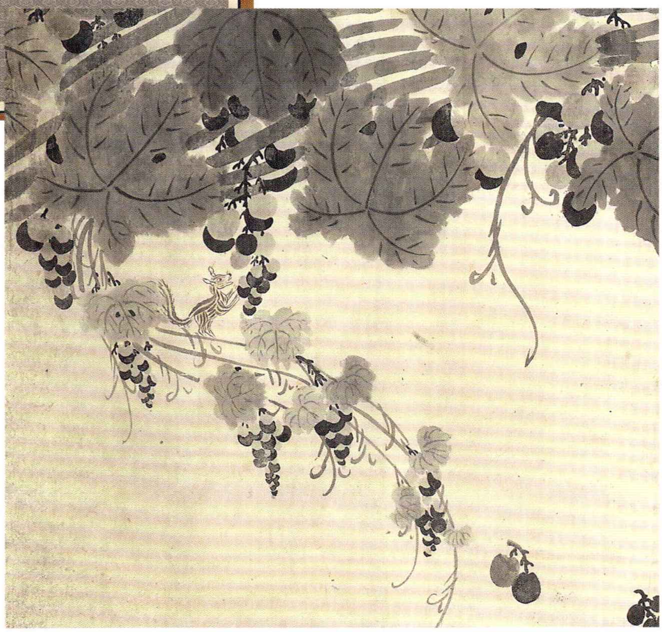

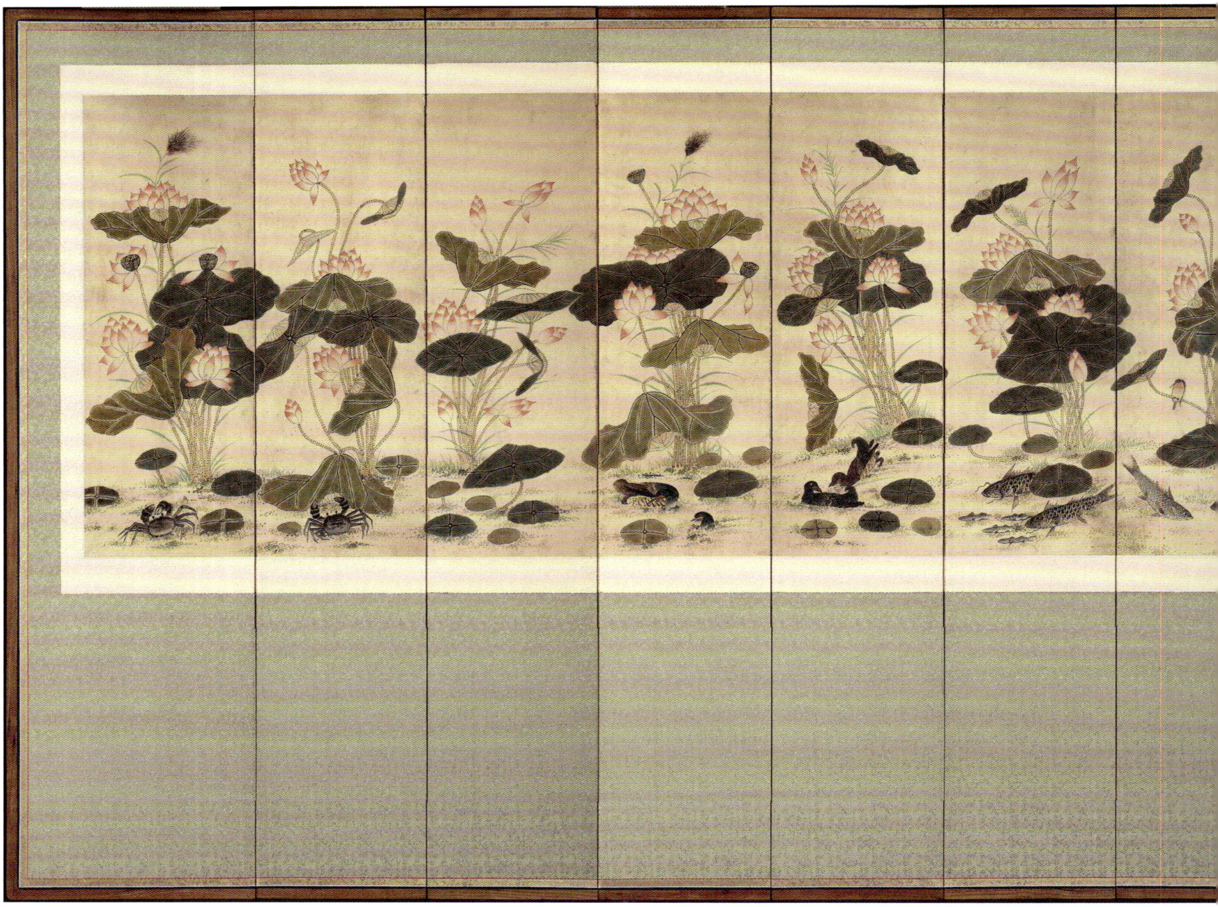

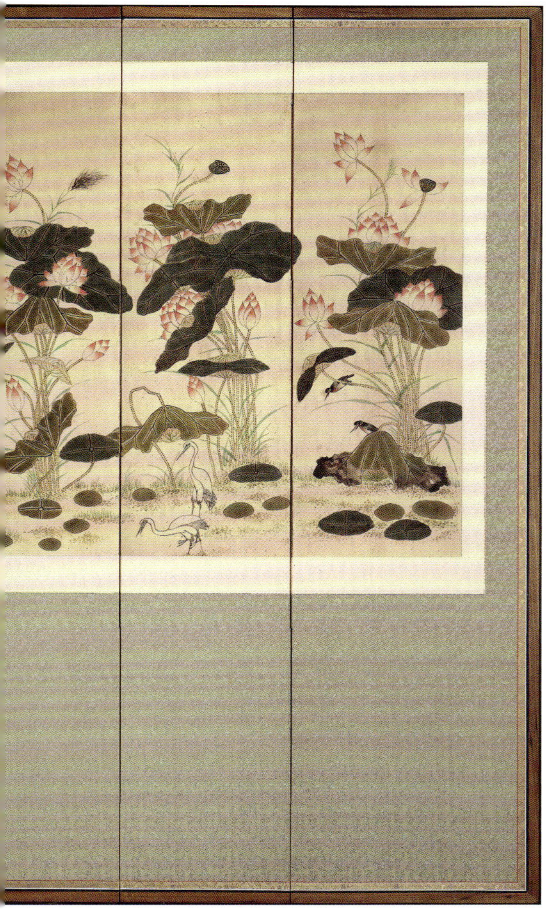

Screen with lotus flowers

Joseon period, late 19th century

Originally a symbol of Buddhist purity and reincarnation, the lotus took on other meanings during the later Joseon period when Buddhism became increasingly mixed up with popular belief. Because the lotus carries a pod full of large seeds within its flower, it signified both femininity and fecundity. It also became a symbol of integrity, because the word for lotus has the same pronunciation in Korean as the word for integrity. Gardens with lotus ponds became very popular among all classes during this period.

This screen of lotus flowers features a bunch of lotus stems on each of its eight panels, which are connected to make a continuous scene. The lotus leaves spill from one panel the next. The pairs of auspicious creatures populating the bottom of the composition symbolize a blissful life and marriage; they include crabs (for a successful career), fish (for wealth), catfish (for daughters), and carp (for sons). The screen may have been a wedding present given with wishes for connubial bliss, many sons and daughters, and wealth enough to afford a lotus garden like the one depicted. It may have been placed in the bedroom of the newlyweds to shield them as their wedding guests performed the custom of mischievously peeping at them on their first night together.

Ten-panel folding screen; ink and color on paper with silk brocade mounting
172.1 x 334 cm (67¾ x 131½ in.)
Keith McLeod Fund 2009.3988

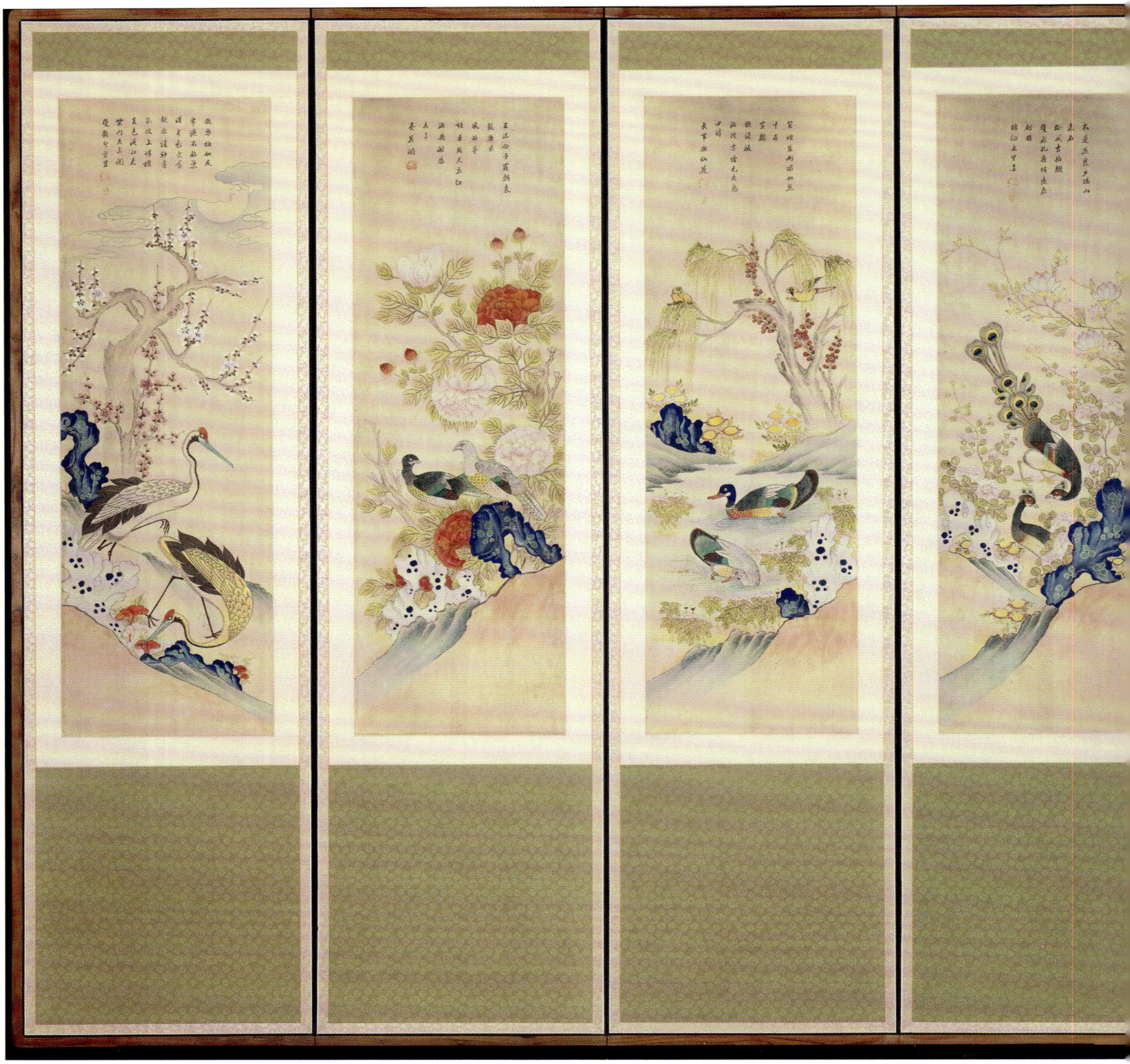

Screen with flowers and birds

Joseon period, late 19th century

Flower-and-bird paintings executed in ink with some color were common during the Joseon period. They usually feature a bird or birds with a flower of choice in a close-range view. Toward the late Joseon period, however, the theme broadened to encompass all sorts of symbolic flora and fauna of an auspicious nature. Well-trained and practiced, painters of the court were able to create elaborate flower-and-bird paintings. This screen is a fine example, made to serve the demands of the royal household. It depicts the Ten Symbols of Longevity—sun, mountain, water, rock, pine, cloud, *bullocho* (an imaginary plant symbolic of eternal life), tortoise, crane, and deer—along with other symbolic creatures and plants, such as a pair of mandarin ducks (for a happy marriage) and a peony (for wealth). All of these auspicious elements are carefully arranged in perspective and illustrated in

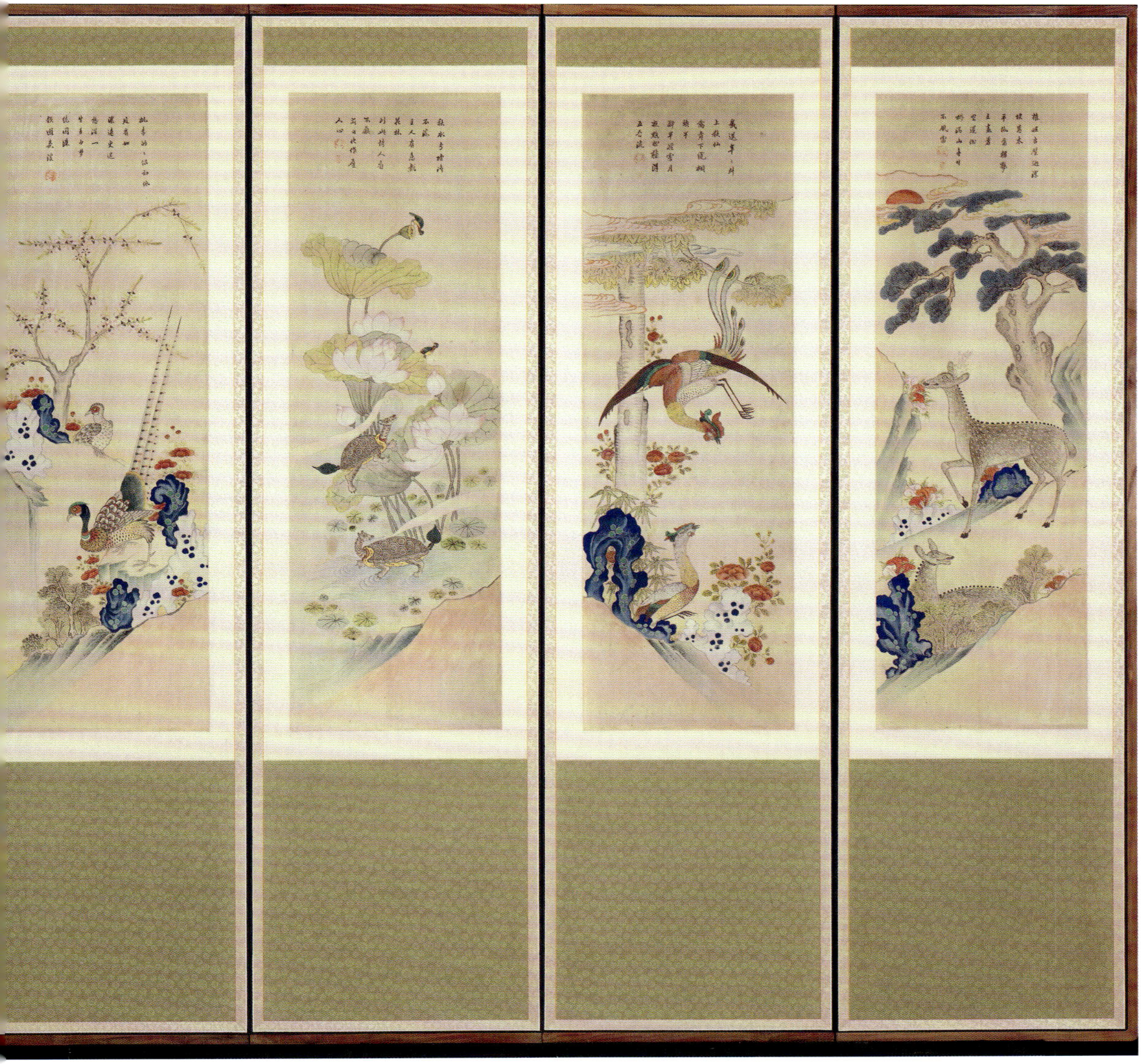

detail to make eight scenes of nature. Although the screen symbolizes the secular wishes of ordinary people, its subdued and elegant style, combined with poems to express the emotions and thoughts evoked by the pictured scenery, would have appealed to aristocratic or royal taste. This screen was most likely created as a gift to celebrate a royal wedding and to adorn the royal couple's bedroom.

Eight-panel folding screen; ink and color on paper with silk brocade mounting
200.7 x 426.7 cm (79 x 168 in.)
Charles Bain Hoyt Fund 2010.754

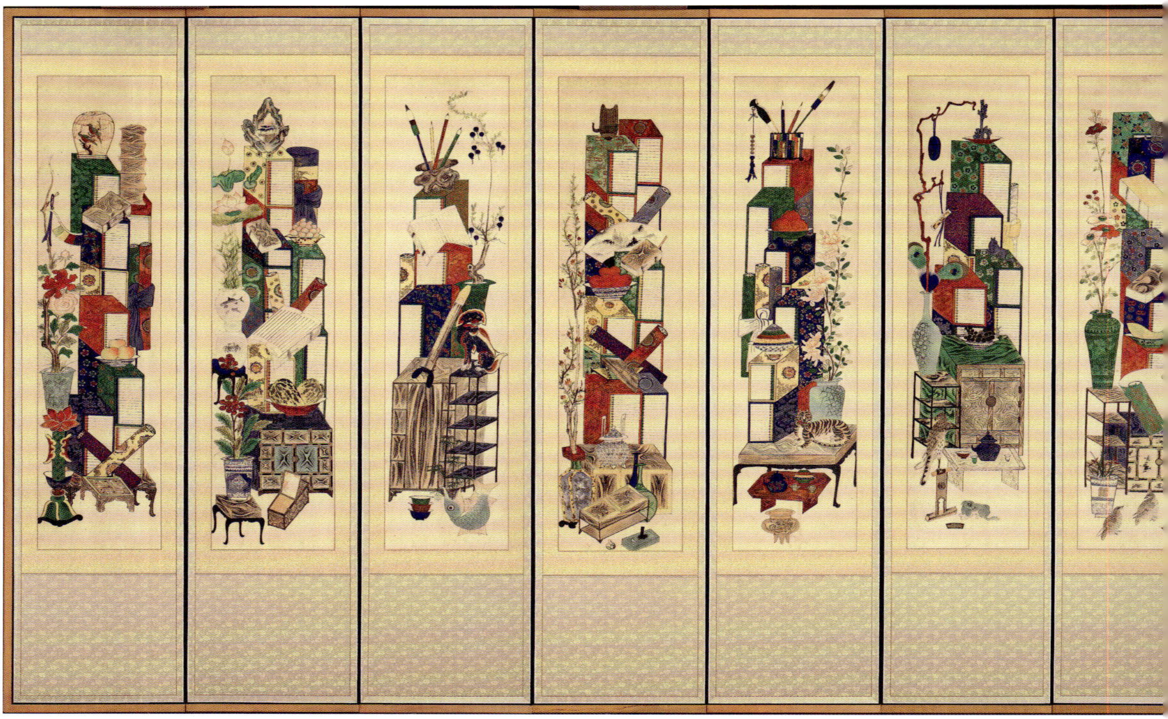

Screen with books and scholar's objects

Joseon period, late 19th–early 20th century

Painted in lively fashion, this screen produced at the turn of the twentieth century depicts a gentleman's library. It includes brush cases, vases, and furniture pieces that are often found in a traditional scholar's study. However, the inclusion of carp and watermelon reflects Korean popular beliefs. The carp symbolizes a successful career because it can leap up a waterfall, just as a successful scholar can pass his examinations, and the fruit holds good luck for the bearing of male heirs. Vases holding flowers denote domestic comfort and harmony, a pun on the pronunciation of the Chinese characters for "vase" and "peace."

King Jeongjo (reigned 1776–1800) was said to have introduced this genre when he ordered his court painters to create an image of his own library in imitation of similar *trompe l'oeil* Chinese paintings. The new subject soon became popular, first among members of the upper class, who saw an opportunity to show off their own prestigious library collections, and then by those in the aspiring middle and lower classes, who became major consumers of visual culture beginning in the eighteenth century.

Ten-panel folding screen; ink and color on paper with silk brocade mounting

173.7 x 420.4 cm (68⅜ x 165½ in.)

Keith McLeod Fund 2009.3989

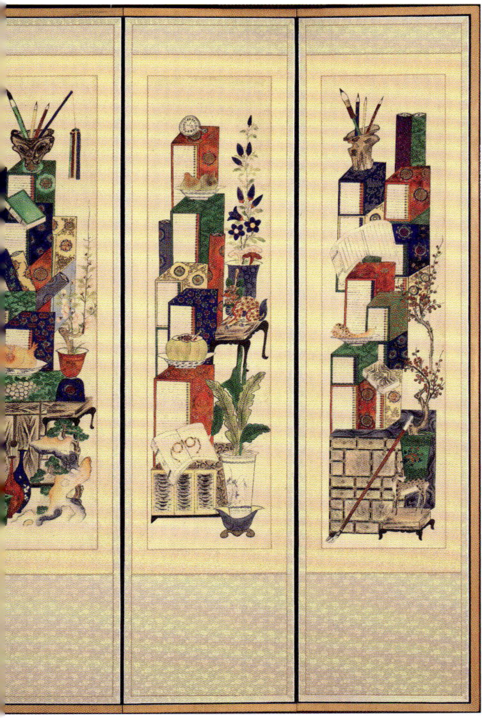

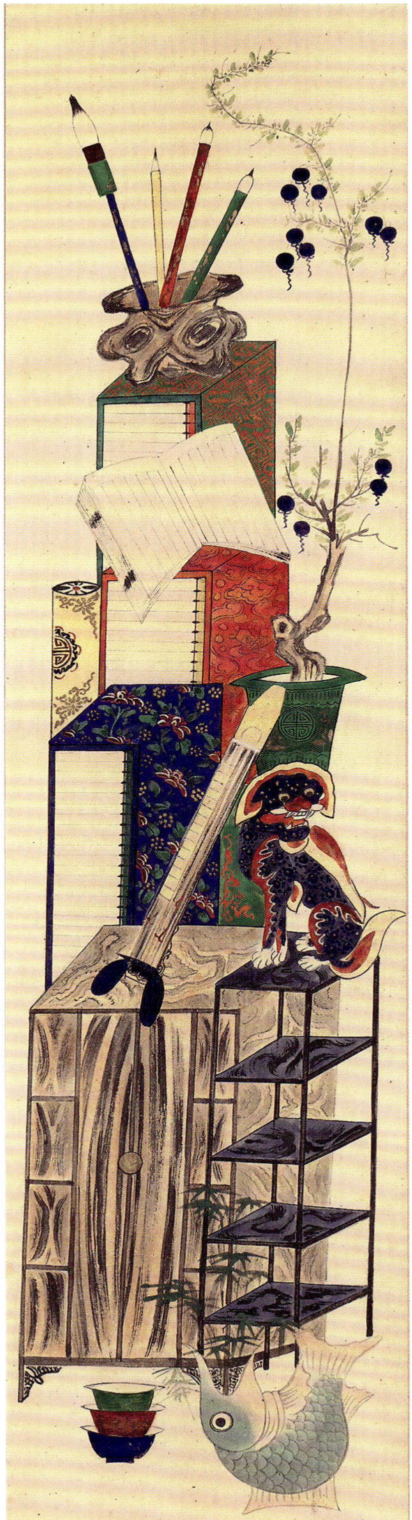

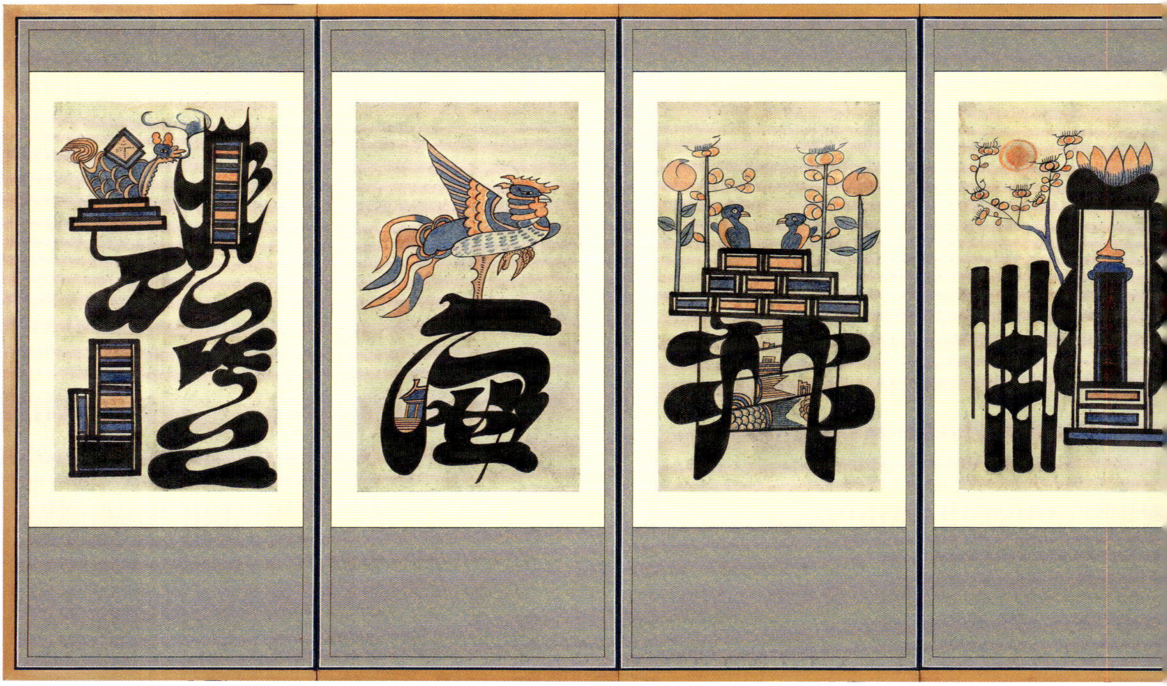

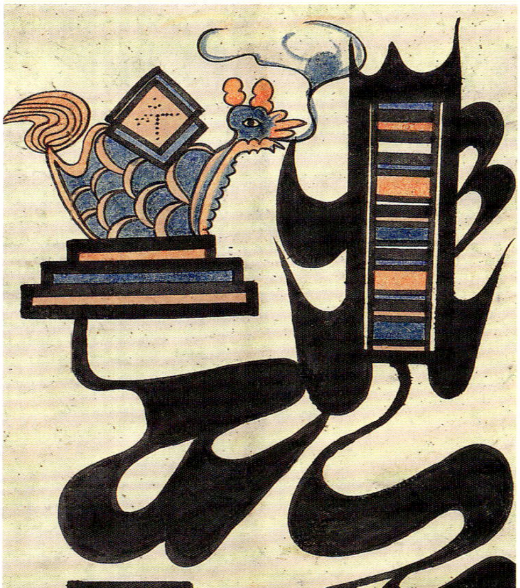

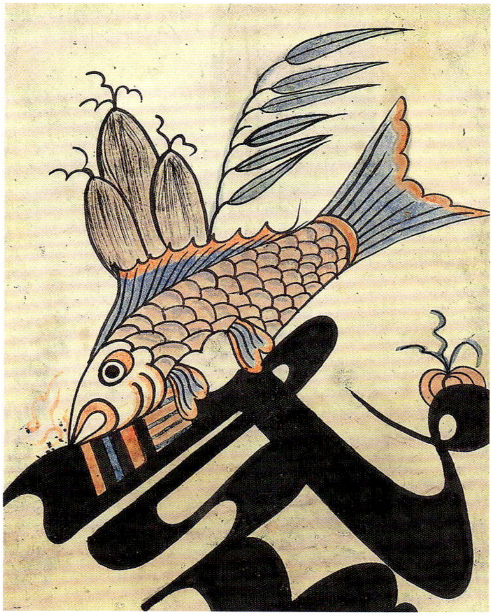

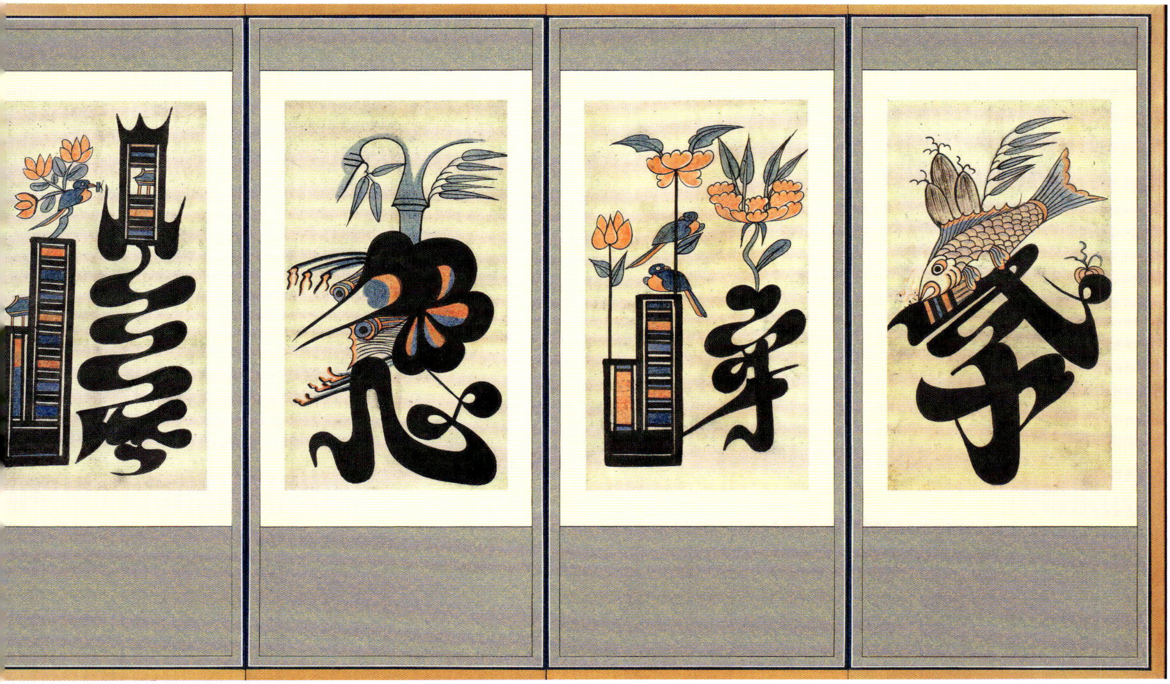

Screen decorated with the eight Confucian virtues

Joseon period, late 19th century

The eight Chinese characters on this screen signify the eight core Confucian virtues: filial piety, brotherly love, loyalty, trust, propriety, duty, integrity, and humility. Called *munjado*, or Chinese Characters Paintings, such screens were traditionally placed in a study or a child's room to remind the occupant of the Confucian codes of conduct. From the mid-eighteenth century onward, numerous illustrated texts, often filled with paintings, were produced widely for general instruction.

This screen uses thick one-tone black calligraphic lines. Simple patterns and popular symbols dominate the picture plane to the extent that the original characters and the associated tales are hardly recognizable. On the far right, for example, only the bottom component of the character for filial piety remains under the extremely stylized carp and bamboo shoots that cover its top.

Eight-panel folding screen; ink and mineral color on paper
110.5 x 381 cm (43½ x 150 in.)
Charles Bain Hoyt Fund 2009.343

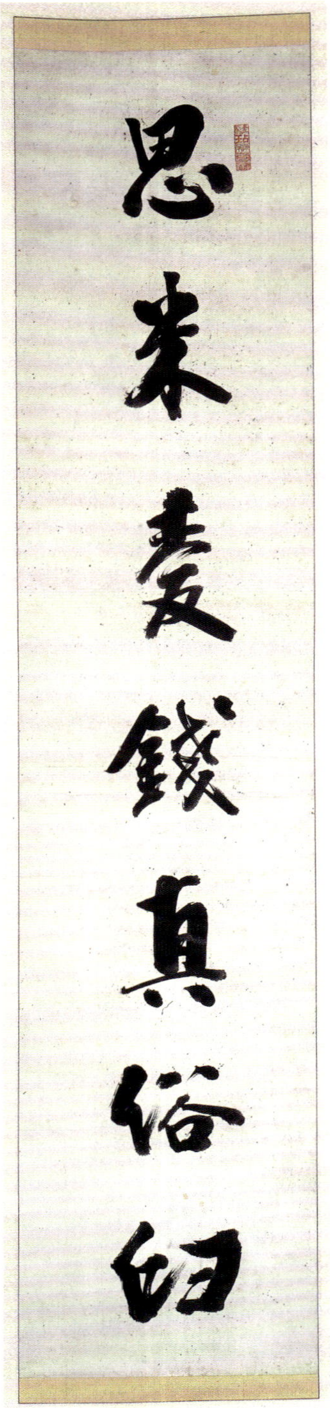

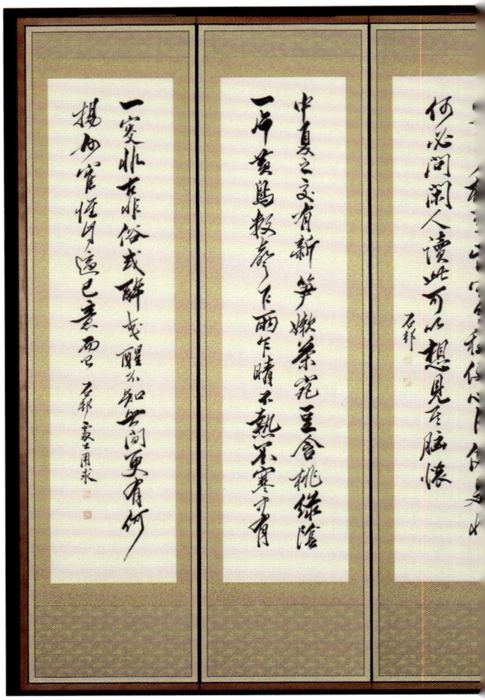

Calligraphy in regular script

Yi Ha-eung (1820–1898)

Joseon period, 19th century

Yi Ha-eung, also known by his official title, Daewongun (Prince Regent), was the father of King Gojong (reigned 1863–1907). An extraordinarily gifted scholar and artist, Yi was best known for his monochrome ink paintings of orchids. He frequently paired his paintings with calligraphy, at which he was also tremendously talented. His calligraphic works demonstrate his mastery of various styles ranging from seal-script to cursive. The verse on this particular scroll is written in running-script style and says: "Questing after riches and pursuing wealth is truly worldly; Farming and fishing are the sole means to put one in communication with otherworldly beings." Judging from the calligraphic style, this work seems to have been completed after Yi's political career had ended. It proclaims his longing for a simple life detached from worldly pursuits.

Hanging scroll; ink on paper
130 x 28 cm (51⅛ x 11 in.)
Gift of Ms. Elizabeth Nicholson, Paul A. Schmid, Sr. family, Mrs. Wu Tung, and Asiatic Curator's Fund in honor of Jan Fontein 1992.431a–b

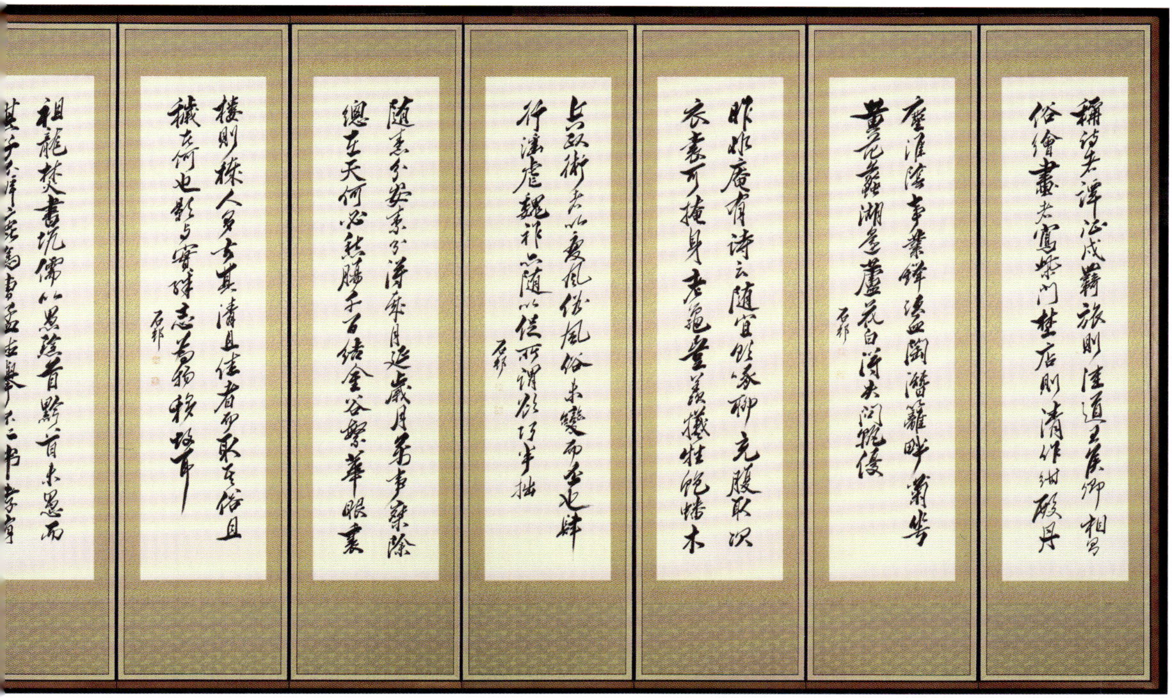

Calligraphy in semi-cursive style

Yun Yong-gu (1852–1939)

Joseon period, mid-19th–mid-20th century

Academic excellence and artistic acumen were highly celebrated during the Joseon period, so both the learned and the illiterate admired calligraphy and painting. Although calligraphy was usually written in Chinese characters and was strongly influenced by Chinese styles, two uniquely Korean styles were created during this period: the style of Han Ho and that of Kim Jeonghui. It was not until the late nineteenth century, however, that Korean-style calligraphy really became popular as an art form.

This ten-panel screen shows the semi-cursive calligraphy of Yun Yong-gu, in the style of Kim. Yun was a literati painter renowned for his bamboo, orchid, and landscape paintings but best known for his calligraphy. He was also revered as a patriot due to his refusal of favorable ministerial posts and a noble title offered by the Japanese during Korea's colonization. Instead of collaborating with the Japanese government, he immersed himself in art and scholarly pursuits. This calligraphy screen expresses his ideals and attitude toward life. The ninth panel (counted from the right), for example, reads, "On an oppressively hot summer day, one plays music on a grass reed pipe, while a nightingale sings joyfully." Each of the other panels has a slightly shorter sentence and bears Yun's seal. This reinforces the rhythm established by his slightly slanted writings and the various tones of his brush—thick and thin and wet and dry.

Ten-panel folding screen; ink on paper with gold-colored silk brocade mounting

184.2 x 461 cm (72½ x 181½ in.)

Gift of Kang Collection of Korean Art 2010.773

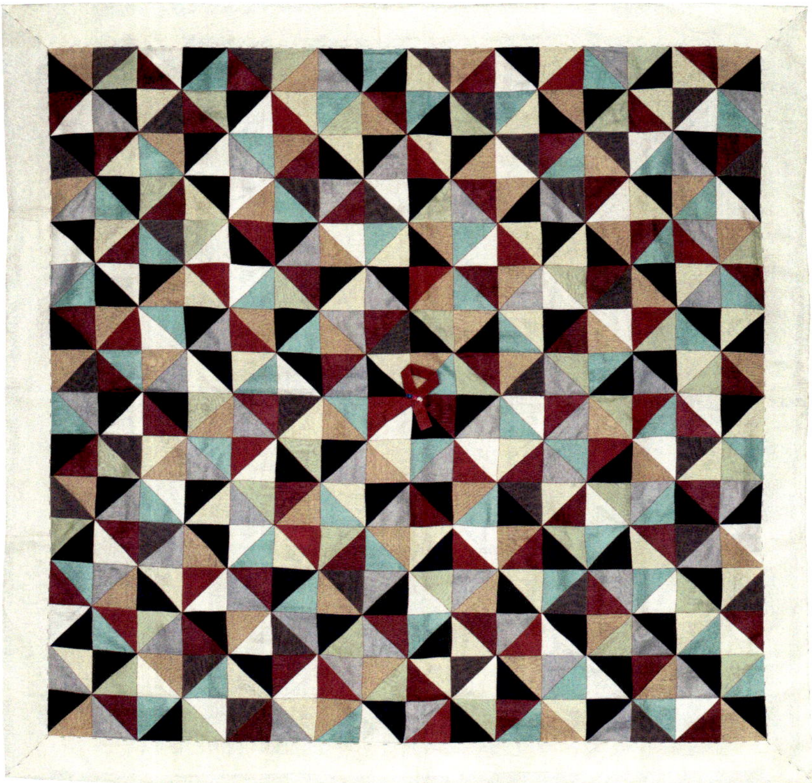

Wrapping cloth (*bojagi*)
Early 20th century

A *bojagi* is a cloth made to wrap, cover, store, or carry objects. Koreans used such cloths as early as the Three Kingdoms period and continue to use them today for wrapping special gifts, such as wedding dowries. These decorative wrapping cloths are occasionally made by renowned artisans or embroiderers, all women, and are increasingly becoming collector's items.

The ribbon in the center of this cloth indicates that it is a table cover to keep food warm and protect it from flying insects. It has a protective lining to keep the fragile silk cover from being soiled by the food, and a band around its four edges to reinforce its durability. The densely woven silk fabric suggests that it was made for the cold season. The geometric design was created by sewing together triangular pieces of nine colors so each side of a triangle meets a different color. Such design appeals to contemporary taste as an abstract work of art.

Silk plain weave; pieced and hand sewn
90.2 x 90.2 cm (35½ x 35½ in.)
Gift of the Keum Ja Kang Collection 2009.4385

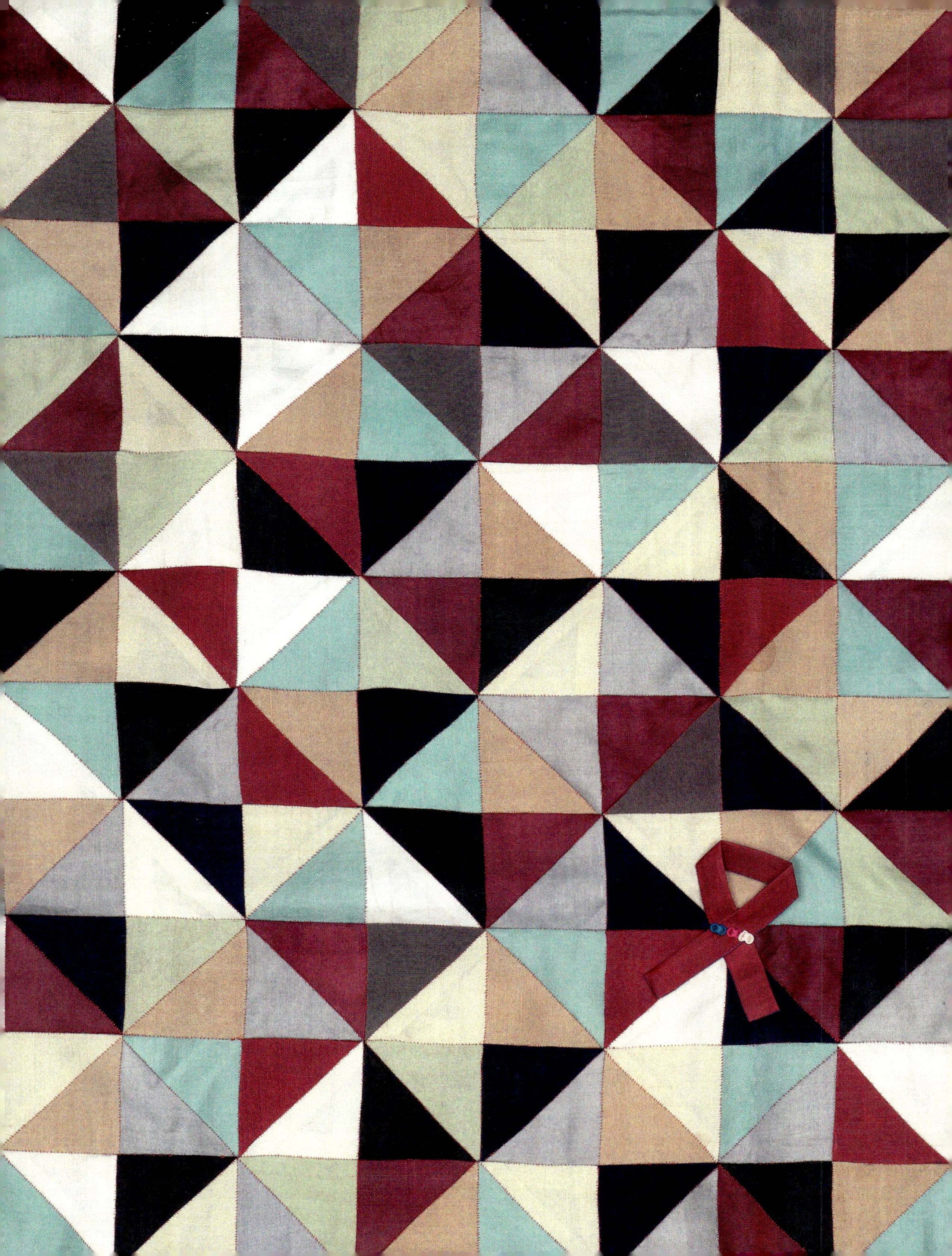

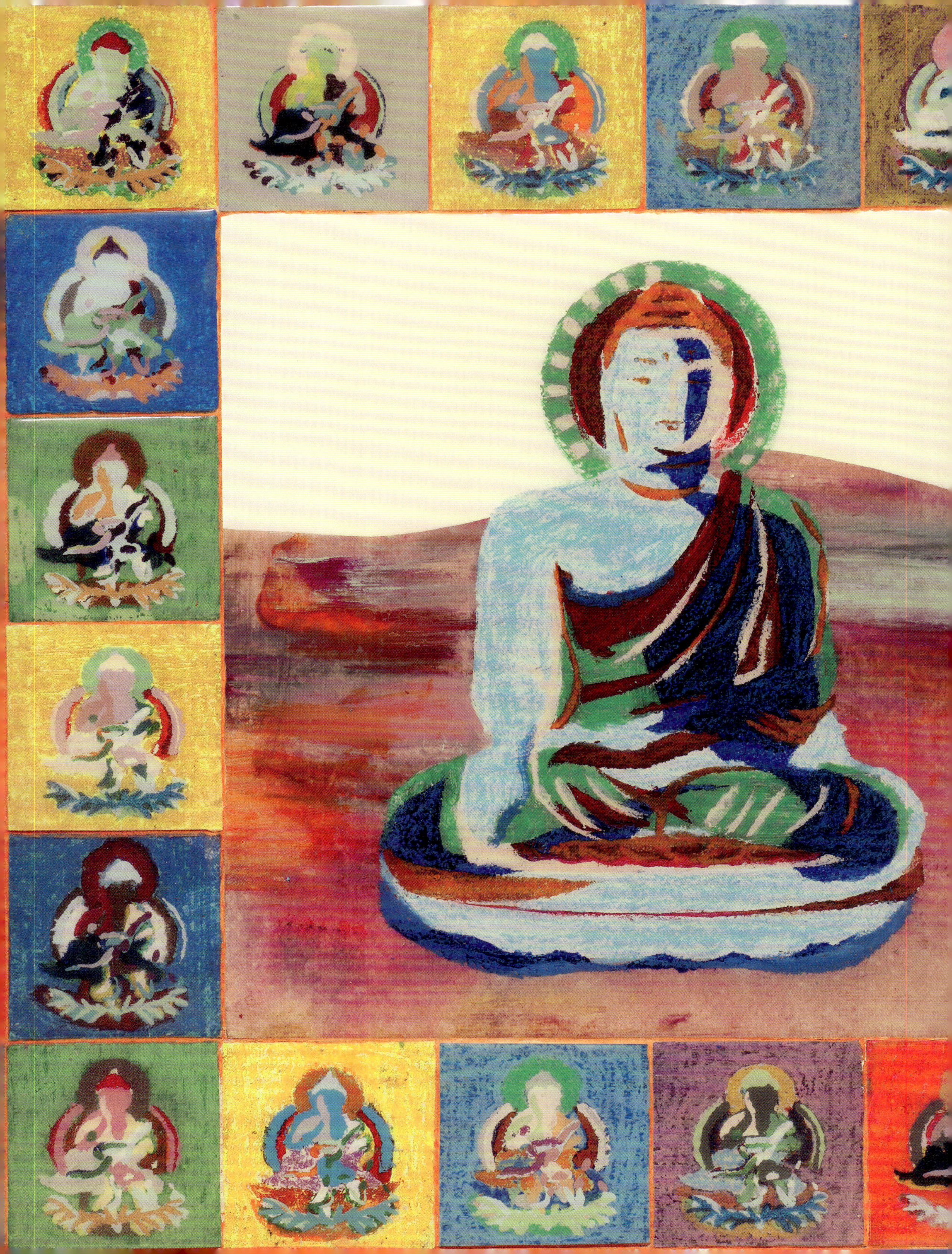

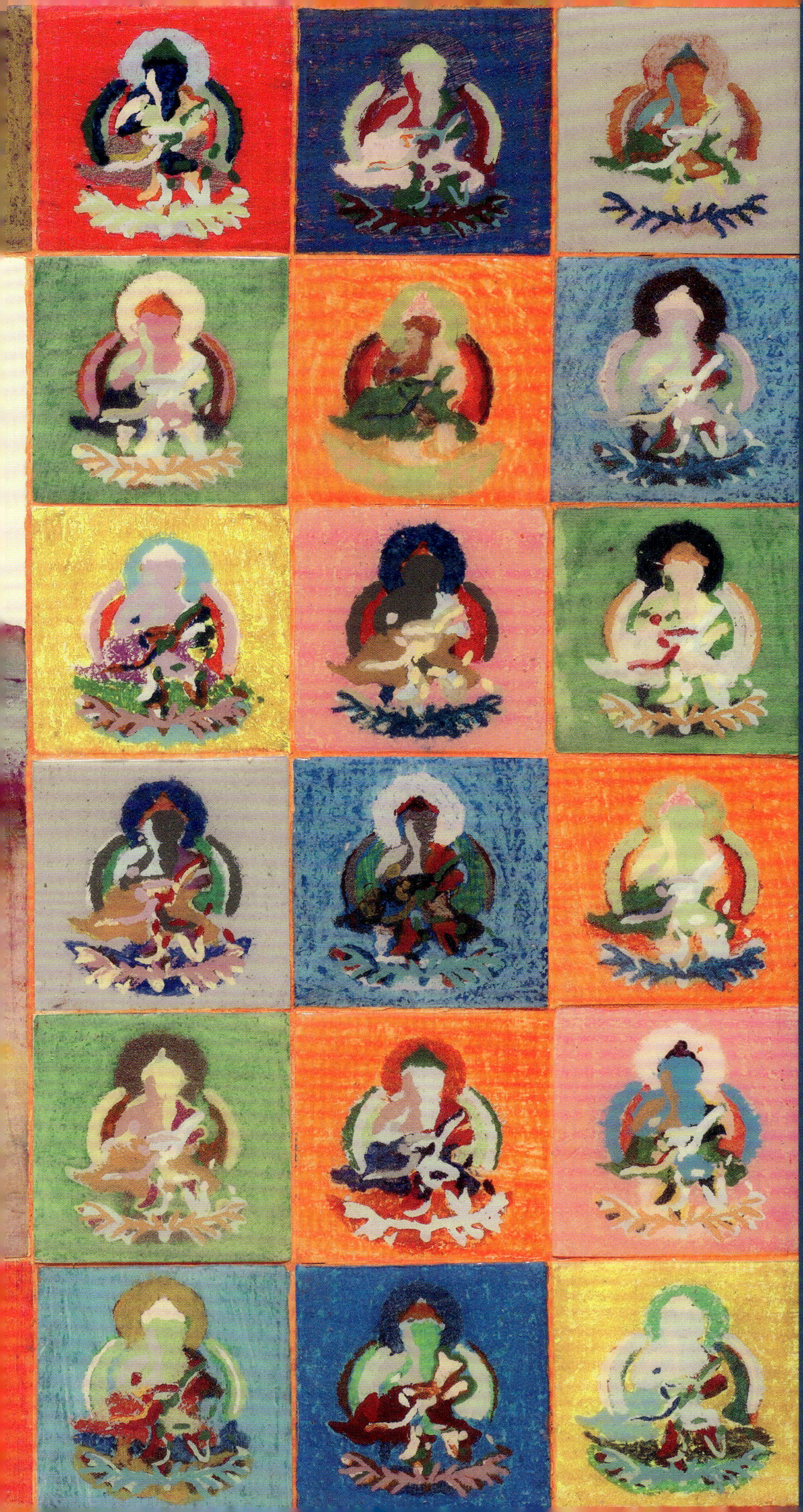

4 MODERN-DAY KOREA

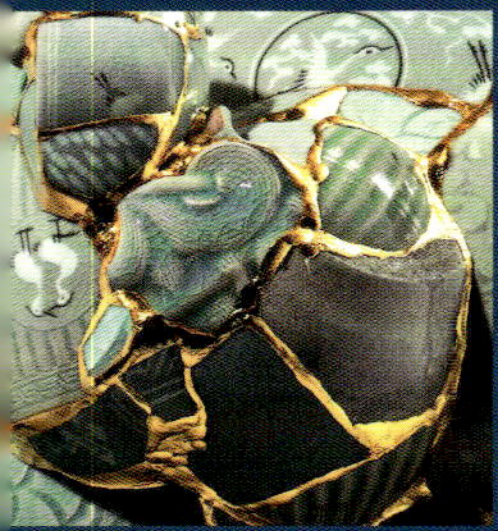
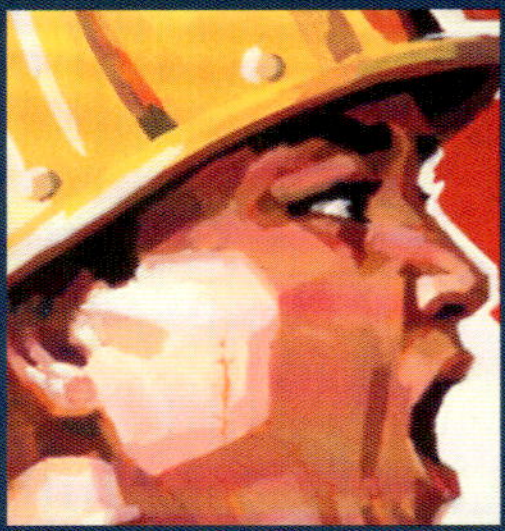
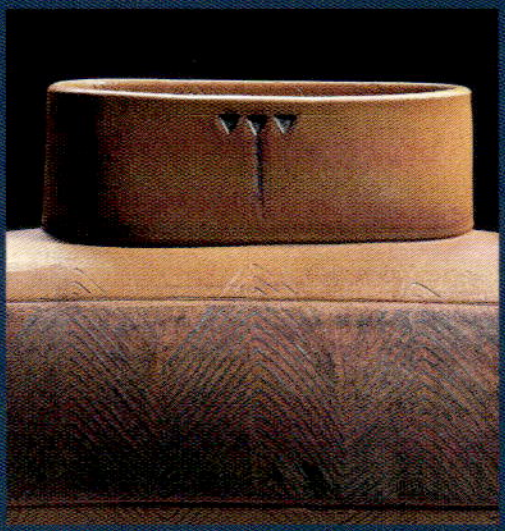
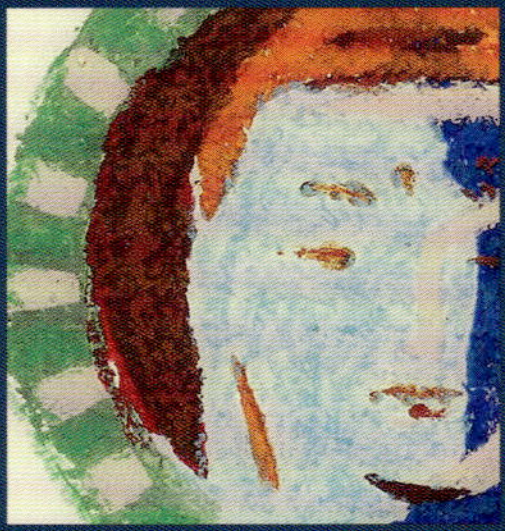
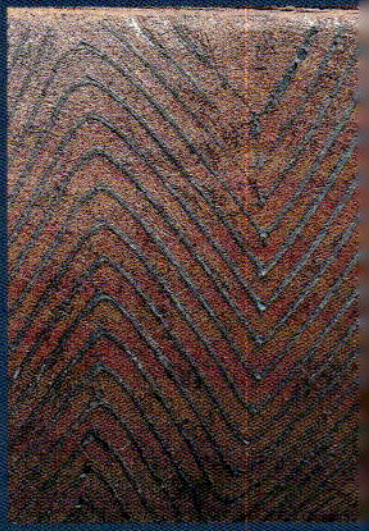

Modern-Day Korea

> The future is now.
>
> Nam June Paik, artist

Korea today is known for its economic development, technological inventiveness, pop and soap culture, and high level of education. However, underlying this success is the shadow of the period of colonial occupation by Japan (1910–45), the Korean War (1950–53), and the subsequent division of the country. North Korea remains stuck in a time warp, politically volatile and economically backward, whereas South Korea has developed in the twenty-first century into a leading world economy and democracy with a vibrant art scene, including a Korean Pavilion at the Venice Biennale since 1995.

Many Korean artists study and live in the United States and Europe and participate in the globalization of contemporary art. Kang Ik-Joong, for example, is a Korean painter living abroad (in New York). He regards himself as a citizen of the world but one whose work still resonates with Korean tradition, as he uses traditional Korean motifs such as moon jars and Buddhas to create contemporary works in nontraditional materials and formats. In the field of ceramics, several leading figures of the post–Korean War generation developed ways of producing innovative works that engage with traditional materials and techniques. Looking back with a contemporary eye to Korea's great ceramic tradition, including ancient tombwares, traditional storage jars, slip-decorated stonewares, and white porcelains, they devised new shapes, sizes, and combinations of decorative techniques to create unique works of art. However, the works they produced are still fundamentally vessels for use, as opposed to the works of a younger generation of artists—such as Yee Sookyung—who are exploring ways of producing ceramic art as installations rather than as traditional vessels.

In contrast to the vibrant and creative art scene in South Korea, art produced in North Korea since 1953 has been dominated by themes that show revolutionary optimism and extol the virtues of the country's leaders. It has been strongly influenced by Socialist Realism as practiced in the Soviet Union and the early years of the People's Republic of China. However, it also retains elements of traditional Korean style and technique, particularly in ink painting and calligraphy. Because artists in North Korea do not have access to international developments in art, their styles are somewhat static. There is no abstract or sexual art in North Korea, for example, nothing that shows frustration or depression. Artists work for and are paid by the State in a system of recognition ranging from Merit Artist to Hero. Although limited in subject matter, the works being produced under the present regime in North Korea provide an important record of society during this part of Korea's history.

Brown Vase

Cho Chung-Hyun (born 1940)

Korean, 1991

In this work, Cho Chung-Hyun, an eminent university professor of ceramics in Seoul who also studied and worked in the United States, responds to the long history of Korean pottery making, particularly the tradition of brown, high-fired pottery called *onggi*. Made from clay containing iron, an element that generates the distinctive dark brick-like color, onggi is the oldest and most commonly used type of pottery known to Koreans. Onggi pots have long been used as storage containers for a variety of staple condiments, such as soy sauce or pickled cabbage (*kimchi*). They may still be seen outside traditional houses, where they are grouped on a kitchen platform, keeping the supplies fresh.

Cho's contemporary interpretation of onggi also refers to ancient burial wares of the Three Kingdoms period. *Brown Vase* recalls the symmetrical, angular proportions of the Silla and Gaya periods' dramatic sculptural funerary stands, which also used openwork and combed decoration. Another source of inspiration for Cho is the inlay technique used in decorating Goryeo celadons; she has explored this aspect of traditional decoration from early on in her career. Here, she carves abstract patterns and fills the carved lines with blue slip. The blue inlay contrasts with the deep brown pottery body. Cho succeeds in creating a totally contemporary work that can be appreciated on its own merits as well as for its subtle references to a number of Korean traditions.

Stoneware with blue slip inlay decoration
H. 30 cm (11 13/16 in.), w. 43.2 cm (17 in.)
Gift of Namhi Kim Wagner 2010.496

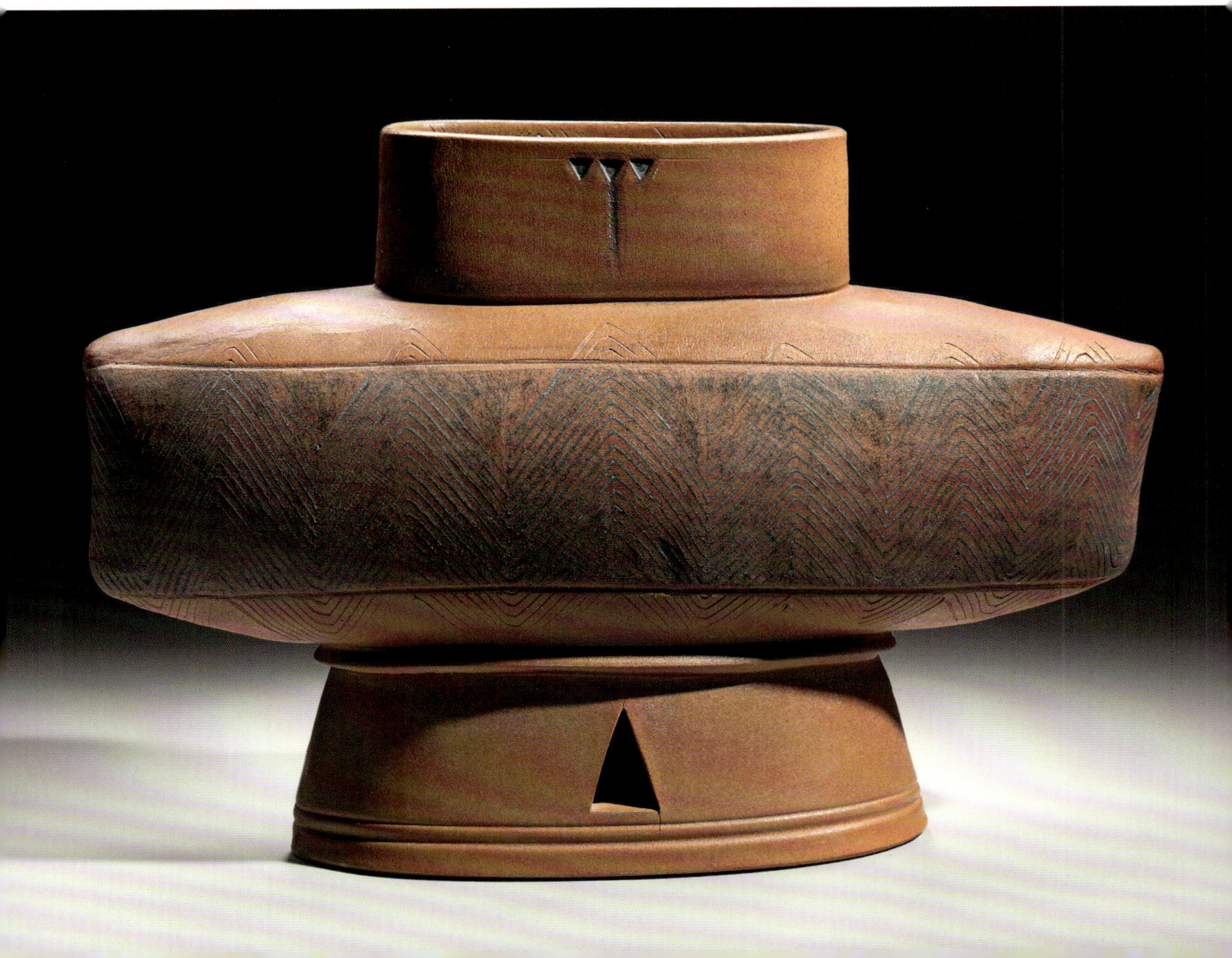

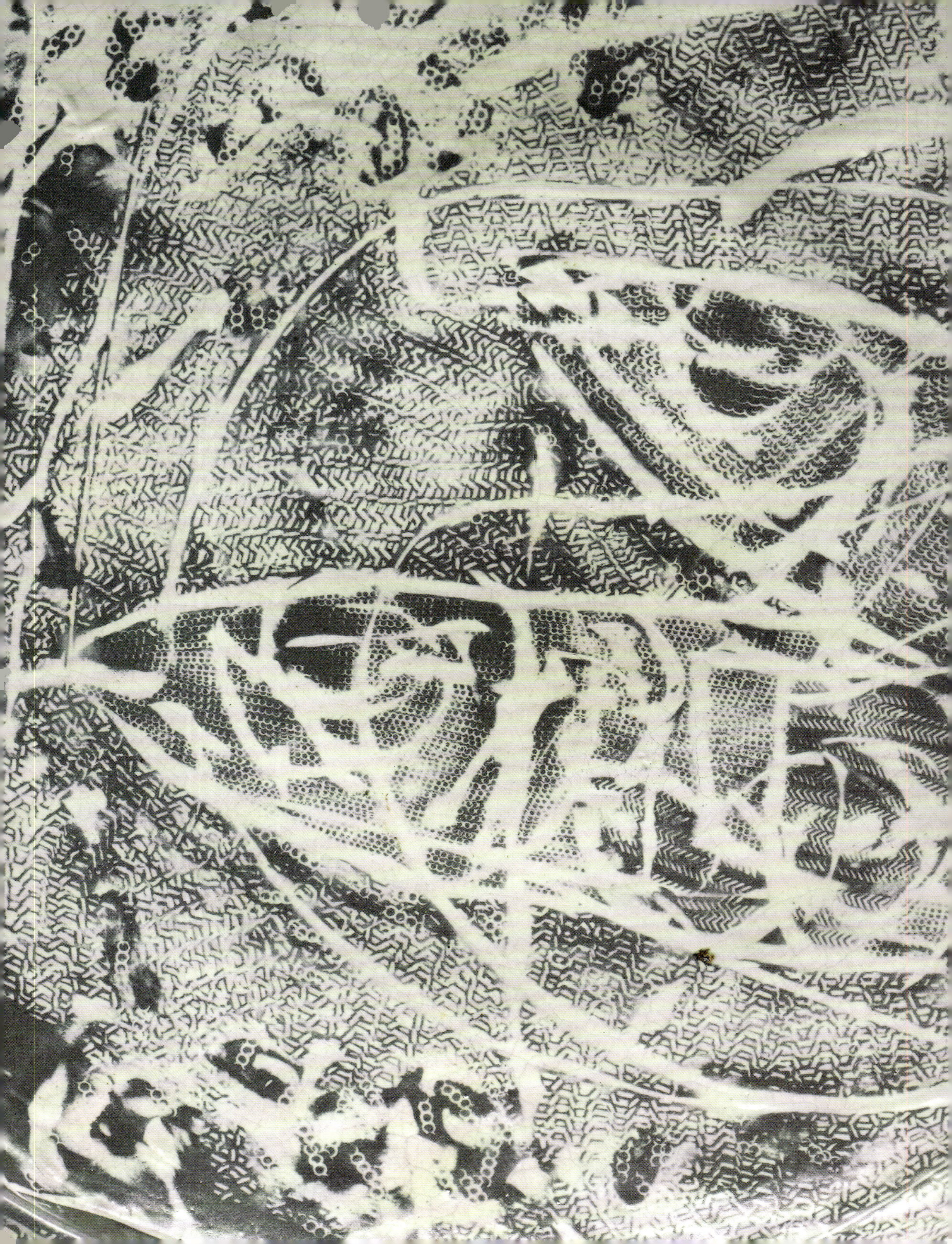

Plate

Shin Sangho (born 1947)

Korean, 1990

Shin Sangho looks back at traditional Korean buncheong slip-decorated gray stoneware of the fifteenth and sixteenth centuries in this work, but at the same time transforms that tradition into something new. Although its size is larger than traditional wares and its platter shape is unusual, the plate's uneven surfaces and inconsistently folded rim successfully capture the rustic, unrefined charm of the buncheong tradition. Shin combines incising, brush painting, and stamped slip decoration, all traditional techniques, although traditional potters did not often explore multiple decorative techniques within a single piece.

The abstract patterns on this work are reminiscent of abstract expressionist paintings of the mid-twentieth century. The two most prominent shapes could be based on fish, an auspicious motif often used in traditional buncheong pottery. Shin's use of irregular pattern sets his work apart from mere repetition of the past tradition.

Stoneware with incised, brushed, and stamped slip decoration in buncheong style
H. 9 cm (3⁹⁄₁₆ in.), diam. 44.5 cm (17½ in.)
Gift of Shin Sangho 2011.38

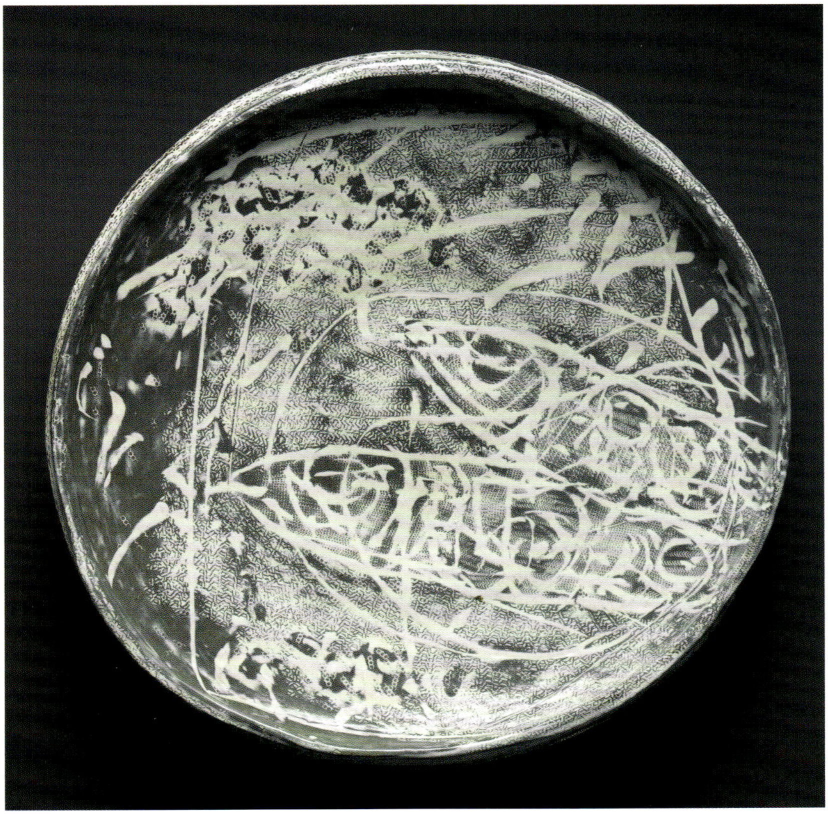

White Dish

Kim Ik-Yung (born 1935)

Korean, 2008

Kim Ik-Yung's works respond to the shape and style of Korean white porcelain from the eighteenth century, a high point in Korean ceramic history in terms of both technique and aesthetics. In this work Kim has produced a bold and strikingly contemporary meditation on the calm and austere Confucian tradition. It is clear that Kim derived her inspiration from Confucian ritual vessels, which trace their origin back to ancient Chinese ritual bronzes. In her interpretation of the traditional ritual ware, she has used a carved faceting technique to add angles to an otherwise smooth surface. This adds a contemporary flavor to the work. She has simplified everything else, except for the protruding ribbed details on each of the vessel's four sides, which represent the intricate flanges typical in Chinese antique bronzes. The gritty texture of the clay, reminiscent of buncheong stoneware, adds warmth to the color where it shows through.

Kim's unique and intelligent interpretation of traditional Korean white porcelain combines her original training as a chemical engineer and studies in the United States, where she says she first learned about potters like Bernard Leach and their appreciation for Korean wares. She has also worked at the National Museum of Korea as a curator of ceramics, which has exposed her to the finest of traditional pieces.

Porcelain with chamotte
L. 49 cm (19 5/16 in.), w. 37 cm (14 9/16 in.), h. 14 cm (5 1/2 in.)
Museum purchase with funds donated by Frank S. Bayley
2011.189

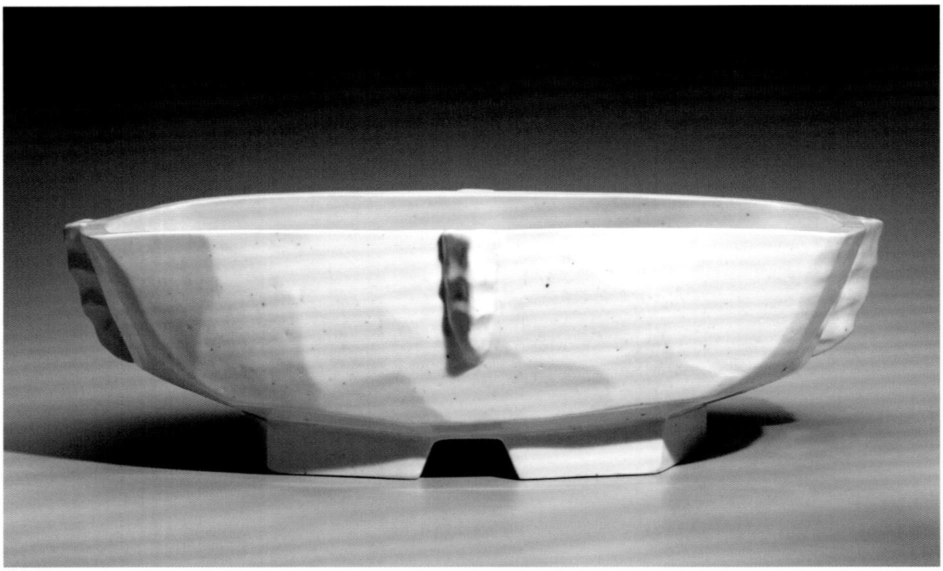

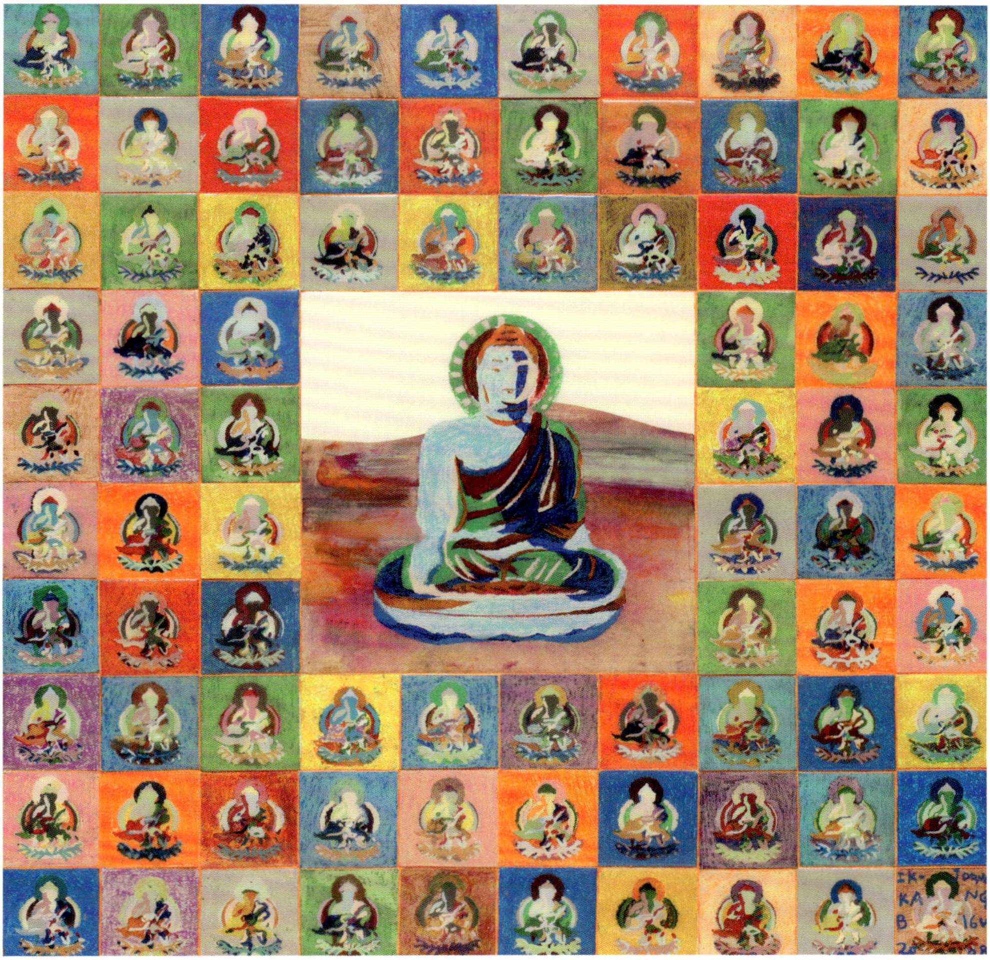

Happy Buddha

Kang Ik-Joong (born 1960)

Korean-American, 2008

Three-inch wooden blocks are signature components of Kang Ik-Joong's work. In *Happy Buddha*, they form a grid of eighty-four squares surrounding one twelve-inch square in the center. Each square features a Buddha sitting in a similar pose but depicted in different colors. From a distance, *Happy Buddha* is similar in effect to an ever-changing video screen of pixels, strongly suggesting the lasting influence of Kang's late mentor, the pioneer video artist Nam June Paik.

The words "Buddha" and "happy" often appear in Kang's work. He once said in an interview that the combination symbolizes nothing more than Kang living life happily. To the artist his three-inch block is "a window to see the universe [where we all are] mixed through the wind and connected via the land." In fact, all his works converge on his political concern over a divided Korea and his constant desire to fill ever-bigger public spaces with his tiny blocks. One of his best-known works is a project in which he covered the main gates of the Gyeongbok Palace with thousands of small blocks painted with white porcelain moon jars.

Crayon and tempera on pine board
76.2 x 76.2 x 5.1 cm (30 x 30 x 2 in.)
Gift of Keum Ja Kang in honor of Jane Portal, Matsutaro Shoriki Chair, Art of Asia, Oceania, and Africa 2009.5115

Translated Vase

Yee Sookyung (born 1963)

Korean, 2011

In a creative process similar to recycling, Yee Sookyung collects and reconstructs ceramic shards into monumental and amorphous masses. She calls the assemblages "my children." This ceramic installation was made with fragments of broken celadons that were rejected by the potters who made them. The work is therefore "green" in both its color and its kindness to the natural environment.

Yee started using ceramic shards in her work when she spotted blue-and-white porcelains that famous potters had broken intentionally because they were not up to their standards. Thinking they were still beautiful, she collected the fragments from the kilns and brought them to her studio. Sticking the irregular pieces together presented quite a technical challenge, particularly with larger constructions. Gilding the glued lines of epoxy was a creative solution that she explains with a pun on the Korean word *geum*: "[I decided to] cover *geum* (lines) with *geum* (gold)." For some viewers, it might recall the way in which precious broken ceramics are repaired with gold lacquer in Japan.

Translated Vase is one of Yee's more recent works made of celadon fragments. The title came about as a result of a translation she did of a poem about porcelain by the Korean poet Kim Sang-ok (1920–2004).

Celadon fragments with epoxy and gold
66 x 64 x 97 cm (26 x 25 3/16 x 38 3/16 in.)
Edward S. Morse Memorial Fund and Charles Bain Hoyt Fund
2011.233

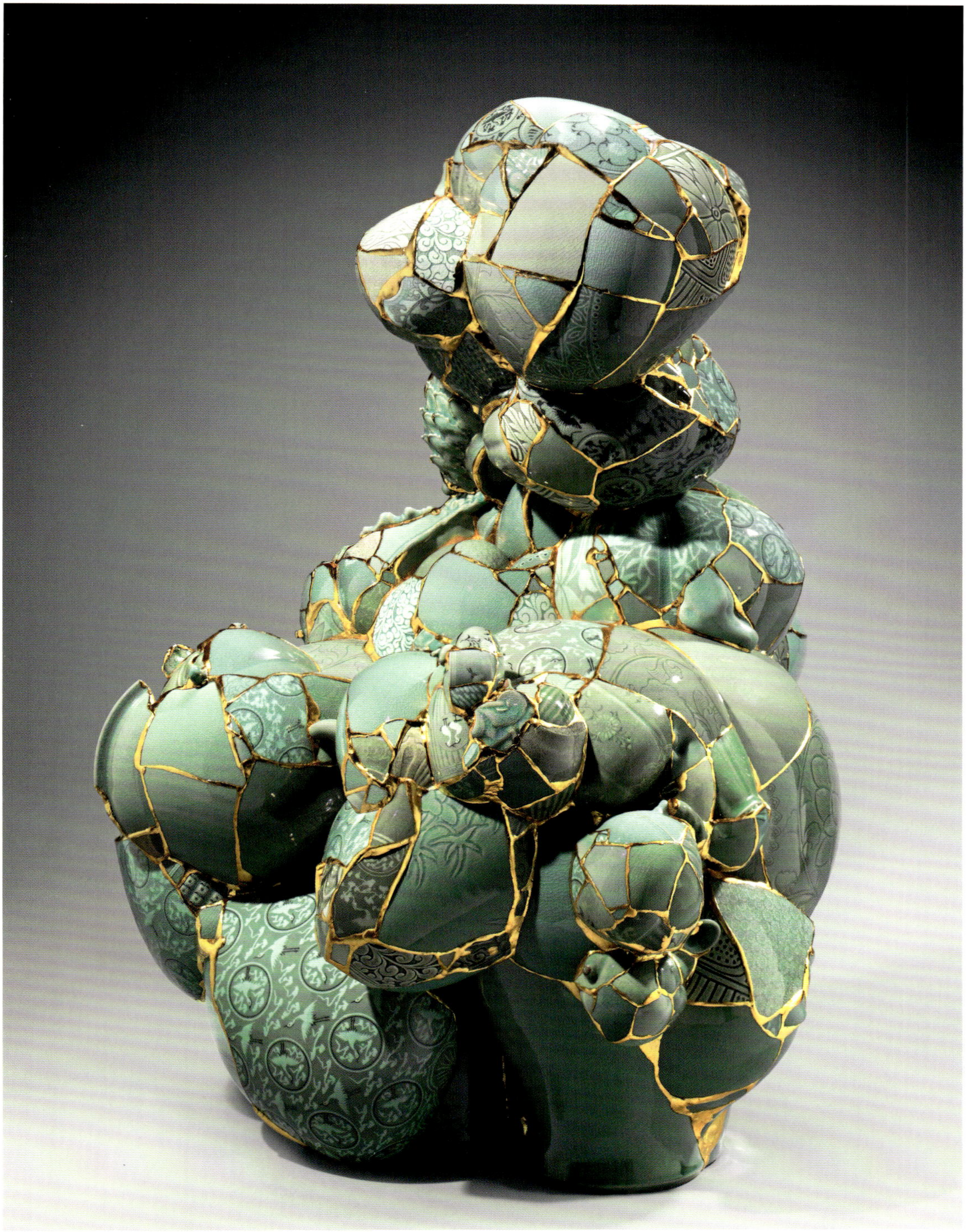

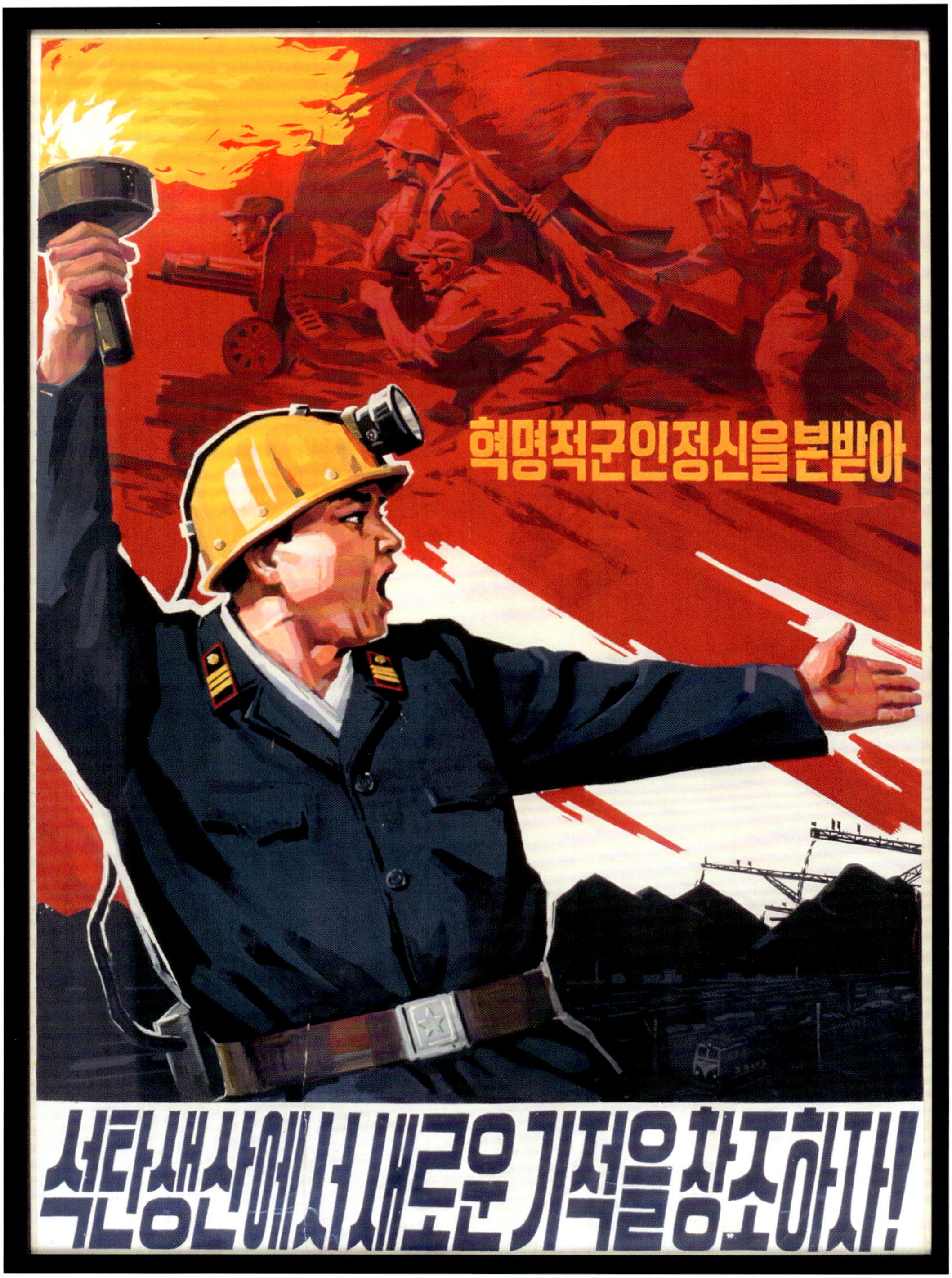
혁명적군인정신을 본받아
석탄생산에서 새로운 기적을 창조하자!

Let's Follow the Spirit of the Great General. Let's Enter a New Phase in Coal Production.

Mansudae Art Studio

Democratic People's Republic of Korea (North Korea), 1990s

This propaganda poster of a coal miner leading workers to greater achievements was produced by artists working at the Mansudae Art Studio, the largest art production studio in North Korea. Founded in 1959, it now employs more than one thousand people. This poster is painted rather than printed, but others like it have been printed in bulk.

The style of the painting is reminiscent of Socialist Realism, the dominant style of posters produced in China during the Cultural Revolution and in the Soviet Union. Socialist Realism became popular in North Korea after the division of the peninsula in 1948 into the communist North and the democratic South. This style is also used on large mural paintings and mosaics on public buildings, such as those in the Pyongyang subway. It stands in contrast to the style of North Korean ink painting, called *Choson-hwa*, which is much more traditional. There is little evidence of any outside influence on art produced in North Korea at present, and all art made there is required to present a positive and easily understood message.

Ink and colors on paper
102 x 70 cm (40 ⅛ x 27 ½ in.)
Promised gift of Dr. Robert Anderson

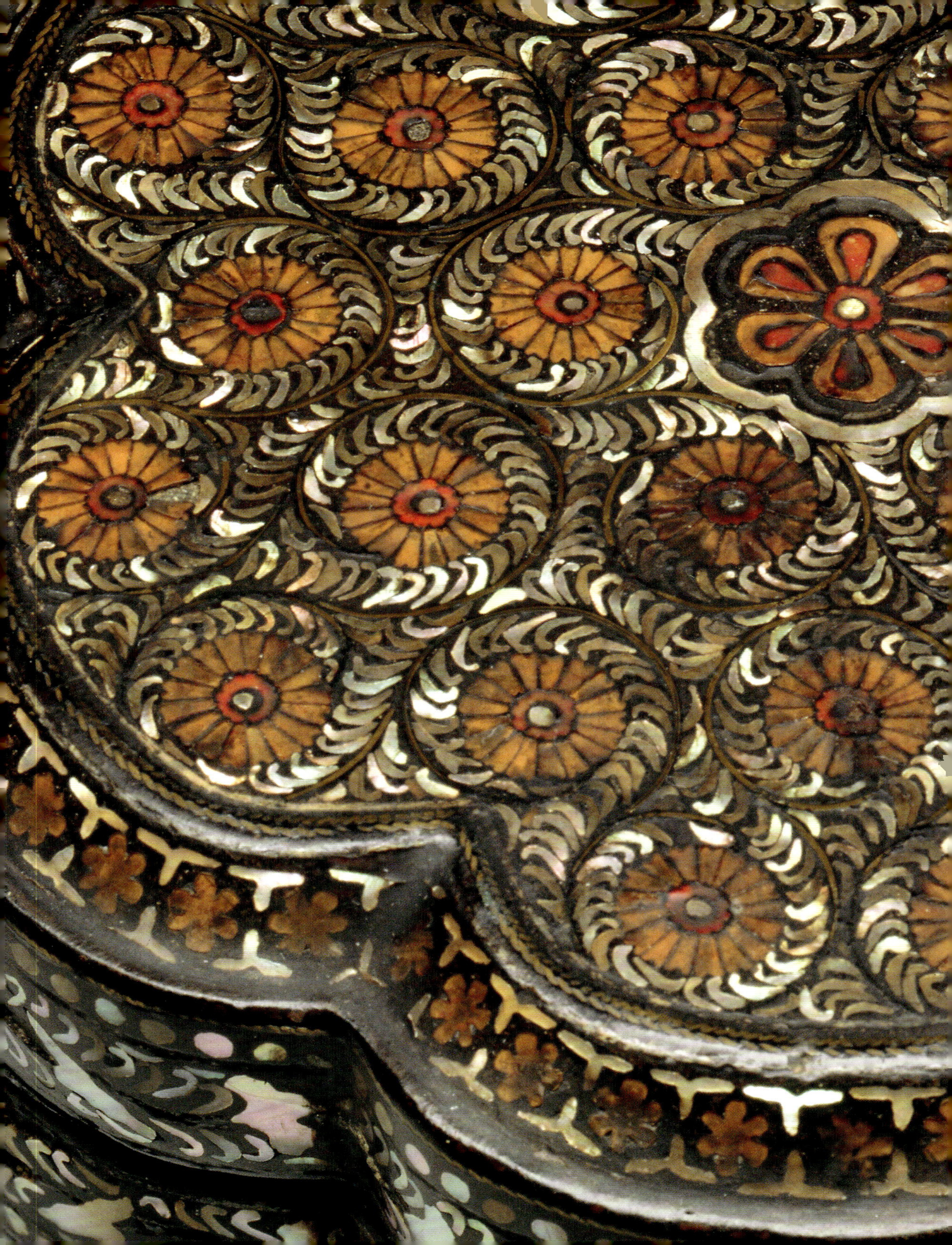

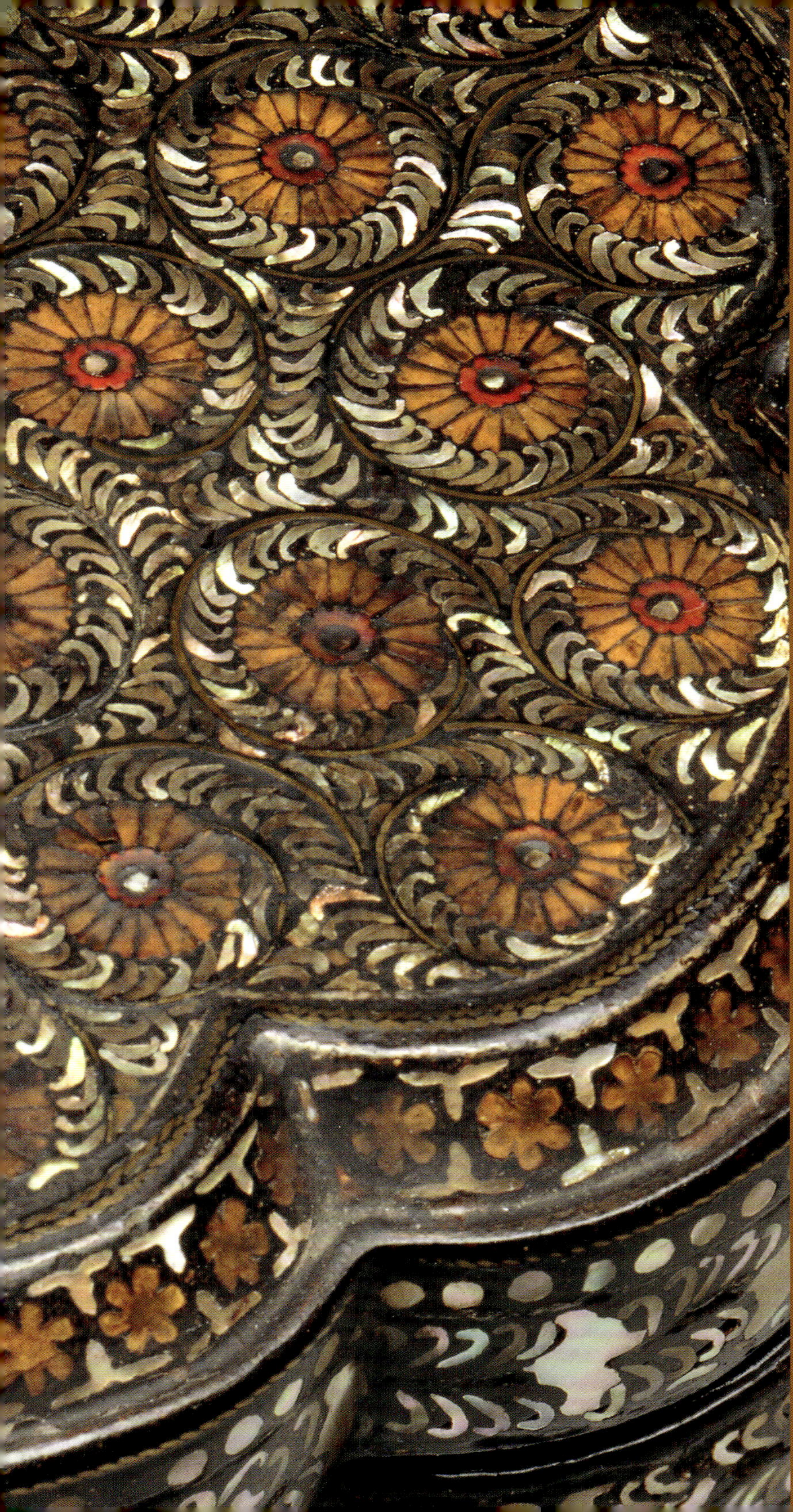

timeline and maps, further reading, index, figure illustrations

Timeline and maps

Neolithic Period (6000–1000 B.C.)

Neolithic people use comb-patterned pottery and live in pit houses. They also produce mounds of discarded shells.

Bronze and Early Iron Ages (1000–1 B.C.)

Advanced farming and rice cultivation develop. Bronze daggers, rattles, and mirrors, some for use in shamanistic rituals, are produced. Plain, undecorated pottery is in general use. Elite members of society are buried with burnished pottery.

Proto–Three Kingdoms Period (A.D. 1–300)

Some stone-lined pit graves contain jar-coffins or wooden chambers. Advanced bronze-casting technology and iron production are practiced. The Chinese establish commanderies and colonies in northern Korea.

Three Kingdoms (57 B.C.–A.D. 668)

Goguryeo (37 B.C.–A.D. 668)

Goguryeo, in southern Manchuria, is the first of the Three Kingdoms to establish itself as a nation-state. Goguryeo tombs from the third century include wall paintings in the style of the Chinese Han dynasty.

313 The Han Chinese colony at Lelang, established in 108 B.C., withdraws

372 Buddhism introduced to Goguryeo via China (earliest in Korea)

Early 600s The Great Tomb at Gangseo constructed

Baekje (18 B.C.–A.D. 660)

The Baekje kingdom is established in the southwest area of the peninsula by emigrants from Goguryeo. There is active international trade and cultural exchange with China and Japan. Baekje craftsmen influence the production of sculpture and architecture in Japan.

384 Buddhism accepted

523 King Muryeong buried with objects that indicate diplomatic or trade relations with southern China

500s Stone pagoda erected at Mireuksa, now the oldest example extant in Korea

Silla (57 B.C.–A.D. 668)

Silla is the first of the Three Kingdoms to set up a dynastic line of rulers. The Silla kingdom is established in the southeastern region of the peninsula. Members of the royal family are buried in tumuli (graves topped by huge mounds of earth and stones), along with precious objects such as gold crowns, belts, earrings, glass vessels, and pottery decorated with clay figurines.

528 Buddhism accepted

562 Silla absorbs the Gaya kingdom

600s Stone observatory constructed at Gyeongju, the Silla capital

Gaya (A.D. 42–562)

Craftsmen of the Gaya kingdom advance pottery production using the wheel and enclosed kilns. They create molded stoneware and wheeled cups. There is also abundant iron production that results in iron armor for men and horses.

Unified Silla (A.D. 668–935)

Silla unifies the southern two-thirds of the Korean peninsula. Buddhism flourishes as the national religion. Gyeongju, the capital, develops into a cosmopolitan hub.

674 Anapji (Lake of Wild Geese and Ducks) completed

751 Bulguksa (Temple of the Buddha Land) and the Seokguram cave temple constructed

Balhae (A.D. 698–926)

Former Goguryeo aristocrats scattered in the north found the Balhae kingdom.

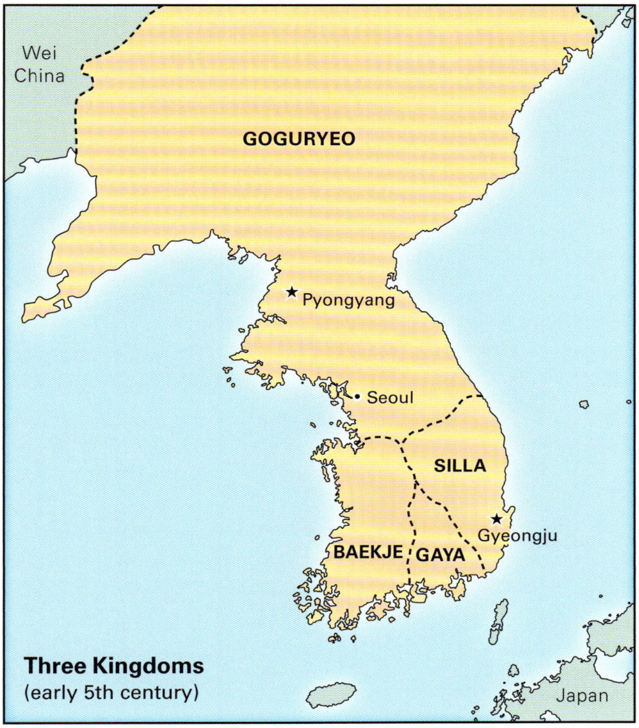

Three Kingdoms
(early 5th century)

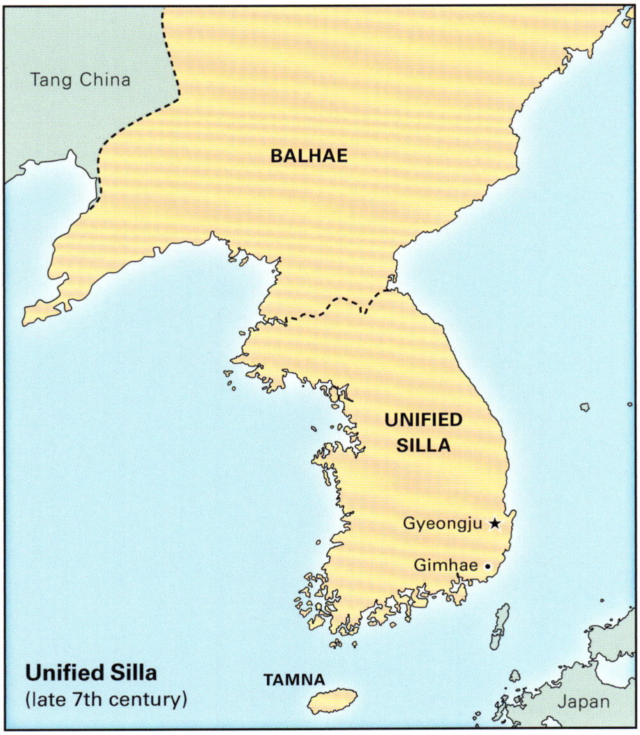

Unified Silla
(late 7th century)

Goryeo (918–1392)

Wang Geon defeats Silla to form a new dynasty, ruling as King Taejo. Buddhism remains the state religion. The capital moves north to Gaeseong (Kaesong). Goryeo painters create beautiful and elegant Buddhist images. Craftsmen develop advanced metal and lacquer inlay techniques. Celadon stonewares reach a highpoint. Metal movable type is invented. Aristocratic society sees the rise of Confucianism and the creation of a literati-official class.

993 Khitan (Liao) forces first invade the Korean peninsula from the north but are forced to retreat

By 1000 Celadon production in Korea begins

1010 and 1018 Khitan (Liao) forces invade Korea again

1123 Xu Jing, an envoy from Song China, visits Goryeo and writes an account of his travels

1145 Kim Busik publishes his *History of the Three Kingdoms* (*Samguksagi*)

About 1150 Inlaid celadon invented by Goryeo potters

1170–1270 Military insurgency

1231–1239 Mongols invade from the north and rule Korea

1234 Metal movable type used for the first time in the world

1236–1251 *Tripitaka Koreana*, the complete Buddhist scriptures, carved on more than 80,000 woodblocks as a prayer against the Mongol invasion

Joseon (1392–1910)

General Yi Seonggye establishes the Joseon kingdom. Neo-Confucianism is the governing ideology but Buddhist art is still produced. Multiple invasions by Japan and Qing China constrain artistic development.

1403 The official Printing Bureau and Painting Bureau established at court

1443 Korean phonetic script (Hangeul) invented

1464 Blue-and-white porcelain produced for the first time in Korea

1467–1468 State-run kilns established at Gwangju

1592–1598 Korean potters emigrate in large numbers to Japan after Japanese forces invade the peninsula

1627 and 1636 Manchus (Qing China) invade Korea

1700s The True View Landscape movement (to paint real places in Korea) and the Genre painting movement develop

1865–1867 Having been burned down during the Japanese invasions, the Gyeongbok Palace in Seoul is reconstructed

1882 Joseon Korea establishes diplomatic relations with the United States of America

1884 Bunwon-ri kiln closes

Modern-Day Korea (1910–present)

1910–1945 Japan rules Korea as its colony

1945–1948 After World War II, the Soviet Union influences the North, where the Democratic People's Republic of Korea is formed; the United States influences the South, where the Republic of Korea is formed

1950–1953 The Korean War leads to a permanent truce with continued division of the peninsula

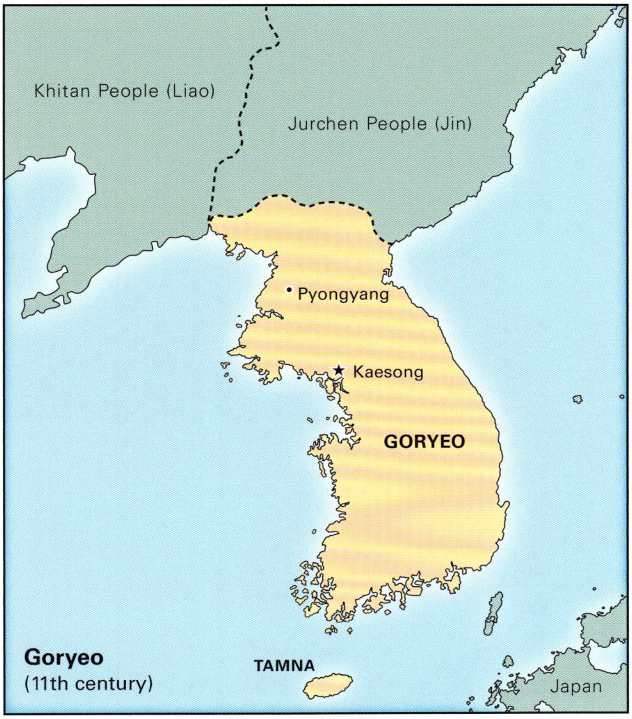
Khitan People (Liao)
Jurchen People (Jin)
Pyongyang
Kaesong
GORYEO
TAMNA
Japan
Goryeo
(11th century)

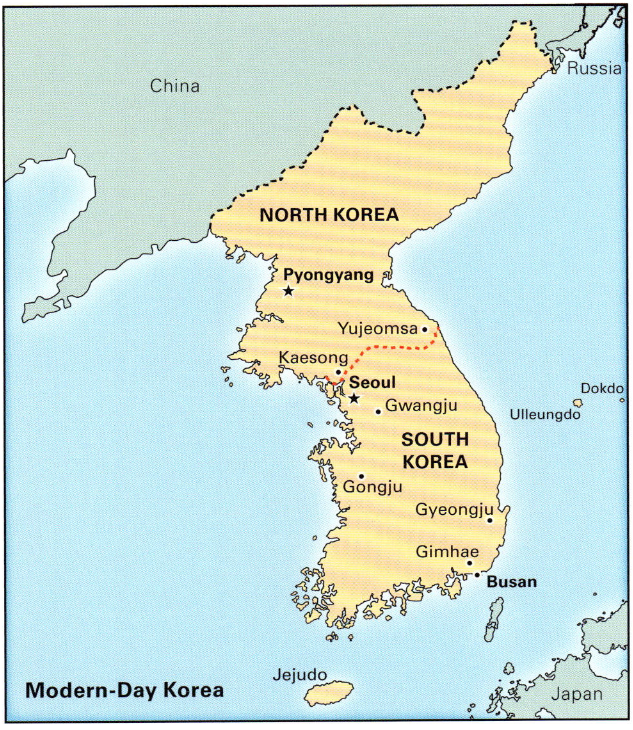
China
Russia
NORTH KOREA
Pyongyang
Yujeomsa
Kaesong
Seoul
Gwangju
Dokdo
Ulleungdo
SOUTH KOREA
Gongju
Gyeongju
Gimhae
Busan
Jejudo
Japan
Modern-Day Korea

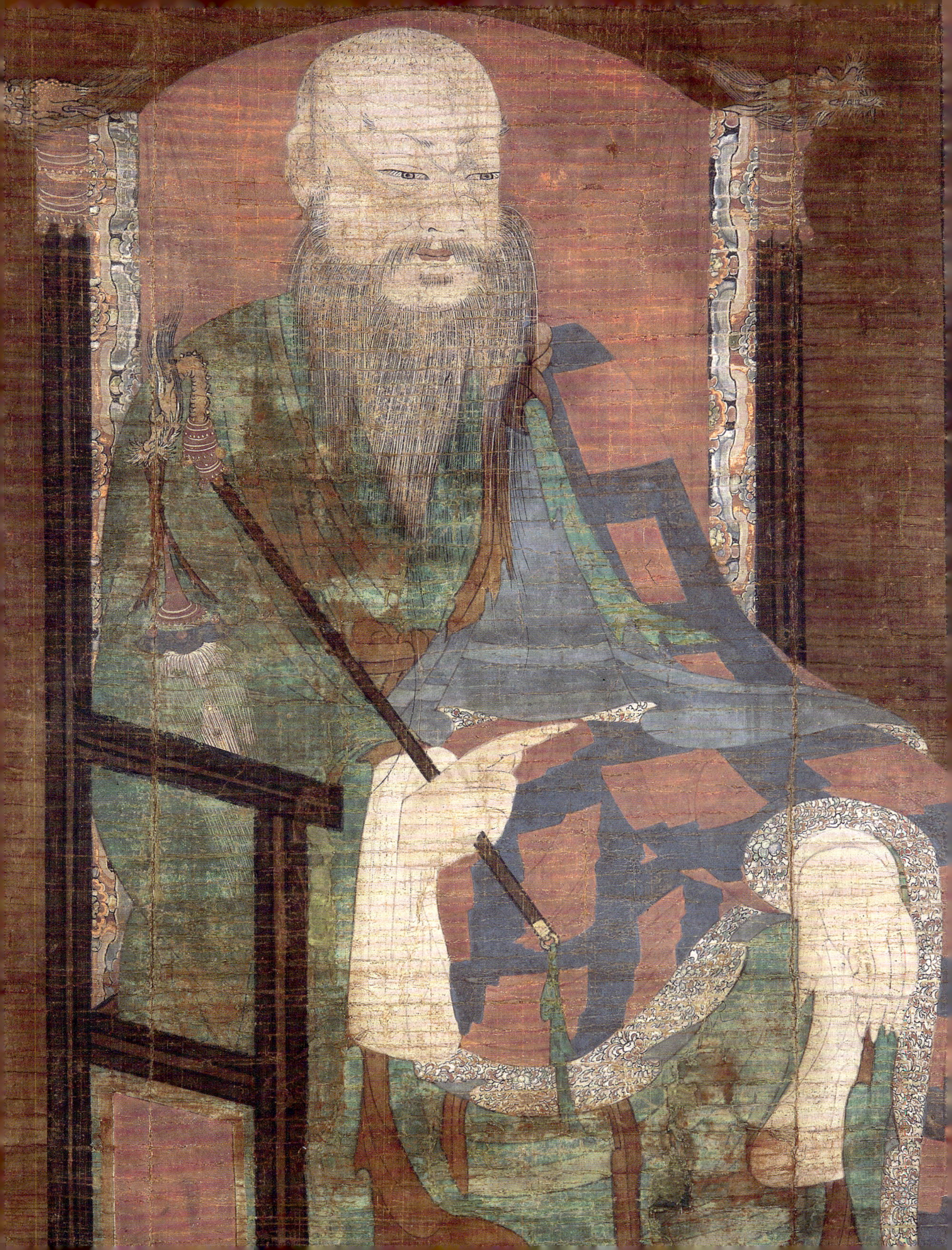

Further Reading

General

Bean, Susan S., and Frederic A. Sharf. *The Korean Collection of the Peabody Essex Museum*. Salem, MA: Peabody Essex Museum, 1999.

Bird, Isabella L. *Korea and Her Neighbours*. New York: Fleming H. Revell, 1879.

Kim, Won-Yong. *Art and Archaeology of Ancient Korea*. Seoul: Taekwang, 1986.

Lautensach, Hermann. *Korea: A Geography Based on the Author's Travels and Literature*. Translated and edited by Eckart Dege and Katherine Dege. Berlin: Springer, 1988.

Lefebvre d'Argencé, René-Yvon, and Diana Turner, eds. *5000 Years of Korean Art*. Exh. cat. San Francisco: Asian Art Museum, 1979.

Lowell, Percival. *Choson: The Land of Morning Calm*. Boston: Ticknor, 1888.

McCune, Evelyn B. *The Arts of Korea: An Illustrated History*. Rutland, VT: Charles E. Tuttle, 1962.

McKillop, Beth. *Korean Art and Design*. London: Victoria and Albert Museum, 1992.

Morse, Edward S. "Korean Pottery." In *Catalogue of the Morse Collection of Japanese Pottery*, 25–31. Boston: Museum of Fine Arts, 1901.

National Research Institute of Cultural Heritage. *Korean Art Collection at the Museum of Fine Arts, Boston*. Seoul: National Research Institute of Cultural Heritage, 2004.

Nelson, Sarah Milledge. *The Archaeology of Korea*. Cambridge: Cambridge University Press, 1993.

Portal, Jane. *Korea: Art and Archaeology*. London: British Museum Press, 2000.

Sands, William Franklin. *Undiplomatic Memories: The Far East 1896–1904*. Seoul: Kyung-In, 1975.

Smith, Judith, ed. *Arts of Korea*. Exh. cat. New York: Metropolitan Museum of Art, 1998.

Whitfield, Roderick, ed. *Treasures from Korea: Art through 5000 Years*. With an introduction by Roger Goepper and contributions by Soon-Taek Choi-Bae, Edith Dittrich, Roger Goepper, Youngsook Pak, Ji Hyun Whang, Roderick Witfield, and Ulrich Wiesener. Exh. cat. London: British Museum, 1984.

Early Period

Barnes, Gina L. *China, Korea and Japan: The Rise of Civilization in East Asia*. London: Thames and Hudson, 1993.

———. "The Development of Stoneware Technology in Southern Korea." In *Pacific Northeast Asia in Prehistory: Hunter-Fisher-Gatherers, Farmers, and Sociopolitical Elites*, edited by C. Melvin Aikens and Song Nai Rhee, 197–208. Pullman: Washington State University Press, 1993.

Cort, Louise Allison. "Korean Influences in Japanese Ceramics." *Orientations* 15, no. 5 (May 1984): 18–29.

Kang, Woo-bang. *The Art of Sarira Reliquary*. Exh. cat. Seoul: National Museum of Korea, 1991.

Kim, Won-Yong. "Philosophies and Styles in Korean Art." *Korea Journal* 19, no. 4 (April 1979): 4–10.

Kwon, Young-pil. "Ancient Glass Trade in Korea." *Papers of the British Association for Korean Studies* 5 (1994): 65–82.

———. "Ancient Korean Art and Central Asia: Non-Buddhist Art prior to the Tenth Century." *Korea Journal* 31 (Summer 1991): 5–20.

Lee, Ki-baek. *A New History of Korea*. Translated by Edward E. Wagner with Edward J. Shultz. Cambridge, MA: Harvard University Press, 1984.

Washizuka, Hiromitsu, Youngbok Park, and Woo-bang Kang. *Transmitting the Forms of Divinity: Early Buddhist Art from Korea and Japan*. Exh. cat. New York: Japan Society, 2003.

Goryeo Period

Gompertz, G. St. G. M. "Hsu Ching's Visit to Korea in 1123." *Transactions of the Oriental Ceramic Society* 33 (1960–62): 1–21.

———. *Korean Celadon, and Other Wares of the Koryo Period*. London: Faber and Faber, 1963.

Griffing, Robert P. *The Art of the Korean Potter: Silla, Koryo, Yi*. New York: Asia Society, 1968.

Hoam Gallery. *Exhibition of Great Treasure of the Goryeo*. Exh. cat. Seoul: Hoam Gallery, 1995.

Itoh, Ikutarō, and Yutaka Mino, eds. *The Radiance of Jade and the Clarity of Water: Korean Ceramics from the Ataka Collection*. With contributions by Jonathan W. Best and Pamela B. Vandiver. Exh. cat. Chicago: The Art Institute; New York: Hudson Hill Press, 1991.

Koh Choo, Carolyn. "A Comparative Scientific Study of the Earliest Kiln Sites of Koryō Celadon." *Archaeometry* 41, no. 1 (February 1999): 51–69.

Lippit, Yukio. "Goryeo Buddhist Painting in an Interregional Context." *Arts Orientals* 35 (2008): 192–232.

National Museum of Korea. *Masterpieces of Goryeo Buddhist Painting*. Exh. cat. Seoul: National Museum of Korea, 2010.

———. *Royal Ceramics of Goryeo Dynasty*. Exh. cat. Seoul: National Museum of Korea, 2009.

Newman, Richard. "A Compositional and Microstructural Study of Korean Celadon Glazes of the 11th to 15th

Centuries." In *Materials Issues in Art and Archaeology II*, edited by Pamela B. Vandiver, James Druzik, and George Segan, 429–40. Pittsburgh: Materials Research Society, 1991.

Paik Kim, Kumja. *Goryeo Dynasty: Korea's Age of Enlightenment, 918–1392*. With essays by Eung-Chon Choi, Seinosuke Ide, Jae Yeol Kim, Juhghee Lee, Youngsook Pak, and Edward Shultz. San Francisco: Asian Art Museum, 2003.

Pak, Youngsook. "Ksitigarbha as Supreme Lord of the Underworld: A Korean Buddhist Painting in the Museum für Ostasiatische Kunst in Berlin." *Oriental Art* 23, no. 1 (Spring 1977): 96–104.

———, and Roderick Whitfield. *Handbook of Korean Art: Earthenware and Celadon*. Seoul: Yekyong, 2002.

Portal, Jane. "Korean Celadons of the Koryo Dynasty." In *Pottery in the Making: World Ceramic Traditions*, edited by Ian C. Freestone and David J. Gaimster, 98–103. London: British Museum Press, 1997.

———. "Some Korean Masterpieces in the Museum of Fine Arts, Boston." *Orientations* 42, no. 4 (May 2011): 65–72.

Seckel, Dietrich. *The Art of Buddhism*. New York: Crown, 1964.

Seinosuke, Ide. "The World of Goryeo Buddhist Painting." In *Goryeo Dynasty: Korea's Age of Enlightenment, 918–1392*, by Kumja Paik Kim, 34–47. San Francisco: Asian Art Museum, 2003.

Vandiver, Pamela B. "The Technology of Korean Celadons." In *The Radiance of Jade and the Clarity of Water: Korean Ceramics from the Ataka Collection*, edited by Ikutarō Itoh and Yutaka Mino, 151–58. Exh. cat. Chicago: The Art Institute; New York: Hudson Hill Press, 1991.

Watt, James C. Y., and Barbara Brennan Ford. *East Asian Lacquer: The Florence and Herbert Irving Collection*. Exh. cat. New York: Metropolitan Museum of Art, 1991.

Wood, Nigel. "Technological Parallels between Chinese Yue Wares and Korean Celadons." *Papers of the British Association for Korean Studies* 5 (1994): 39–64.

Yun, Yong-i. *Korean Art from the Gompertz and Other Collections in the Fitzwilliam Museum, Cambridge*. Edited by Regina Karhl. Translated by Youngsook Pak and Roderick Whitfield. New York: Cambridge University Press, 2005.

Joseon Period

Ahn, Hwi-Joon. "Korean Painting: Influences and Traditions." In *Koreana: Korean Cultural Heritage Vol. 1, Fine Arts*, by the Korea Foundation, 38–47. Seoul: Korea Foundation, 1994.

Black, Kay E., and Edward W. Wagner. "Chaekkori Paintings: A Korean Jigsaw Puzzle." *Archives of Asian Art* 46 (1993): 63–75.

Cho, Sunmie. "Korea's Portrait Paintings." *Koreana* 6, no. 3 (Autumn 1992): 34–41.

Chung, Yang-mo. "The Merit Lay in 'Absolute Purity': White Porcelain of the Chosun Dynasty." *Koreana* 5, no. 3 (1991): 46–49.

Cort, Louise Allison. "Korean Influence in Japanese Ceramics: The Impact of the Teabowl Wares of 1592–1598." In *Ceramics and Civilization, Volume II: Technology and Style*, edited by W. D. Kingery, 331–62. Columbus, OH: The American Ceramics Society, 1986.

Deuchler, Martina. *The Confucian Transformation of Korea: A Study of Society and Ideology*. Cambridge, MA: Harvard University Press, 1992.

Gompertz, G. St. G. M. *Korean Pottery and Porcelain of the Yi Period*. London: Faber and Faber, 1968.

International Exhibitions Foundation. *Auspicious Spirits: Korean Folk Paintings and Related Objects*. Exh. cat. Washington, DC: International Exhibitions Foundation, 1983.

Itoh, Ikutarō. *Color of Elegance, Form of Simplicity: The Beauty of Korean Ceramics from the Rhee Byung-chang Collection*. Exh. cat. Osaka: Museum of Oriental Ceramics, 1999.

Jungmann, Burglind. *Painters as Envoys: Korean Inspiration in Eighteenth-Century Japanese Nanga*. Princeton: Princeton University Press, 2004.

Kang, Kyung-sook. *Korean Ceramics*. Translated by Cho Yoon-jung. Korean Culture Series 12, edited by Edward Adams and Lorrie Kim. Seoul: Korea Foundation, 2008.

Kim, Hongnam, ed. *Korean Arts of the Eighteenth Century: Splendor and Simplicity*. New York: Weatherhill, 1993.

Kim, Jae-yeol. *Handbook of Korean Art: White Porcelain and Punchong Ware*. Translated by Moonjung Choi. Seoul: Yekyong, 2002.

Lee, Soyoung. *Art of the Korean Renaissance, 1400–1600*. With essays by JaHyun Kim Haboush, Sunpyo Hong, and Chin-Sung Chang. Exh. cat. New York: Metropolitan Museum of Art; New Haven: Yale University Press, 2009.

———, and Seung-Chang Jeon. *Poetry in Clay: Korean Buncheong Ceramics from Leeum, Samsung Museum of Art*. Exh. cat. New York: Metropolitan Museum of Art, 2011.

Paik Kim, Keumja. "Bamboo and Grapes in Choson Dynasty Painting and

Porcelain Decoration." *Korean Culture* 13, no. 2 (Summer 1992): 18–25.

———. "A Celebration of Life: Patchwork and Embroidered Pojagi by Unknown Korean Women." *Oriental Art* 45, no. 4, (Winter 1999/2000): 52–58.

———, and Kay E. Black, with Edward W. Wagner. *Hopes and Aspirations: Decorative Paintings of Korea*. Exh. cat. San Francisco: Asian Art Museum, 1998.

Yoon, Yeolsu. *Folk Painting*. Translated by Wonjun Nam. Handbook of Korean Art. Seoul: Yekyong, 2002.

Modern-Day Korea

Cho, Chung-Hyun. *Tradition Transformed: Contemporary Korean Ceramics*. Exh. cat. Washington, DC: International Arts and Artists, 2006.

Ciclitira, Serenella, ed. *Korean Eye: Contemporary Korean Art*. Milan: Skira, 2010.

Jungmann, Burglind. *Life in Ceramics: Five Contemporary Korean Artists*. Exh. cat. Los Angeles: Fowler Museum at UCLA, 2010.

Kim, Youngna. "Modern Korean Painting and Sculpture." In *Korean Art Tradition: A Historical Survey*, edited by Young Ick Lew, 151–200. Seoul: Korea Foundation, 1993.

Portal, Jane. *Art under Control in North Korea*. Chicago: University of Chicago Press; London: Reaktion Books, 2005.

Roe, Jae-Ryung. *Contemporary Korean Art*. St. Leonards, New South Wales: Australian Humanities Research Foundation, 2001.

Van Gucht, Bie. *Nature et religion dans la céramique coréenne contemporaine: Collections du Musée royal de Mariemont*. Morlanwelz, Belgium: Musée Royal de Mariemont, 1996.

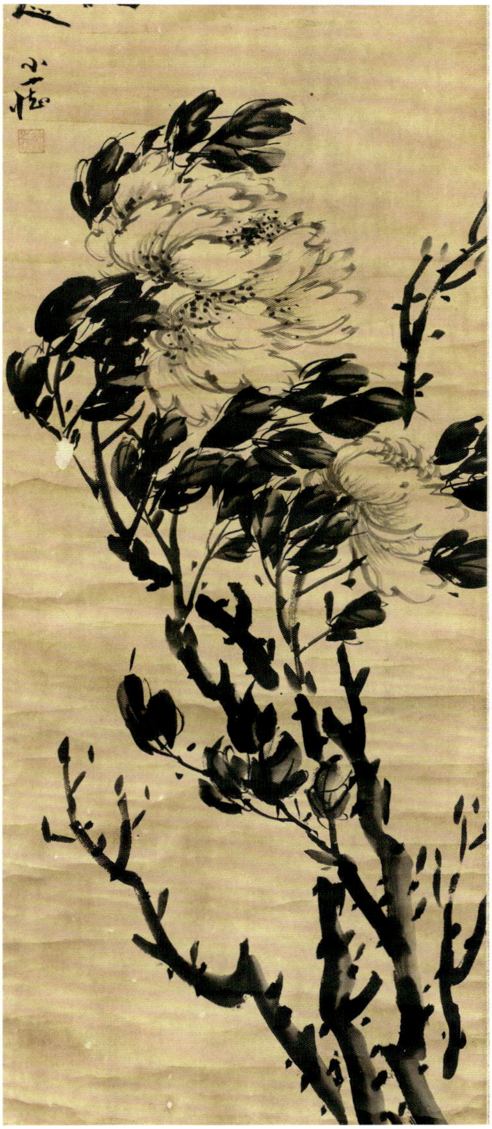

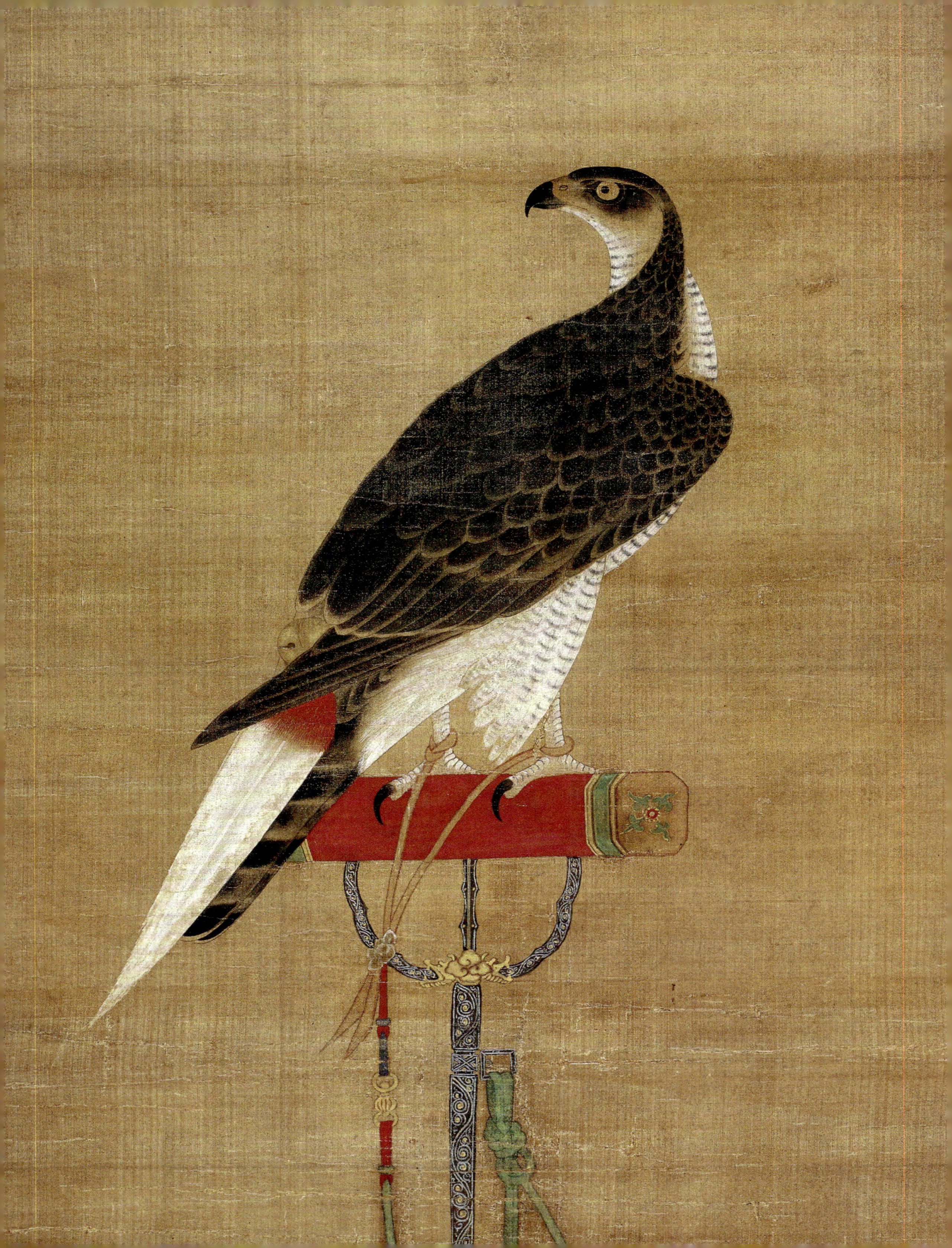

Index

Page numbers in italics refer to illustrations.

Figure Illustrations

1
Bernard Leach (British, 1887–1979)
Bottle, 20th century
Ceramic
H. 36.2 cm (14¼ in.); diam. 18.2 cm (7⅛ in.)
Charles Bain Hoyt Fund 58.33

2
Early Korean ceramics in the Edward Sylvester Morse Collection, Museum of Fine Arts, Boston
Photograph
Reproduced from *Catalogue of the Morse Collection of Japanese Pottery* (Boston: Museum of Fine Arts, 1901), plate 1

3
Percival Lowell (American, 1855–1916)
His Majesty the King of Korea, 1884
Photograph
Boston Photograph Library 2003.718

4
The Korean embassy to the United States, 1883
Photograph
Peabody Essex Museum